COOKING IN

ALASKA

THE LAND OF THE MIDNIGHT SUN

COOKING IN ALASKA

THE LAND OF THE MIDNIGHT SUN

by Pat Babcock & Diane Shaw

A Division of Schiffer Publishing
4880 Lower Valley Rd.
Atglen, PA 19310 USA

Book Design by
Sherri Faye Dugan

Cover Design by
Lori Shantz

Published by Whitford Press
A Division of Schiffer Publishing, Ltd.
4880 Lower Valley Road
Atglen, PA 19310 USA
Phone: (610) 593-1777 Fax: (610) 593-2002
E-mail: schifferbk@aol.com
Please write for a free catalog.
This book may be purchased from the publisher.
Please include $3.95 postage.
Try your bookstore first.

Libraray of Congress Cataloging-in Publication Data

Babcock, Pat, 1941-
Cooking in Alaska: the land of the midnight sun/by Pat Babcock and Diane Shaw.
P. cm.
Bibliography; p.
Includes Index.
ISBN: 0-89865-628-1 (pbk.)
1. Cookery, American.   2. Cookery--Alaska. 1. Shaw, Diane, 1948-
II. Title
TX715.B132   1988
641.59798--dc19   87-36425
CIP

Copyright © 1988 by Pat Babcock & Diane Shaw

ISBN: 0-89865-628-1
Printed in United States of America

edication

To the family of cooks at the top of the world.

$\mathcal{T}$able of Contents

Illustrations and Photos

Introduction

Logos for recipes: by April Kelley, Rachel Levine, and Pat Babcock

Logo Map: prepared by cartographer Ann Schell

Beverages *The Inupiat*

Appetizers *The Central and St. Lawrence Island Yupik*

Poultry   *The Aleut*

Desserts   *Tlingit*

Preserved Foods   *Haida*

ℱ oreword

Cooking in Alaska: The Land of the Midnight Sun has a different approach because Pat Babcock and Diane Shaw took the time and effort to divide our great state into seven regions, touching on the many people of different dialects from North to South and East to West. In it they give some description of each people's region while also describing the terrain and beauty of that section of Alaska.

Interesting facts and some history are added throughout the book. Intermingled are the beautiful illustrations by April Kelley, Rachel Levine, and Marionette Stock. One can enjoy a valuable book of recipes and also have an informative trip through the state of Alaska.

I feel that this book would be treasured as a gift not only to the new bride, but to people from other states or countries who would like to learn the Alaskan style of cooking. They will also become familiar with the native people that inhabit our forty-ninth state along with our pioneers and the many animals, birds, fish, and some of the wild flowers of Alaska.

In this book Pat Babcock and Diane Shaw have captured the Alaskan spirit of preparing good nutritious food as simply and as quickly as possible. In the early days, miners, prospectors, and trappers would return from a hard day's work, often in inclement weather, to a cold cabin. They would start a fire in the wood stove and then cook what was on hand the easiest and quickest way.

This cookbook contains sophisticated recipes that I am sure came later, but Pat and Diane have included a few of the original native recipes. These help give this book a more vivid feel for the people who were creative enough to make something edible with so very little to work with.

Pat Babcock is a well-known Alaskan artist and writes a gardening column for the Fairbanks *Daily News-Miner*. Diane Shaw is a well-known gourmet cook, freelance writer, and director of a Northern Testing Laboratory. She has had recipes published in national magazines. Being pioneers of our time they understand the necessity to cook quickly and simply to satisfy the hungry Alaskan appetite. The recipes are written clearly so even beginning cooks should have no trouble.

As you use these recipes I hope that you will think of Alaska and its people who used them during cold winter days and on warm mosquito-infested evenings.

Happy *Cooking in Alaska: The Land of the Midnight Sun!*

Edna Wilder

About Edna Wilder

Well-known artist and author Edna Wilder was born in Bluff, Alaska, at that time a small mining community just northwest of Rocky Point. She is the daughter of the late Minnie Nedercook and Arthur Samuel Tucker.

Sam Tucker came over from England to cross Chilkoot Pass. On the other side of the pass were the Klondike and the 1898 gold rush. Soon afterward, gold was found on the beaches of Nome. Tucker floated down the Yukon River on a raft, going to Nome. At this time Minnie Nedercook was a young woman in the village of Rocky Point.

Edna is one of Sam and Minnie Tucker's five children.

Edna paints in watercolor and oil, and sculpts with wood and soapstone. She has instructed classes in skin-sewing and basket-weaving at the University of Alaska, Fairbanks. Her art appeared in the A-67 Centennial Exposition in Fairbanks in 1967, and the Fairbanks Art Association show in 1969. In 1980 her paintings and sculptures were shown at the Charles and Emma Frye Museum in Seattle.

She has written two books: the first, Secrets of Eskimo Skin Sewing; the second, Once Upon An Eskimo Time.

$\mathscr{A}$cknowledgments

More than five dozen people contributed to this book. Some gave recipes, others tales of gathering abundance, and the rest a lot of invaluable support. Rachel Levine, April Kelley, and Marionette Donnell Stock provided us with lovely illustrations. Ann Schell produced the fine introductory maps to Alaska. Marge Haggland, Ellen Ayotte, Dorothy Beistline, Mary Dial, Evolyn Melville, Phelpsie Sirlin, Jane Neidhold and Jeanette Wrede shared volumes of Alaskan recipe books. Elisa Jones, Randall Jones, Priscilla Kari, Rusty Heurlin, Effie Kokrine, and Betty Starr gave us knowledge about Alaskan native people. Wynola Possenti helped us with wise counsel and suggestions for the index. We are indebted to DeAnna Gladieux for her editing and final proofreading. The black and white photographs are from the University of Alaska Archives and the Fairbanks *Dairy News-Miner* photo library and personal contributions. Special thanks to our husbands and children for their patience, enthusiasm, and inspiration.

Elsie Adams, Rachel Adams, Patricia Babcock, Marion Blossom, Emily Ivanoff Brown, Mrs. Minor Bruce, Vicky Cooper, Paul Coray, Elsie Cresswell, Diane Crocy, Mary Daubersmith, Mathilda Davidson, Dolores Dodson, Dieter Doppelfield, Betty Doyle, Karen Encelewski, Helen Finney, Mary Hamilton, Frances L. Hardy, Mary Hawkins, Fedora Hedrick, Virginia Doyle Heiner, Alice Kitkun, Ida Knabel, Jean Kurtz, Sanna LeVan, Helen Malcolm, Emily Marten, Janie Meckel, Audrey Meyers, Roswitha Miller, Ree Nancarrow, Lorna Nelson, Sophie Nickolle, Bessie Osuruk, Gladys Parker, Irene Peyton, Wynola Possenti, Diane Shaw, Patricia Shields, Sophie Sherebernikoff, Phelpsie Sirlin, Mrs. J. A. Sutherland, Susie Swaim, Millie Terwilliger, Lola Tilly, Ruth Towner, Bobbie Truax, Jeanette Trumbly, Evelyn Valentine, Jeannie Wenstrom, Ada Wien, Brenda Wilbur, Dorothy Wilbur, Mariel Wilbur, Charlotte Wilbur, and Marion Wood contributed the recipes for our book.

$\mathcal{P}$reface

Throughout Alaska, an abundant variety of delicious and nutritious natural foods are enjoyed. For many years the Indians, Eskimos, and early settlers have eaten well. Through their influence, there is a simplicity in food preparation that characterizes all of Alaska's cuisine.

We have tried to provide a cookbook that will touch every season in Alaska and introduce the flavor of the state through its geography, history, and culture.

There have been many sources for this cookbook: excellent cooks from throughout the state, various cookbooks printed from the turn of the century onward, and the University of Alaska's Cooperative Extension Service. We also provide a fine bibliography at the end of the cookbook.

We wish to give grateful acknowledgment to Rachel Levine, April Kelley, and Marionette Donnell Stock for preparing beautiful pencil illustrations throughout the book. We also wish to thank the University of Alaska Archives and Fairbanks *Daily News-Miner* for providing the photographs. We offer special thanks to the many contributors of recipes that comprise the book. We appreciate the personal communication and guidance from the following special people: Ellen Ayotte, Marge Haggland, Rusty Heurlin, Linda Hulbert, Elisa Jones, Randall Jones, Priscilla Kari, Effie Kokrine, Wynola Possenti, and Betty Starr.

The State of Alaska: An Introduction

Alaska is a vast and beautiful state, sparkling with the pristine beauty of snow-capped mountains, raging rivers, and miles of unspoiled wilderness. The villages and cities are separated by great and incomprehensible distances. It offers a kaleidoscope of variety to the people who live in the various regions.

One of the ways to introduce Alaska is by the regions. The Arctic, Western, Southwestern, Aleutian Island, Gulf Coast, Interior, and Southeastern regions of Alaska are different in their own mountain systems, water systems, or linguistic groups. The different regions of Alaska play an important role in the different lifestyles of the many people living here. In this cookbook we will travel along with

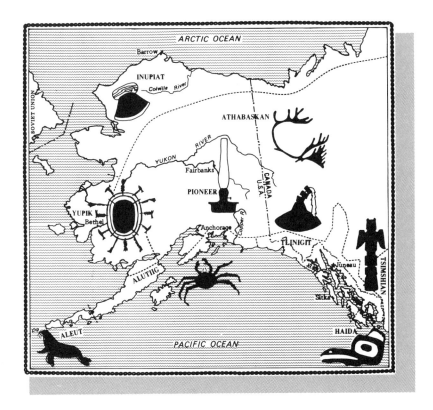

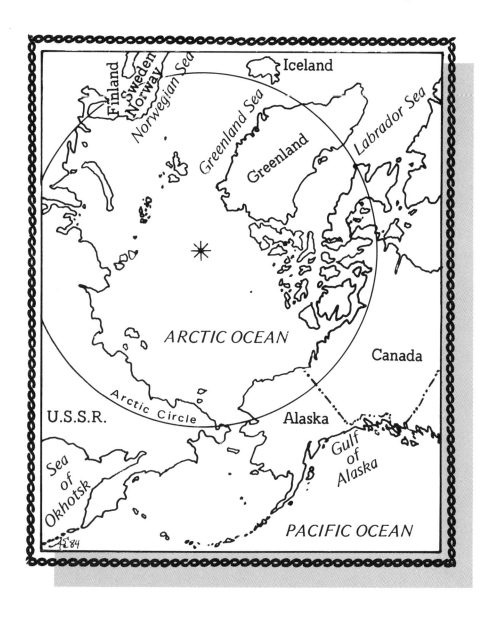

you through all seven Alaskan regions. You will find recipes from all the native Alaskan linguistic groups, pioneers, and new settlers.

Whether it be for subsistence living, survival, aesthetics, or jobs, Alaskans endure and enjoy our huge state which partially lies within the Arctic Circle along with Northern Canada, Greenland, Norway, Sweden, Finland, and Northern Siberia. The logos from the Alaskan map will show you from where a certain recipe

Arctic Ponds and Lakes
Fairbanks Daily News-Miner

originates.

The Arctic region encompasses about the top third of the state, going from the southern flanks of the Brooks Range north to Point Barrow. There are hundreds of miles of alpine tundra pocked with many ponds and lakes. The surface water flows from "breakup" which is the time when snow and ice melt, causing muddy conditions, to "freezeup," when the waters turn to ice and the ground is covered with snow. Permafrost, or permanently frozen ground, is found to depths of two thousand feet. At Point Barrow the sun stays above the horizon for eighty-five days in summer and sixty-seven days in winter. The soils never permanently thaw out here, since the temperature during the summer stays between thirty and forty degrees Fahrenheit. During the winter, the chill factor from the cold and wind brings the temperature to far lower than minus sixty degrees Fahrenheit. Pack ice is abundant in the Arctic Ocean. Moose, brown bear, grizzly bear and Dall sheep, along with caribou, live here. Smaller mammals, such as snowshoe hares, weasels, lynx, shrews, and lemmings also live in the Arctic. The icy waters of the nearby Arctic Ocean support populations of polar bears, walrus, bowhead and beluga whales, and various sorts of seals. The native inhabitants, the Inupiat, make their

Arctic Pack Ice
University of Alaska Geophysical Institute

home here and traditionally subsist upon the land by hunting, fishing, and gathering wild greens and berries during the summer. They supplement their diet from local grocery stores. Development of the oil fields located in this region has provided jobs for the people living in the Arctic.

The Western region encompasses the Seward Peninsula, which reaches out towards Siberia. At the point of the peninsula, Little Diomede Island is only three miles away from Big Diomede Island on Soviet ground. Although there are a few mountainous areas, there are also many lakes, ponds, and hills, as well as the Kobuk and Noatak rivers, which wind through the area. This region borders on the Arctic. Therefore, the winters are harsh, and summer temperatures hover around forty to sixty degrees Fahrenheit. The sea coast is made up of tundra vegetation, underlaid with several feet of permafrost. Nome, a center for an early 1900s gold rush, is the major community. Some of the Inupiat speaking people who live here herd reindeer as part of their economy, and fishing is also a part of their subsistence economy. Villages are linked by air, water, dog sled, or any machine that can cross the snow.

The Southwestern region, which is south of the aforementioned Seward Peninsula, is a broad lowland in which the Kuskokwim and Yukon rivers wind to the Bering Sea to form a huge delta area. There is an abundance of waterfowl, fish, and mammals in this region, on which some of the native Central Yupik speaking people subsist by fishing, hunting, and trapping. In Bethel, the major community center, the summer temperatures average around fifty degrees Fahrenheit, with winter temperatures averaging around zero degrees Fahrenheit. In the southern

Akutan Volcano, Aleutian Islands
by John Reeder

part of this region the Bristol Bay sockeye salmon runs are world-famous. Sheefish and whitefish are utilized also. Fishing is an important source of income and food, but berry picking, along with gathering different greens is also a part of the lifestyle here. Saint Lawrence Island, home of the Siberian Yupik speaking people, lies off the coast.

The Aleutian Island region arcs for more than one thousand miles into the Pacific Ocean, pointing toward Japan. There are more than one hundred islands in the region, some of which are highly mountainous and include many volcanic peaks. The temperature averages about fifty degrees Fahrenheit in the summer and twenty degrees Fahrenheit in the winter. There are constant winds and fog is common. The islands are sparsely populated with Aleuts and other settlers. Sea otters, Steller sea lions, and many species of sea birds make their homes here. Fishing for crab, salmon, shrimp, herring, and bottom fish is the major industry, while small, sheep ranching ventures struggle on some of the islands.

The Gulf Coast region, located in the Gulf of Alaska in the southernmost portion of the state, is noted for its fishing industries—crab, shrimp, and salmon. Some areas are rich with razor clams, herring, and halibut. Shoreline areas serve as a base for harvesting and extracting offshore resources. The vegetation ranges from spruce-hemlock forest to spruce and birch forests. Sea birds and sea mammals

Southeastern Alaska Small Boat Harbor
Fairbanks Daily News-Miner
Mark Kelley

Cook Inlet Oil Exploration
Fairbanks Daily News-Miner

Alaska Range Glacier
Fairbanks Daily News-Miner

Denali
University of Alaska Archives
Edby Davis Collection

abound in this region and the Alutiiq speaking people subsist here by utilizing the fishing industry and by hunting.

The Interior region, located in the middle of Alaska, contains both the largest area of any of the regions in the state and the towering Alaska Range. Here Mount McKinley, called "Denali, the Great One," by the Athabaskan Indians, looms at 20,320 feet. The Interior contains the large river valleys of the Yukon, Tanana, Kuskokwim, and Koyukuk. The winters are cold, clear, and have little wind. Temperatures have reached minus sixty degrees Fahrenheit in the winter.

Hydraulic Mining for Placer Gold
University of Alaska Archives
Wm. B. Ballou Collection

Summers are warmer here than in any other region of Alaska, and high temperatures have been above ninety degrees Fahrenheit. There are only twelve inches of precipitation annually, making it somewhat desert-like. Forests of spruce, aspen, birch, and cottonwood roll on for many miles. In some areas the highlands are covered with moss, grass, and brush, and the lowlands are marshy. Fairbanks, a transportation and business center, is the main city of the Interior and it serves as a supply source for many outlying areas. It is also home to the University of Alaska main campus. Placer mining for gold has been a heavy mineral industry in the Interior for years. Grain farming and other agricultural ventures are expanding

Southeastern Alaska Waterfall
University of Alaska Archives
Barret Willoughby Collection

here. Electricity for the Interior is generated from coal mines near Healy, which is about one hundred miles south of Fairbanks. Populations of moose; caribou; Dall sheep; black, brown, and grizzly bears; mountain goats; and other small mammals like the snowshoe hare, lynx, wolverine, and fox exist here. King salmon, silver salmon, chum salmon, whitefish, northern pike, sheefish, and grayling abound in different rivers and streams. The native Athabaskan speaking people traditionally subsist on the many varieties of fish and game, along with the many types of berries found here.

The Southeastern region, pointing toward the northwestern part of the state of Washington, extends from the southern tip of Prince of Wales Island to Yakutat Bay. Here there are many glaciated mountains, islands, fjords, and waterfalls. This region is heavily forested with spruce, hemlock, and cedar, and has a wide variety of edible berries and edible plants. The summer temperatures are between fifty and sixty degrees Fahrenheit, while winter temperatures hover around forty degrees Fahrenheit in January. There is heavy precipitation—some areas near the coast see two hundred inches annually. Fishing, lumbering, and tourism are the major industries, providing an economy for the Tlingit, Haida, and Tsimshian speaking people and the settlers of the area. Airplanes and ferries provide the means of transportation. Juneau is the state capital.

In Alaska the foods which people eat are determined by where they live. For the most part, it is the game—moose, caribou, rabbits, deer, birds, fish, plus wild plants, and berries—that spells survival to the people living here. If you live in the Southeastern region, the food you eat would be different from that eaten in the Interior of the state.

The introduction of new foods into the aboriginal diet pattern began as soon as the native Alaskans came into contact with explorers, sailors, colonizers, traders, and others, but the Russians were the first to make a change in the diet of the native people. The foods they introduced were brown and white sugar, tea, flour, crackers, rice, salt, butter, and canned fruits. They also introduced gardening. Some of the vegetables grown were potatoes, rutabagas, and onions.

After the United States purchased Alaska from Russia, more Americans, such as whalers, sailors, miners, traders, missionaries, teachers, and servicemen came into the country. The American people are responsible for introducing canned milk, oatmeal, cornmeal, baking powder, candy, lard, margarine, hydrogenated fats, cookies, coffee, macaroni, dried fruit, and beef tallow. Today there is a whole array of foods available for everyone who lives here.

We hope you will enjoy journeying along with us through the Alaskan cuisine found in the different regions of our glorious state! The recipes will surely offer you a true taste of Alaska.

HOUSEHOLD HINTS FROM
FAIRBANKS COOKBOOK CIRCA 1910

To prevent fingers from being stained when peeling potatoes or apples, use a silver knife.

When baking potatoes, wash and dry them and rub them over with some kind of grease. When baked they will have a rich, satiny look, and the outer skin will peel off as thin as tissue paper, leaving the rich nutritious part beneath to be eaten instead of wasted, as usual.

To keep cheese from molding after it is cut, wet a cloth in vinegar, wring it out, and smooth it over cut portion.

To prevent mush from sticking to kettle when making corn meal mush, grease the kettle with fresh lard. Make a batter of the meal with luke warm water, and it will not be lumpy.

Put a pinch of cream of tartar in frosting or fudge to prevent it from going to sugar. It will be nice and creamy.

When peeling oranges, the white substance will remain. Dip in cold water and scrape with a sharp knife. It will disappear like magic.

When eggs are frying, add a little boiling water and cover with a lid just during the last moment of their cooking. This will create the pretty, pink, glazed-over look that is so desirable.

To remove the grease from soups without waiting for it to get cold, dip a cloth in ice cold water and pour the soup through it. The chilled cloth will congeal the grease, while the soup will pass through readily.

When stirring sugar and butter together for a cake, instead of using a spoon, use a wooden masher and see how much quicker and easier it is done.

Use a string for cutting hot brown bread. Turn the loaf on its side, using both hands to draw the string.

Pastry should be cooled off in a warm room. Taking it suddenly from the oven to a cold place will make it heavy.

To take the odor of fish from a frying pan or baking pan, place a good handful of potato peelings in it, pour boiling water on, and let them boil 10 to 15 minutes.

—Dr. Dora Fugard-Kirkpatrick

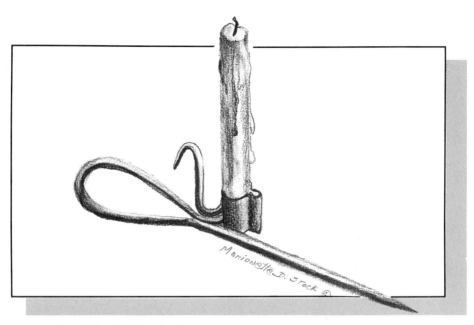

Gold Miner's Candle: by Marionette Donnell Stock

THE INUPIAT

The Inupiat Eskimos are a hospitable people. They love singing, dancing,

Dancing to the Drumbeat
by April Kelley

clowning, and mimicry. They love the wild laughter of children, as well as the children themselves. The Inupiat are a subsistence people who often share their bounty with their neighbors. For instance, a bowhead whale feeds entire villages.

Generation Upon Generation
by Rachel Levine

They are a resourceful people, using as much of each animal as possible: the fur is used for winter clothing, and all of the meat is used for food. The Inupiat are located in the Arctic Slope and Bering Straits regions of Alaska. Since they lead a subsistence lifestyle, they depend upon the different seasons for land animals such as caribou; sea mammals such as bowhead whale, and seal; birds; eggs; berries; and roots and greens. There are available grocery stores, stocked yearly by summer visits of freighters, and more frequently by air service from larger villages and cities. Simple preparation of the foods available in their environment is the norm, whether they boil, eat raw, or fry their foods. They can live off the land cleverly—they are true survivors.

Every spring the Inupiat watch over the edge of the ice pack for bowhead whales, which migrate north to the Arctic Ocean. The whales provide needed meat for the people of many villages. With light walrus-skin boats called umiaks beside them, the hunters are ready at all times in the event a whale is sighted. This pattern is repeated in the fall, when the whales return home on their migration to warmer waters. During the whaling seasons, hunters are often on the watch twenty-four hours a day until the whales are spotted. While waiting, they drink a lot of strong tea and coffee and eat a lot of frozen caribou meat, or fish, called quak. After the whale is harpooned and killed, it is towed by a string of umiaks to

Successful Whale Hunt
by Rachel Levine

the edge of the ice pack where a heavy rope is used to winch it by the tail onto the ice where it is butchered. After the whale is cut up and divided among the villagers, it is stored in ice cellars deep in the permafrost where huge ice wedges, centuries old, lie hidden.

The traditional feast which follows the taking of the whale is called *kuqruk*. People of Point Hope and visitors from neighboring villages welcome the feast annually. It brings together families separated by many miles of ice and tundra, for a real family reunion. The tradition is preserved from the early-day Eskimos as a "Great Sharing Feast," which celebrated the grace of the animal and the skill of man.

The feast begins on a very formal note with first choice sections of the whale being given to the captain of the successful whaling crew. Then the crew members and their families receive shares. Finally, visitors and guests may claim their share. Usually the tail portions of the bowhead whales are given to no one. They are saved for special village feasts.

The bulk of the whale is then cut into large chunks and lowered into ten- or twenty-foot-deep permafrost pits, which act as a deep freeze year around. An ample portion is then cut up and cooked in pots for the *kuqruk* feast. Whale meat tastes somewhat like beef. It is often referred to as the "cow of the ocean."

Muktuk, which is the thick black layer near the blubber or fat layer, has a fishy, almond taste. Watching a woman at work with her *ulu,* a woman's knife, it is hard to believe that she is really working on a hunk of whale insted of beef. Whale heart tastes a lot like beef also.

$\mathcal{B}$ EVERAGES

All over Alaska unique beverages are made from local wild and garden plants, and from berries. They serve as welcome warm-ups, refreshments, and nourishment, as well as being ideal accompaniments for Alaskan-style meals. In keeping with the climate, many of our beverages are served hot, and the drinks such as hot spiced juices and "teas" show that, in Alaska, a hot drink can be much more varied than plain coffee or tea.

In native cultural groups throughout the state, beverages are traditionally quite simple: plain water with most meals, or perhaps hot meat broths or tea. Tea was actually introduced to north and west coast Eskimos by early Russian explorers. Local plants and herbs (spruce tips, Labrador tea, *etc.*) are also made into tea for enjoyment, or for medicinal purposes, and some of these drinks are very high in vitamin C. There are regional specialties, of course: in southern coastal regions, clam juice is considered a tasty treat.

As you will see in every chapter of this book, the influence of Scandinavian cooking is very strong in Alaska. This is due to the similar regional foods and to the many people of Scandinavian heritage who settled here. The same trend is seen in the heavy influence of Russian and German cooking. These cuisines have a common style which is shared by Alaskan cooking: they are simple, colorful, hearty foods which are not elaborately seasoned or garnished. They make use of salted, pickled, and smoked foods which have stemmed from the need to preserve the food supply. Native Alaskan methods of food preservation (drying, packing in oil, freezing, smoking, *etc.*), have been very popular with all Alaskans and contribute favorite flavors to many of our foods.

So for now, begin your journey into Alaskan cuisine by preparing one of these special beverages—either hot and spicy, or cool and sweet—which you will find in this chapter.

Snowy Owl
by April Kelley

Rose Petal Tea

Yield: 1 serving

Even many Alaskans are not aware that our beautiful, pink wild rose petals can be steeped for a delicate tea, or to make syrup or jelly. The infusion looks gray or brownish, but add a bit of lemon juice and it turns bright pink!

2 tablespoons loosely measured wild
   Alaskan rose petals
1 cup boiling water

1 teaspoon lemon juice
Sugar or honey to taste

Pour boiling water over the rose petals and steep for 5 minutes. Rose petals will lose their color completely. Add lemon juice (watch it turn pink) and sweeten to taste with sugar or honey.

Rose Hip Tea

Yield: 1 serving

1 tea bag
1 tablespoon dried rose hips
3 or 4 whole cloves

1 cup boiling water
Sugar or honey to taste

Steep tea bag, rose hips, and cloves in boiling water for 5 minutes. Strain, and reheat if desired. Sweeten to taste with sugar or honey.

Wild Rose
by Rachel Levine

Mrs. Egleston's Russian Tea

Yield: 1 gallon

3 oranges
1½ tablespoons whole spices
   (cloves and cinnamon)
Juice of 3 lemons

16 cups water
1/3 cup tea
2 cups sugar, or to taste

Peel and juice the oranges. Tie spices in a cheesecloth bag and boil for a few minutes, in a small quantity of water, along with the orange peel (colored rind only). Combine the liquid with the orange and lemon juices and the sugar. Use the remaining water to brew tea in a non-metallic vessel. Cover and let stand 5 minutes. Strain tea and add to fruit juices and sugar. Chill or serve hot.

From the *Golden Heart Cookbook,* Fairbanks

In many Arctic villages the families get melt water from ice that is cut from the many lakes found in their vicinities. Children in Point Hope have historically had a six day school week, so they can participate in the annual spring bowhead whaling season.

Instant Russian Tea

1¼ cups instant orange-flavored breakfast drink mix
1 cup iced tea mix (with sugar and lemon)
1 teaspoon cinnamon
1 teaspoon allspice
1 teaspoon cloves

Combine all ingredients and store in a covered container. Mix as you would instant tea with boiling water.

Athabaskan Spruce Needle Tea

Spruce Needles
Water

Boil spruce needles in water. This is traditionally drunk to cure kidney problems or to obtain spirit power from the spruce. The infusion can be applied to the skin to heal dry skin or sores.

Eskimos of the past hunted, killed, and ate in one place only for as long as they found the game to do so. When game disappeared, they moved on. If they didn't, starvation would set in—and then death.

Raspberry-Rhubarb Hot Spiced Tea

Yield: 2 quarts

4 cups wild raspberries
4 cups thinly sliced rhubarb
2 cups water
3 sticks cinnamon
12 whole cloves

1 teaspoon nutmeg
Cheesecloth
1 cup sugar
2 tablespoons lemon juice
4 cups freshly brewed tea

In a saucepan cook the raspberries, rhubarb, and water together with the cinnamon, cloves, and nutmeg (tied in cheesecloth). Let simmer for 5 minutes. Strain through cheesecloth in a colander. Reheat liquid with the sugar, lemon juice, and tea, stirring to dissolve the sugar; serve hot.

Polar bears come ashore along the northern slope region of the Arctic in the coastal areas to prepare dens deep in the snowdrifts. Here they have their cubs, which are born in the darkness of December. A breathable area is made by the mother bear in the top surface of the den, by clawing away the icy coating of her den. The mother bear and cubs emerge from their den in the spring and head for the ice pack of the Arctic Ocean.

Eskimo Blanket Toss
by Rachel Levine

Nulakatuk *is the Inupiat word for blanket toss. It means "up in the air." Blanket tossing is always a highlight of the whaling festivals, which are held to send off the whale's soul. This is always a time for prayers of thanks, feasting, dancing, and sports. Blanket tossing, first by the children and then by the adults, goes on for several hours following the feast. Wrapping up the evening activities, traditional Eskimo dancing livens up the night.*

Even though it is perpetually dark in the winter months, the summer sun shines for eighty days without setting in Prudhoe Bay, which is in the northern slope region of the Arctic. In the summer, wild flowers of various species bloom spectacularly for a short time. During the early summer the ground thaws and becomes fragile. A vehicle traveling over the surface can leave permanent scars.

Northern Potpourri Tea

This is a colorful tea made from northern wild plants. Gather together the plants of your choice:

Fireweed leaves
Rose hips and seeds
Rose petals
Strawberry leaves
Raspberry leaves

Blue violets
Bearberry leaves
Sage
Chamomile
Water

Dry the plants, then grind or pulverize them. To make tea, pour boiling water over them and steep for 10 minutes.

Alaskan Cranberry Tea

Yield: 1 gallon

1 quart lingonberries or 1 pint
   lingonberries and 1 pint high bushcranberries
2 sticks cinnamon

3 quarts water
6 tablespoons lemon juice
2 cups orange juice
2 cups sugar

Cook berries, cinnamon sticks, and water until the berries are just tender; strain. Add the lemon juice, orange juice, and sugar. Heat just enough to dissolve the sugar; serve hot. May be kept refrigerated indefinitely.

—Irene Peyton, Fairbanks

Jade comes from the Jade Mountains and Kobuk area of the Arctic. It is also found along the Dall and Shungnak rivers. It is used in jewelry making and in larger pieces such as coffee tables, clock faces, and book ends.

Hot Cranberry Tea

Yield: 12 cups

1 pound fresh or frozen cranberries or
  lingonberries
2 quarts water
2 tablespoons grated orange peel
8 cinnamon sticks

12 whole cloves
4 cups orange juice
1 cup lemon juice
1½ cups sugar

Combine in a large saucepan the cranberries, water, orange peel, cinnamon sticks, and cloves. Cook until the cranberries are soft; strain. Add orange juice, lemon juice, and sugar; heat until sugar is dissolved. Serve hot.

Since there are always prevailing winds on the north slope, the ice can blow into shore. Therefore, it can block barges from coming into the coastal villages from time to time. The trick of the trade is to get into port, unload and leave before the ice pinches the boats between its icy fingers.

Blueberry Syrup

Yield: about 2 quarts

2 quarts wild blueberries
4 cups sugar
¾ cup cold water

Pick over and mash the fruit; sprinkle with the sugar, cover and let stand overnight. Add water. Cook slowly to the boiling point, and cook for 20 minutes. Force mixture through a double thickness of cheesecloth, and again bring to the boiling point. Fill small glass jars, and adjust the covers. Use as a foundation for beverages, ices, or sauces.

—University of Alaska, Cooperative Extension Service.

Spiced Cranberry Juice

Yield: 2 quarts

1 teaspoon whole allspice
2 2-inch sticks cinnamon
12 whole cloves

2/3 cup brown sugar, packed
2 quarts cranberry juice
Ground nutmeg

Tie allspice, cinnamon, and cloves together loosely in cheesecloth. In a large saucepan combine cranberry juice and brown sugar; heat. Add spice bag and simmer for 10 minutes or until juice is spiced to taste. Remove bag. Serve hot in mugs with a dash of nutmeg in each. This is delicious made ahead of time and reheated.

—University of Alaska, Cooperative Extension Service

Low-Bush Cranberry Juice #1

Yield: 2 gallons

40 cups or 10 pounds lingonberries
3 quarts water
1 ounce cream of tartar
$\frac{1}{2}$ cup hot water
5 pounds sugar (approximately)

Grind the cranberries into a large non-metallic container. Add the 3 quarts water and stir. Dissolve cream of tartar in the $\frac{1}{2}$ cup hot water and add to cranberries, stirring well. Let stand 2 days, stirring occasionally. Strain through a jelly bag or a cheesecloth-lined strainer. Measure juice and add one-half as much sugar as you have juice. Stir well; strain if necessary, and pour into sterilized bottles or jars.

At Point Hope and other north slope region areas, the winter windchill can be minus one hundred degrees Fahrenheit with the prevailing, eternal winds.

High Bushcranberry-Rhubarb Drink

Yield: 1 quart

High bushcranberries are not really cranberries at all—they are the bright red fruit of a Viburnum, which grows plentifully in Alaskan forest edges, thickets, and clearings as far north as the Brooks Range. The berries contain a large flat seed, so they are nearly always used in recipes as juice or strained pulp rather than as whole berries.

1 quart high bushcranberries	3 cups water
1 quart finely chopped rhubarb	Sugar to taste

Simmer and mash at the same time the cranberries, rhubarb, and water. Strain the juice through a wet jelly bag. Return the juice to the preserving kettle, adding 1 cup of sugar for each quart of juice, or to taste. Reheat to 170 degrees F., which is the pasteurization point, or simmer just below the boiling point if you have no thermometer. Maintain this temperature for 2 minutes. Pour into sterilized bottles and cap. Cool quickly and store in a cool, dark place until needed. This juice may be sealed in sterilized canning jars and processed for 15 minutes in a boiling water bath. It makes an excellent punch by diluting it 1:3 (or 1:1) with lemon-lime soda or ginger ale.

—University of Alaska, Cooperative Extension Service

In the Kobuk river area archaeologists have discovered one of the most important sites found in the Arctic at Onion Portage—the remains of Eskimo cultures eighty-five hundred years old.

Delicious Rhubarb Drink

Yield: 1 quart

1 lemon, juice and rind	1 cup finely chopped rhubarb
¾ cup sugar	4 cups boiling water

Squeeze the juice from the lemon and finely chop the rind. Add the sugar and the rhubarb. Pour the boiling water over this, and allow to stand for two hours. Drain and chill the liquid.

This makes a delicious drink and can be sealed while hot in sterilized jars and saved for winter use.

—From the *Golden Heart Cookbook*, Fairbanks

Tanniktuk is the Inupiat word for "white man's food." This can be anything purchased in the grocery store that is not natural to the Inupiat diet.

Alaskan Raspberry-Vinegar Drink

Yield: Depends on amount of berries gathered

Fresh wild raspberries
White vinegar, to almost cover raspberries
Sugar

Pour vinegar over raspberries in a non-metallic container. Crush the berries and let the mixture stand, covered, overnight. Strain the liquid and measure it into a saucepan. Add 1 cup of sugar for each cup of liquid, and heat to 190 degrees F.; maintain at this temperature for 5 minutes. Pour into sterile bottles. To serve as a drink, combine 1 part of the bottled mixture with 3 or 4 parts cold water. This raspberry vinegar won a blue ribbon at the Tanana Valley State Fair.

—Mary Hamilton, Fairbanks

In the arctic, loose fitting, dry clothing is a must for keeping warm in the winter.

Snow drinks are wonderful, slushy mixtures of clean snow, sweetening, and cream or canned milk. They are very popular with children and adults all over Alaska. Here are two variations.

Chocolate Snow Drink

Fill a chilled quart bowl with new, dry fine snow. Add canned milk and chocolate and beat vigorously with an egg beater until the mixture is the consistency of a thick ice cream shake. Eat with a spoon. If desired, garnish with chopped nuts and a cherry.

Maple Snow Drink

For each person, fill a styrofoam cup with clean, fresh snow. Put about 1 tablespoon of pure maple syrup and about 2 tablespoons heavy cream into each cup. Stir gently and "eat" with a spoon. Children always eat their lunches when they know they can go outside and gather their cup of clean snow for this treat afterwards!

The game refuge in the Arctic is called the Arctic National Wildlife Refuge, and it contains over eighteen million acres. The most important mammals here are the caribou, polar bears, grizzly bears, wolves, and Dall sheep. Peregrine falcons, snowy owls, and rock ptarmigan are residents here also.

Easy Oven Yogurt

1 envelope unflavored gelatine
1 cup boiling water
1 tablespoon honey
3 cups instant powdered milk in dry
  form

5 cups barely warm water
1 13-ounce can evaporated milk
3 tablespoons plain yogurt, for starter

Dissolve gelatine in the boiling water. Add honey and let the mixture cool slightly. Preheat oven to 275 degrees F. Mix the powdered milk with 3 cups barely warm water in a large bowl. Add 2 more cups water, the evaporated milk, and the gelatine mix. Add yogurt starter and stir thoroughly. *Turn oven off.* Cover bowl, and place mixture in the warm, dark oven. Leave overnight, or 8 to 10 hours. Then transfer to covered containers and refrigerate. Save some yogurt as a starter for your next batch.

In the village of Noatak, people enjoy a prosperous life of subsistence living off both the sea and the land. They go to Kotzebue Sound in the spring to hunt seals and whales; they fish on the Noatak River for various species of fish in the summer; and they hunt caribou in the fall and winter.

Alaskan Punch

1 cup lingonberries
1 cup ripe wild rose hips
½ cup water
1 cup wild raspberries

Dash of salt
1 cup sugar
Orange slices

Cook the lingonberries and the rose hips in the water until fruit is soft. Add raspberries and cook until they are soft, too. Drain through a wet jelly bag and squeeze to get all possible juice. Drain again to clarify the juice, but do not squeeze the bag this time. Add the sugar and salt; stir until all the sugar is dissolved. Pour over cracked ice in tall glasses. Float a thin slice of orange on top of each glass.

The Arctic coastal plain is underlaid by continuous permafrost and dotted with thousands of oriented lakes, polygons, pingos, and marshes.

Red Christmas Punch

6 cups lingonberries
6 cups sugar

1 liter of lemon-lime soda
3 cups vodka

Combine juice and sugar in a saucepan. Bring quickly to a boil and boil until syrupy—about 5 or 6 minutes. Cool to lukewarm. Stir in the soda and the vodka and chill in the refrigerator for a few hours before serving.

Low-Bush Cranberry Juice #2

Cranberries
Water

Boil cranberries with one-half as much water as berries; cook until berries pop and become soft, about 5 minutes; strain.

In the Colville River area there have been bones of the wooly mammoth, wild horse, giant bison, ground sloths, and camels found. These mammals disappeared thousands of years ago.

Raspberry Punch

Yield: 1 quart

2 cups raspberry juice, canned,
    bottled, or fresh
1 teaspoon cornstarch
¼ cup sugar

5 cloves
1 2-inch stick cinnamon
1 cup orange juice
¾ cup grape juice

Boil raspberry juice with the cornstarch, sugar, and spices. Remove spices. When cool, add orange and grape juices. Serve over cracked ice, or freeze the mixture and serve it as a sherbet.

—University of Alaska, Cooperative Extension Service

When a person walks over the Kobuk River sand dunes, he might think he was in the middle of the Gobi desert. The dunes in some places are one hundred feet tall. Here plants found during the time of the wandering mammoth still exist.

Rhubarb Punch #1

Yield: 1 gallon

3 pounds red rhubarb
Water
1½ cups sugar (or to taste)

1 12-ounce can frozen pink lemonade
2 cups ginger ale

Cut rhubarb into 1-inch lengths, cover with water, and simmer until very tender. Extract rhubarb juice by straining through cheesecloth. Add extra water to juice, if needed, to make 3 quarts. Dissolve sugar in 1 cup water and cook for 10 minutes. Add this syrup to the rhubarb juice, then add the pink lemonade (diluted according to directions on the can); chill. Add the ginger ale before serving.

—Brenda Wilbur, Fairbanks

In 1976 a fifty-five gallon drum of fuel oil cost $60.50 in Point Hope and $70.00 in Wainwright, Alaska. A twenty-pound sack of commercial dog food costs around $40.00 a bag. A dogteam can eat fifty pounds of food a week.

18

Rhubarb Punch #2

Yield: 6 to 8 servings

2 cups sliced rhubarb
1 cup sugar
$^{1}/_{2}$ cup water

$^{1}/_{2}$ cup pineapple juice
$^{1}/_{4}$ cup lemon juice
27 ounces ginger ale or lemon-lime soda

Cook the rhubarb, sugar, and water until rhubarb is very tender. Drain the juice from the rhubarb and add to the rest of the ingredients.

—Patricia Shields, Fairbanks

In White Mountain on the banks of the Fish River, people hang plentiful supplies of fish for drying during the summer months. Rivers in this area abound with salmon, rainbow trout, grayling, and pike. In the fall the people hunt seals, ducks, geese, and moose. This village is located eighty miles east of Nome, and is not far from Norton Sound.

Alaska Pink-and-Blue-Skies Champagne

Winter in Alaska means dwindling hours of daylight, with long periods of "sunrise" and "sunset" sky. On clear days, with the sun very low on the horizon, the sky is bright blue, and the clouds and snowy tops of the spruce trees are a beautiful pink. I like to serve twin glasses of this champagne drink, one pink and one blue, as a truly Alaskan version of champagne.

Alaskan cranberry liqueur
Alaskan blueberry liqueur
Very dry champagne

For each (twin) serving, pour a few teaspoons of cranberry liqueur into one champagne glass and a few teaspoons of blueberry liqueur into another. Fill glasses with chilled champagne and serve immediately.

—Diane Shaw, Fairbanks

Baleen is the stiff material that lines the mouth of certain kinds of whales. It strains out plankton, called krill. It was once used for buggy whips and corset stays, creating an Arctic whaling industry which lasted for several years in the latter part of the eighteenth century. Baskets are made from it nowadays.

Dry Cranberry Wine

Approximately 6 quarts

4 quarts rhubarb, chopped
1½ lemons, thinly sliced
Boiling water

2 quarts lingonberries
1 quart water

*   *   *   *   *   *

2 quarts warm water
4 pounds sugar
2 packages active dry yeast, dissolved in 1 cup warm water

Cover rhubarb and lemons with boiling water and let stand for two days. Strain the juice. Boil the cranberries and the 1 quart water together until the berries pop; strain. Cool the juice. Combine rhubarb juice, cranberry juice, 2 quarts warm water, sugar, and dissolved yeast. Use a large, glass, stainless steel, or earthenware container. Mix together thoroughly; cover with a cloth and let stand until it stops "working," about 3 to 4 weeks. Bottle and cap the mixture and let it stand in the bottles until it is clear.

—University of Alaska, Cooperative Extension Service

The outer skin layer of whales is called muktuk. *It comes from the bowhead and beluga whales. It can be eaten fresh, cooked, frozen, or pickled.*

Blueberry Wine

8 quarts blueberries
8 quarts cool water
8 cups sugar

2 ounces moist (cake) yeast
1 slice toasted whole wheat bread

Mash the blueberries in a large kettle, using a potato masher. In a second kettle mix 4 quarts of water and the sugar. Bring to a boil, and boil hard for 7 minutes. Pour this syrup over the crushed berries to set their color. Add the remaining

4 quarts water, stirring well. Moisten the yeast with enough water to make a paste; spread yeast on the toast. Float toast, yeast side down, on surface of the blueberry mixture. Allow to ferment at room temperature for two weeks, stirring gently, but thoroughly, every 24 hours. Strain through a jelly bag, squeezing to remove all of the liquid. Let stand another 3 days in a kettle for the sediment to settle. Siphon into sterilized bottles and cork lightly. When the fermentation has ceased—3 to 4 weeks—cork bottles tightly and seal the corks with paraffin. Store for 6 months. After a year's storage, the wine will be even more mellow.

The annual plants that grow in the cold soils are shallow rooted and have a short growing cycle. There are eighty-five days of continual daylight, which aids the growth process. Perennial plants have tough roots, branches, and stems to withstand the long desert-like dryness of the Arctic.

Red Currant Wine

10 pounds red currants, crushed
6 pints water
Sugar

Sodium bisulfite
Active dry yeast

Mix the crushed currants and the water in a large fermentation vessel. Weigh out 1¾ pounds of sugar for each gallon of the mixture. Add one-half the sugar to the fruit; stir to dissolve. Set remaining sugar aside. Add 1/3 ounce sodium bisulfite for each *10 gallons* of the mixture. Then add 1/3 teaspoon of yeast for each gallon of mixture. Cover with cheesecloth, and let stand to begin fermentation. Add the remaining sugar in 3 daily batches, and when all sugar is added, strain out the pulp and bottle the mixture. Let fermentation continue in the bottles—*do not seal* bottles until fermentation is complete. When there is no more bubbling, or "working" of the mixture, fermentation is complete. Seal the bottles. Lay them on their side in a large cooking vessel. Fill vessel with hot water and heat slowly to 130 degrees F. Remove from the heat and let set for 10 minutes. Set bottles on a rack to cool, then store them in a cool, dark place until ready to serve.

—University of Alaska, Cooperative Extension Service

Whaling Vessel: Caught in the Ice
University of Alaska Archives
Barret Willoughby Collection

Cranberry Wine Punch

Yield: approximately 30 servings

1 pound lingonberries, or regular cranberries
1 quart boiling water
2 cups sugar
1 bottle (750 ml) Burgundy or other red dinner wine, chilled
1 6-ounce can frozen orange juice concentrate
1/3 cup lemon juice
1 2-liter bottle sparkling water, chilled

Cook cranberries in boiling water until they pop; strain through a fine sieve. Add sugar; stir over low heat to dissolve. Chill. At serving time, mix the cranberry juice, wine, orange juice concentrate, and lemon juice in a punch bowl. Add a large block of ice and sparkling water; stir well. This is also good as a wine cooler, served over ice cubes in tall glasses.

—University of Alaska, Cooperative Extension Service

In 1897 the ice pack off of Point Barrow closed in on many whaling vessels with crews numbering in the hundreds. The survivors were very hard pressed to keep from starving to death during the encroaching winter. Miraculously, the commander of a rescue cutter called "The Bear" drove a large herd of reindeer to Point Barrow in the latter part of the winter. He saved the day for many hungry people.

Dandelion
by April Kelley

Dandelion Flower Wine

Yield: 8 pints

4 quarts dandelion flowers
4 quarts boiling water
1 envelope active dry yeast

3 pounds sugar
3 oranges, diced
3 lemons, diced

Select fresh flowers and be careful all the stems have been removed. Pour boiling water over the flowers and let stand three days. Strain the juice into a glass, stainless steel or earthenware container; add the remaining ingredients and let stand for three weeks, until fermented. Strain, bottle, and seal the mixture.

—University of Alaska, Cooperative Extension Service

Low-bush Cranberry Liqueur

Yield: 3 fifths

This recipe is well known all over Alaska and we have found it in many people's recipe collections and in several different books. Diane remembers being served this liqueur within days of arriving in Alaska. It preserves the true berry flavor very well and always brings back memories of cranberry picking (in your well-guarded secret cranberry patch) on a cold, bright September day.

3 quarts lingonberries
1 fifth 190-proof alcohol

6 cups sugar
3 cups water

Crush or grind the berries into a 1-gallon stainless steel, glass or earthenware pot. Let them stand for 24 hours in a cool place. Add the alcohol, cover, and let stand for another 24 hours.

Strain the juice and alcohol so that no pulp remains. (First use a sieve, then a jelly bag or a triple layer of cheesecloth). Cook the sugar and water together briefly to make a clear syrup. Skim off any scum that forms on the surface while cooking. Cool the syrup, and mix it with the juice-alcohol solution, stirring very well. Bottle the liqueur, cap, and set aside to "age" for a minimum of 3 months.

Kuspuk is the Eskimo parka worn by women. They are made of brightly colored calico material. Infants can be carried inside the loosely cut back.

Wilderness Cream Liqueur

Yield: 1 quart

1¼ cups Irish whiskey
1½ teaspoons instant coffee powder
¼ teaspoon almond extract
2 egg yolks, lightly beaten

1 14-ounce can sweetened
   condensed milk—*not* evaporated!
1 cup heavy cream

Combine all ingredients thoroughly with a whisk, or beat lightly with a mixer. Keep refrigerated.

Stone lamps were used traditionally by the Inupiat. The people burned seal oil in stone lamps or stoves, using moss along the edge as a wick. In order to make fire, drill sets were used until matches were obtained in more recent years.

Lighting a Stone Lamp
by April Kelley
reference: Fairbanks Daily News-Miner

Hot Buttered Rum Mix

1 pound butter, softened
1 pound light brown sugar
1 pound powdered sugar
1 teaspoon vanilla

1 teaspoon nutmeg
Dash of allspice
1 quart vanilla ice cream, softened

Mix all ingredients together by hand or using a mixer. Store in the freezer. To use for hot buttered rum: for each cup place 1 tablespoon of the mix into a mug. Add 1 jigger of rum, and fill the mug with boiling water. Stir and serve hot.

Christmas Spiced Brandy (Glogg)

Yield: 12 or more servings

1 750-milliliter bottle of claret or
   burgundy wine
10 cardamon seeds
6 whole cloves
1 stick cinnamon
1 cup whole blanched almonds

1 cup raisins
$^1/_2$ cup candied orange peel, sliced
$^1/_2$ pound sugar cubes
1 750-milliliter bottle of brandy,
   aquavit, or cognac

Mix all ingredients, except sugar cubes and brandy, in a large suacepan. Cover and heat just to boiling point. Lower heat and simmer for a few minutes. Place sugar cubes in serving kettle. Warm 1 cup of the brandy and pour over sugar cubes; ignite with a match and let burn until sugar is melted. Add remaining brandy, then stir in the heated wine mixture. Serve warm. May be served ahead, cooled, and heated in the amounts needed.

Sod homes have been replaced by framed ones in this modern day. The sod homes provided insulation and protection from the severe winter winds that sometimes could bring on a chill factor of minus one hundred degrees Fahrenheit in the early half of this century.

Fairbanks Martini

Make your favorite martini. In place of a cocktail onion or olive, use a tiny, home-pickled green tomato.

Traditionally, wood fires were used to melt permafrost cellars. This would take months or years for success. Nowadays, steam boilers are used. Using this method, it takes about a month to make a useable cellar.

Johnny Busia's Home Brew

Johnny Busia was very well known for his home brew, and very reluctant to give out his recipe, but he relented sometime in 1949 or 1950. Johnny shared his home brew with visitors both in winter and in summer. It was well-aged and good in the winter, and slightly green in the summer—sometimes just bottled, in fact!

½ 16 oz. package hops
4 gallons water
7 pounds sugar
1 can malt extract

5 gallons cold water
¾ teaspoon yeast
Additional sugar

Boil the hops in the 4 gallons water for 30 minutes. Add the sugar and the malt; boil for 30 minutes more. Put into a crock and add the 5 gallons of cold water. Stir in the yeast very thoroughly and let set in a warm place 3 days, or until mixture stops bubbling. Put 1 teaspoon of sugar in each quart bottle, and bottle the beer. Keep filled and capped bottles in a warm place for 3 days and then store in a cool place.

—Ree Nancarrow, Denali National Park

Freeze-up is the term applied to the freezing of rivers, lakes, and ground in the fall and early part of the winters.
Break-up is the general term applied to the melting and disappearance of ice from rivers, lakes, sloughs, and tundra in the early part of spring.

THE CENTRAL AND ST. LAWRENCE ISLAND YUPIK

The Yupik Eskimos are a happy people, closely bound to family and village life.

Yupik Finery
by April Kelley

Elders from the communities have great respect among people. It is from the elders that traditional dances and ways of life are passed from generation to generation.

Like the Inupiat Eskimos, they love their children and laughter. Like all people in remote areas of Alaska, they have adapted well to the use of the snowmobile, computer, CB radio, and satellite communications to television sets in their living areas. They live in a modern world but still are a subsistence people, making use of living off the land each season of the year to a good extent.

The Siberian Yupik live on Saint Lawrence Island. The Central Yupik live in an area which encompasses the Southwest Coastal Lowlands and extends east into the Upper Kuskokwim River area. Saint Matthew and Nunivak islands are included in their area. Both the Yukon delta area and the Kuskokwim delta areas, containing thousands of lakes and ponds, provide a variety of waterfowl, fish, and game animals for the Yupik subsistence economy. The majority of this area is a treeless tundra, although some forested areas are found along the Yukon and Kuskokwim rivers.

Another area in which the Central Yupik live is Bristol Bay, which includes the drainages of the Togiak and Nushagak rivers, Illiamna, Naknek, and Becharof lakes, plus the area of the Alaska Peninsula to the 160th meridian. This region is dominated by two mountain ranges which curve around Bristol Bay. They are the Ahklun Mountains to the west and north and the Aleutian range to the southeast. These two mountain systems and the Nushagak-Big River Hills to the northeast form the watershed for the valuable river and lake systems that are the nursery for the famous Bristol Bay salmon runs.

The Bristol Bay area is known worldwide for its annual salmon runs, which produce about thirty percent of the total Alaska salmon pack. Moreover, nearly ninety percent of the Bristol Bay pack is made up of the highly-valued red salmon. People come from all over Alaska and other states to participate in the Bristol Bay salmon fishing season, working in canneries, and fishing the bay, with small gill net boats.

Fishing and trapping are very important to the Yupik economy of subsistence, especially if there is no cash economy to depend upon. Bethel is the primary city in the area. It acts as a service and distribution center, attracting natives from the surrounding villages for better employment opportunities, health and hospital facilities, schools, and housing. Dillingham, located at the head of Nushagak Bay, is the largest village in the Bristol Bay area. Around Bristol Bay is outstanding sport fishing. The area's lakes offer several varieties and sizes of fish, unexcelled anywhere in Alaska. Thousands of fishermen visit the area each year in spite of its relative inaccessibility. Most of the recreational fishing has been in the King Salmon area in past years. Today increased attention is being paid to Lake Illiamna and the more remote Wood River and Tikchik lakes.

The Yupik are a happy and genuine people, bound to areas of bountiful natural resources, that are a great part of their traditional subsistence lifestyles.

Jigging For Tomcod
by Rachel Levine

Jigging for tomcod is a popular activity in the early winter. Tomcod livers can be made into a delicious paté.

$\mathcal{A}$ PPETIZERS

Appetizers mean party foods, for the most part. Since so many Alaskan specialties are rich seafood delicacies, or spicy pickled and smoked foods, these may be
many people's favorites. Many a party has been given, potluck style, just for a
chance to sample the otherwise sinful goodies: "Bring some of that Chitina
salmon you smoked last summer!" and similar requests are heard often.

Traditional native potlatches are particularly welcome parties for Alaska natives
who have moved out of the villages to a city. This is a chance to sample the
traditional foods, delicacies, and treats (usually a whole meal), as well as a time to
join in dancing, singing, storytelling, and visiting. While an "appetizer" in traditional
native meals would have no special meaning, some native recipes in this chapter
might be called "appetizers" because they are specially prepared delicacies eaten
in small amounts as a treat or as a party food.

You will notice the large number of seafood recipes in this chapter. There is
plenty of logic in this, as Alaskan seafood is expensive, unless you gather it
yourself. It makes sense to serve luxury foods such as crab and shrimp either on
special occasions, such as parties, or in smaller amounts as hors d'oeuvres or a first
course. Of course, no one should turn up his nose at a good crab casserole (and
there are several in the Seafoods chapter), but for the most part, luxury foods are
best "shown off" as appetizers.

Again, with appetizers such as pickled herring or pickled beets, we see the
Scandinavian and Russian influences on Alaskan cooking. And many traditional
native dishes, such as salmon eggs or smoked salmon, have become equally
popular throughout the state.

Alaskan Smoked Salmon

Smoked salmon is served literally hundreds of ways in Alaskan cooking. Although it was once most important as a staple food, with the smoking used as a food preservation method, this tasty delicacy now shows up most frequently with party foods or on buffet tables. Many Alaskans smoke their own freshly-caught salmon, using their own "secret" brine solutions and smokehouses or portable smokers. It's always a treat to sample the smoked salmon prepared by different people with different varieties of salmon, or fish, caught in different regions of the state.

Here is the basic method of smoking salmon: Smoke only fish that is absolutely fresh. As soon as possible after it is caught, remove the head, fins, and entrails, then wash in salt water. Cut each side of the fish into two strips the length of the fish. Do not remove the skin. You may allow the ends to hold together, not cutting entirely through the flesh, so that you may hang the strips over a pole in the smokehouse, or you may cut entirely through the flesh and tie a string through the end to tie on the ridge of the pole.

Soak in a brine of ½ cup salt to 1 gallon of water for 4 hours. Rinse in clear, cold water; drain and dry.

Hang the strips over a rack in the smokehouse. Use a smoldering fire of non-resinous wood such as alder. *Do not* let the fish become hot enough to drip fat. Keep a steady fire for about 100 hours (four days and nights), so that the fish will be dry and evenly smoked. It should be a dark brown color. Store by wrapping in oiled paper and hanging in a bag in a cool place. Do not wrap it airtight, as this has caused food poisoning under some circumstances. Smoked salmon may also be wrapped in freezer paper and stored frozen. Serve in slices cut paper-thin, with cream cheese and toasted sourdough French bread.

Salmon Party Ball

This is a well-known recipe, and one that is always popular.

1 1-pound can red salmon
1 8-ounce package cream cheese, at room temperature
1 tablespoon lemon juice
2 teaspoons grated onion
1 teaspoon prepared horseradish

¼ teaspoon salt
¼ teaspoon Liquid Smoke*
1/3 cup finely chopped nuts (pecans, walnuts, or almonds)
3 tablespoons minced parsley
Crackers for serving

Drain and flake the salmon, removing skin and bones. combine salmon with the cream cheese, lemon juice, onion, horseradish, salt, and Liquid Smoke. Mix thoroughly, then cover and chill several hours. Combine nuts and parsley in a shallow dish. Mold salmon mixture quickly into a ball and roll in the nuts and parsley. Keep refrigerated until ready to serve as a spread with crackers.

*Instead of salt and Liquid Smoke you may use ¼ teaspoon of hickory smoked salt.

> *In the spring, smelts, blackfish, whitefish, pike, king salmon, sheefish, dog salmon, silver salmon, herring, flounder, and sculpin are caught. Ground squirrels, black bear, muskrats, birds, eggs, mink, and beluga are also eaten. Sourdock and marsh marigold are two popular spring-time traditional greens. During this time of the year beaver trapping begins. Most trappers take their furs to Dillingham in March for the annual "Beaver Round Up," for sale to fur buyers.*

*Half Man-Half Animal (Red Fox) Mask
by Rachel Levine*

The halo mask is a traditional mask of the Central Yupik speaking people.

Special Salmon Quiche

Yield: 6 to 8 appetizer servings

CRUST

1 cup whole wheat flour
2/3 cup shredded cheddar cheese
1/4 cup chopped almonds

1/2 teaspoon salt
1/4 teaspoon paprika
6 tablespoons salad oil

Preheat oven to 400 degrees F. Mix all ingredients well. Reserve 1/2 cup of crumbs and press the remainder into a 9-inch pie plate. Bake at 400 degrees F. for 10 minutes. Remove from the oven.

SALMON FILLING

3 beaten eggs
1 cup sour cream
1/4 cup mayonnaise or salad dressing
1 1-pound can salmon, flaked and
  bones removed

1/2 cup liquid from canned salmon
1/2 cup shredded sharp cheddar cheese
1 tablespoon grated onion
1/4 teaspoon dried dillweed
3 drops hot sauce

Lower oven temperature to 325 degrees F. Whisk together the eggs, sour cream, and mayonnaise. Stir in remaining ingredients until well mixed. Spoon filling into crust (see directions above), sprinkle with reserved 1/2 cup crust crumbs, and bake at 325 degrees F. for 45 minutes.

—Lorna Nelson, Anchorage

Yupik Eskimos braid herring and grass into ropes, which are put over fish racks. The grass and fish dry at the same time, after which the fish heads are broken off and left with the grass. The remainder of the fish is stored in open grass baskets for future use. The Yupik utilize everything around them, traditionally. In past years, when furs were scarce, bird skins were used for boots, gloves, and hoods. Seal-gut rain gear and sealskin pants and boots were often used. Grass served as an insulation for boots and as fibers for ropes and baskets.

Alaska Salmon Nuggets

Yield: 6 servings

1 1-pound can salmon
1 tablespoon grated onion

Dash pepper
1 egg, well beaten

¹/₄ teaspoon salt
¹/₄ teaspoon celery salt
1 teaspoon Worcestershire sauce
¹/₂ cup mashed potato
1 tablespoon butter or other fat

¹/₄ pound sharp cheese, cut into ³/₈-inch
  cubes
1 cup dry bread crumbs
Oil or fat for deep frying

Drain and flake the salmon. Combine all ingredients except cheese and crumbs, and mix thoroughly. Shape mixture into balls the size of walnuts. Insert a cheese cube into the center of each ball and reshape. Roll in bread crumbs. Fry in deep fat, 375 degrees F., for 3 to 4 minutes or until golden brown. Serve hot, plain, or with a sauce.

—University of Alaska, Cooperative Extension Service

Salmon
by Rachel Levine

Gravlax with Mustard Sauce

This dish is nearly as popular in Alaska as it is in Scandinavia, where it originated. Fresh dill grows very well in Alaskan gardens, or it can be found in grocery stores during "canning" season.

4-to-5-pound piece of salmon, cut in half and boned (leave skin on)
¼ cup coarse salt
¼ cup sugar
2 tablespoons peppercorns (preferably white), crushed or coarsely ground
2 large bunches fresh dill
2 loaves thinly sliced whole wheat pumpernickel bread
Mustard Sauce (see recipe below)

To cure the salmon: Put half the salmon, skin side down, in a glass dish. Combine the salt, sugar, and pepper and sprinkle on the fish, covering the whole side. Spread the dill over the seasonings. Put the other half of salmon over the dill, skin side up. Cover with plastic wrap. Put a smaller dish on top of the salmon and weigh it down with a heavy object. Refrigerate for 3 to 4 days, turning the salmon every day. To serve, remove the fish from the marinade. Wipe clean and pat dry. Slice each side on the diagonal into thin pieces, much as you would smoked salmon. Serve on half-slices of whole wheat pumpernickel, topped with Mustard Sauce.

Mustard Sauce

4 tablespoons Dijon mustard
1 teaspoon dry mustard
3 tablespoons sugar

2 tablespoons white vinegar
1/3 cup light vegetable oil
1 small bunch dill, finely chopped

Combine the mustards, sugar, and vinegar in a bowl or food processor. Whisk or process in the oil, drop by drop, until mixture is thick. Stir in the dill. Refrigerate until ready to use—up to 3 weeks.

—Virginia Doyle "Bunny" Heiner, Fairbanks

In the summer, ducks, geese, herring, flounder, tomcod, muskrats, cloudberries, pike, whitefish, seal, dog salmon, red salmon, king salmon, and sheefish are available for subsistence use. After the salmon are caught they are dried on racks for winter use. If the fish is used for human consumption, the backbone is usually taken out by filleting. If the fish is used for dog food, the backbone is left in.

Picking Berries
by Rachel Levine

The harvesting of cloudberries, crowberries, blueberries, and low-bush cranberries is continuous throughout the fall in southwest Alaska tundra areas.

Canape Fillings Using Alaska Kippered Salmon

Russian Canape: Mix kippered salmon with mayonnaise to a paste; spread on thin slices of onion and place on toast or rye bread. Garnish with paprika.

Alaska Canape: Mix kippered salmon with chopped hard-boiled egg, or mashed hard-boiled egg yolk, and enough mayonnaise or salad dressing to moisten. Spread on unbuttered toast.

Yukon Canape: Mix kippered salmon with mayonnaise to a paste; spread on toast. Top with a piece of bacon to cover. Brown in a hot oven until bacon is crisp.

—University of Alaska, Cooperative Extension Service

Salmon Doughnuts

Yield: 15 appetizers

1 1-pound salmon, drained and flaked
½ cup mashed potatoes
1 tablespoon lemon juice
½ teaspoon Worcestershire sauce
½ teaspoon salt

Dash of pepper
1 egg, beaten
1 tablespoon grated onion
1 cup dry bread crumbs

Combine all ingredients except bread crumbs; chill 1 hour. Roll and cut with a doughnut cutter. Roll in bread crumbs. Fry in deep fat, 375 degrees F., for 5 minutes or until golden brown. Drain on absorbent paper and serve hot, with a tartar or cocktail sauce.

—*Alaska Seafood Recipes,* Ketchikan

Alaskan Caviar-Filled Eggs

Hard-boiled eggs
Red salmon caviar (or whitefish caviar)
Anchovy paste

Capers, chopped
Vinegar
Olive Oil

Cut hard-boiled eggs lengthwise and replace the yolks of half of them with red salmon caviar or whitefish caviar, or both. Arrange on a platter with lettuce, alternating colors of yolk and caviar. Mash yolks with a little anchovy paste, chopped capers, vinegar and olive oil; serve as a sauce with the eggs.

—U.S. Bureau of Fisheries

Salted Salmon Eggs

Fresh salmon eggs
Table salt to taste

Soak fresh salmon eggs in cold water until hard (1 hour for eggs not in a membrane, as long as overnight for eggs in a membrane). Drain water from the eggs and add table salt to taste.

Eskimo Salmon Egg Appetizer

Salmon eggs
Rock salt
Water

Wild onions, chopped
Fresh bread

Soak salmon eggs in 100% brine, made from salt and water, for 10 minutes. Drain. Chop fresh, wild onions and add to the drained eggs. Serve on fresh bread.

Hot Shrimp Dip

Yield: Serves a party

3 8-ounce packages cream cheese
1 pint cottage cheese
1 pound cooked shrimp (fresh or
   frozen)

1 cup chopped onion
1 cup chopped tomatoes
1 4-ounce can green chili, chopped
Drops of hot sauce, optional

Mix all ingredients. Heat slowly in a double boiler to blend flavors. Serve with wheat crackers.

—Wynola Possenti, Fairbanks

Salmon Eggs and Herring Eggs

Salmon eggs
Herring eggs
Seaweed

Grease
Mayonnaise
Soy or Worcestershire sauce

Clean eggs with water. Cook in boiling, salted water until eggs are medium soft. Serve salmon eggs mixed with some seaweed and a little grease. Or mix salmon eggs with mayonnaise and put into a salad.

After cooking, herring eggs are good served with melted butter or ooligan grease, and some soy sauce or Worcestershire sauce.

—Tsimshian recipe, Metlakatla

Hot Crab Dip

8 ounces cream cheese, at room
    temperature
1 tablespoon milk
1 6½-ounce can crab meat
2 tablespoons finely chopped onion

½ teaspoon prepared horseradish
¼ teaspoon salt
¼ teaspoon pepper
Blanched slivered almonds

Mix all ingredients except the almonds in a small, ovenproof casserole, or dish which can be placed on a candle warmer. Top with slivered almonds. Bake at 375 for 15 minutes, or until bubbly and creamy. Keep warm, and serve with melba toast or substantial crackers.

—Alaska Airlines is Cookin, Anchorage

Chevak Dancers
by April Kelley

Dance masks of the Chevak and Marshall Yupik dancers are wonderfully expressive. The Yupik dancers show a lot of whimsy and grace while wearing wolverine hats during their traditional cultural dances, which portray hunting and other parts of their subsistence lifestyle.

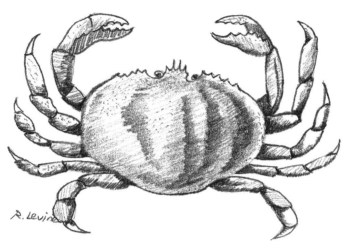

Crab
by Rachel Levine

Crab Mold

8 ounces cream cheese, at room
  temperature
1 cup mayonnaise
1 6½ or 7-ounce can crab meat
1 cup celery

2 or 3 scallions, chopped
1 can cream of mushroom soup
1 envelope unflavored gelatine
2 tablespoons cold water

Beat the cream cheese until smooth, and stir in the mayonnaise. Stir in the crab meat, celery, and scallions. Heat the can of soup until bubbly. Soften the gelatine in the cold water; stir into the soup until gelatine is dissolved. Stir this into the cheese/crab mixture. Lightly oil a 1-quart mold. Fill the mold with the mixture and refrigerate for at least 3 hours to set. Unmold and serve with crackers.

—Lorna Nelson, Fairbanks

Crab Salad in Puff Shells

Yield: approximately 36 filled puffs

1 cup crab meat
½ cup finely chopped celery
1 teaspoon lemon juice

¼ teaspoon celery salt
½ teaspoon salt
Dash of pepper

1 teaspoon grated onion
1 tablespoon chopped sweet pickle

¼ cup mayonnaise or salad dressing
36 small puff shells (see recipe below)

Pick apart crab meat and combine all ingredients except puff shells; mix well and chill. Before serving, cut tops from puff shells and fill with crab mixture. Replace tops and garnish as desired.

Puff Shells

½ cup boiling water
¼ cup butter or margarine
⅛ teaspoon salt

½ cup flour
2 eggs

Preheat oven to 450 degrees F. In a saucepan combine boiling water, butter, and salt. Heat until butter is melted. Add the flour all at once, and stir vigorously until the mixture forms a ball and leaves the sides of the pan. Remove from heat. Add the eggs, one at time, beating thoroughly after each addition. Drop by teaspoons onto a greased baking sheet. Bake at 450 degrees F. for 5 minutes; reduce heat to 350 degrees F. and bake 10 minutes longer. Makes about 36 one-inch puff shells. Baked shells may be frozen. Reheat in a moderate oven to re-crisp shells that were frozen, or baked long before serving.

—University of Alaska, Cooperative Extension Service

Crab Mousse

Yield: one party dip

1 envelope unflavored gelatine
3 tablespoons cold water
1 can cream of mushroom soup
8 ounces cream cheese, at room
  temperature

1 cup mayonnaise
1 cup finely chopped celery
6 to 8 finely chopped scallions
8 ounces crab meat

Soften gelatine in the cold water. Heat the soup and add to the gelatine, stirring to dissolve. Add remaining ingredients and mix well. Pour into a lightly oiled mold. Refrigerate until set. Unmold and serve with crackers—Japanese rice crackers are especially good.

—Jane Pryor, Fairbanks

Pastry Crab Puffs with Mustard Dip

Yield: 3 dozen crab puffs

¹/₂ cup water
¹/₈ teaspoon salt
2 tablespoons butter or margarine
6 drops liquid hot pepper seasoning
¹/₂ cup all-purpose flour

2 eggs
1 tablespoon finely chopped fresh or
   freeze-dried chives
1 8-ounce cup crab meat
Salad oil for deep frying

Bring water, salt, butter, and liquid hot pepper seasoning to a full boil in a covered, 2-quart saucepan. Remove lid and add flour all at once; remove from heat and stir vigorously until the mixture forms a ball and leaves the sides of the pan. Beat in eggs, one at a time, until mixture is very smooth. Add chives and crab; stir until blended.

In a deep saucepan, heat 1¹/₂ to 2 inches of salad oil to 370 degrees F. Drop teaspoons of dough into the hot oil and fry, turning occasionally, until golden brown on all sides. Remove from oil and drain. Serve warm, with cocktail picks and Mustard Dip (see recipe below).

Crab puffs may be cooled and frozen. To reheat: Thaw puffs, place on a baking sheet and bake, uncovered, in a 350 degrees F. oven for about 7 minutes or until hot.

Mustard Dip

¹/₂ cup sour cream
2 tablespoons Dijon mustard
1 teaspoon lemon juice

Stir ingredients together until blended.

Crab Dip

1 8-ounce package cream cheese
Small amount of milk
¹/₂ cup sour cream
1 cup crab, drained well and broken
   apart

2 teaspoons lemon juice
1¹/₂ teaspoons Worcestershire sauce
Dash of Accent (optional)
Dash of garlic powder

Soften the cream cheese with a small amount of milk and mix in the remaining ingredients. Refrigerate, and serve with crackers or chips.

—Charlotte Wilbur, Fairbanks

Walrus
by April Kelley

    Traditionally, walrus has been the mainstay of the diet on Saint Lawrence Island for centuries, along with greens, eggs, seal, and fish.

Kodiak Deviled Crabs

Yield: 6 servings

3 slices bacon chopped
1/2 cup chopped celery
1/2 cup chopped onion
1/2 cup chopped mushrooms
Salt and pepper
1 tablespoon flour

1 cup water
2 tablespoons soy sauce
3 cups fresh or canned crab meat
Hard crab shells or ramekins
Cracker crumbs
Melted butter

Braise bacon until brown; add celery, onion, mushrooms, salt, and pepper; sauté until tender. Sprinkle with the flour, and let cook for one minute. Add water and soy suace, and bring to a boil to thicken the mixture. Add the crabmeat and mix well. Fill hard crab shells or ramekins with the mixture. Sprinkle with cracker crumbs and drizzle with melted butter. Bake or broil in a hot oven until browned on the top.

—What's Cooking in Kodiak, Kodiak

Eggs Stuffed with Crab

Yield: 24 stuffed eggs

2 cups crab meat (or 2 8-ounce cans
  crab meat)
1 tablespoon chili sauce
1 teaspoon chopped pimiento
1 teaspoon chopped green pepper

1 teaspoon grated onion
1 cup mayonnaise or salad dressing
1 dozen hard-boiled eggs
5 tomatoes
Lettuce

Remove any shell or cartilage and chop crab meat. Add chili sauce, vegetables, and mayonnaise; chill. Cut eggs in half lengthwise and remove yolks. Fill egg whites with crab mixture. Serve on tomato slices on a bed of lettuce. Garnish with grated egg yolk.

—Alaska Seafood Recipes, Ketchikan

Curried Crab or Shrimp Dip

Yield: one party dip

8 ounces cream cheese, at room
  temperature
1/8 teaspoon salt

2 teaspoons lemon juice
1/2 teaspoon Worcestershire sauce
3/4 cup sour cream

⅛ teaspoon curry powder
1 tablespoon grated onion

1 pound crab or shrimp meat (or 2 7-ounce cans)

Mix cream cheese very well with seasonings and sour cream. Stir in crab or shrimp; chill. This is an excellent dip for vegetables.

—*Alaska Airlines is Cookin,* Anchorage

Spicy Seafood Cocktail

Yield: 4 to 6 servings

1 pound cooked shrimp, crab, or chunks of fish such as halibut
Lettuce leaves
¼ cup finely minced celery
1 8-to 10-ounce bottle chili sauce
1 tablespoon fresh lemon juice
2 heaping teaspoons prepared horseradish
1 tablespoon finely minced onion
1 tablespoon Worcestershire sauce
¼ teaspoon hot sauce
Dash of salt

Arrange seafood attractively on lettuce leaves on chilled small plates or bowls. Combine remaining ingredients and serve over the seafood as an appetizer course.

Shrimp Cocktail
by Rachel Levine

Shrimp with Garlic-Rum Sauce

Yield: approximately 24 appetizer servings

2 pounds medium-raw shrimp with tails, shelled
1/4 pound butter or margarine
1 garlic clove
1/2 cup light rum
3 tablespoons finely chopped parsley
1/2 teaspoon salt
Freshly ground pepper
1 small loaf French bread, sliced

Rinse shrimp in cold water and pat dry with paper towels. Melt the butter in a skillet. Add the garlic, rum, and parsley. Place shrimp in the butter-rum sauce, turning until well-coated. Cook shrimp for 5 to 7 minutes, stirring once or twice until just cooked through. Remove garlic clove. Stir in salt and pepper.

Set shrimp in a dish over a warming candle or other warming tray. Serve with cocktail forks or toothpicks with a basket of thinly sliced French bread along side for catching the sauce.

—Alaska Airlines is Cookin, Anchorage

Marinated Shrimp or Mushrooms

1 1/2 to 2 cups cooked shrimp or 2
   6-ounce cans whole mushrooms
1 medium onion, sliced into rings
2/3 cup tarragon vinegar*
1/2 cup salad oil
1 clove garlic, minced

1 tablespoon sugar
1 1/2 teaspoons salt
2 tablespoons water
Freshly ground black pepper
Dash of hot sauce

Mix and let marinate at least 8 hours. Drain and serve with toothpicks.

*If you are using the shrimp, try using *Alaskan raspberry vinegar* (see Beverage chapter) instead of the tarragon vinegar.

—Bobbi Truax, Fairbanks

Shrimp Cheese Sandwich Triangles

Yield: 6 servings

1/2 pound cooked shrimp

1/4 cup chopped ripe olives

6 ounces cream cheese	1 tablespoon lemon juice
1/2 cup toasted slivered almonds	6 slices buttered white bread
1/2 cup drained crushed pineapple	6 slices buttered whole wheat bread

Chop shrimp. Combine all ingredients except bread. Spread the white bread slices evenly with the shrimp mixture; cover with the whole wheat bread slices. Cut each sandwich diagonally into 4 triangles.

—University of Alaska, Cooperative Extension Service

Splitting a Walrus Hide
by Rachel Levine

Walrus hides are split to make resilient, bendable coverings for the boats used to move through icy areas on walrus-hunting trips.

Pickled Bidarkis

Bidarkis (chitons) are used for food in the Aleutian Islands. They are gathered by scraping them off rocks with a knife.

Clean bidarkis
Worcestershire sauce
Garlic powder
Sliced onion

Soy sauce
Salad oil
Vinegar

Mix all together to your own taste, then store in a jar.

Hot Clam Hors d'oeuvre

Yield: 1 dozen

1 can finely chopped clams, well drained
3 ounces cream cheese, at room
   temperature
1 tablespoon finely chopped onion
1 tablespoon Worcestershire
   sauce

2 drops hot sauce
3 slices bread, crusts trimmed
Butter
Paprika

Mix all ingredients except bread and paprika. Butter bread slices and cut each into 4 squares. Put them under the broiler to toast on the buttered side. Spread the clam mixture on the untoasted sides of the bread. Sprinkle with paprika and put them under the broiler until bubbly and brown.

—Marion Wood, Fairbanks

Abalone Ceviche

1 pound abalone, removed from shell
$1/2$ cup lime juice
1 tablespoon salad oil
$1/2$ teaspoon salt

$1/8$ teaspoon finely chopped garlic
$1/2$ teaspoon white pepper
$1/8$ teaspoon cayenne pepper
Lettuce

1 tablespoon finely chopped onion   Lime slices

Pound abalone until it is paper thin, being careful not to break through the flesh. Cut into bite-sized pieces and place in a deep bowl. Combine lime juice, oil, salt, onion, garlic, pepper, and cayenne pepper in a jar; shake well. Pour over abalone and mix well. Refrigerate for 24 hours. Line a salad bowl or cocktail glasses with lettuce and fill with abalone mixture. Garnish with lime slices, and serve as an appetizer.

—Coffman Cove, Prince of Wales Island

Tiny Bear Meatballs in Sherry Sauce

Yield: 1 pint

1 pound lean bear meat or 1 pound
   very lean pork
2 small "boiling" onions
1 clove garlic
2 tablespoons finely chopped parsley
$1/2$ teaspoon nutmeg
$1/4$ teaspoon cinnamon
$1/4$ teaspoon allspice

1 tablespoon Golden sherry
1 teaspoon salt
$1/4$ teaspoon pepper
1 cup water
1 stick cinnamon
2 whole cloves
$1/2$ cup brown sugar
2/3 cup Golden sherry

Grind bear meat, onions, garlic, and parsley together in a meat grinder or a food processor. Mix in the nutmeg, cinnamon, allspice, 1 tablespoon sherry, salt, and pepper. Chill the mixture, then shape into marble-sized balls. (These may be placed on a cookie sheet and frozen at this point, if desired.) Before serving, bring remaining ingredients to a boil in a large saucepan. Drop in meatballs (thaw if frozen) and cook over medium-high heat, uncovered, until most of the liquid is gone and a syrupy, deep brown sauce remains. Turn onto a rimmed plate, and serve hot with cocktail picks.

High Bushcranberry Pemmican

Dried cranberries

Dried moose meat or caribou meat

2 tablespoons lard per pint of meat

$1/4$ teaspoon sage per pint of meat

Dry cranberries in sunshine or in the oven on low heat. Use one part meat to three parts berries and grind together. Melt lard and pour over the mixture. Add sage and stir well. Place in plastic bags and freeze, or smoke.

Cooking up a Storm, Homer

Oven Method Jerky

3 pounds venison, caribou, or moose

$1/2$ teaspoon Liquid Smoke, in 2 tablespoons water

Uniodized salt to taste

Pepper (optional)

Slice meat $1/4$-inch thick and remove all fat. Lay out in a single layer on a counter surface. Dab each piece with a brush dipped in the Liquid Smoke and water. Salt generously. Sprinkle with pepper if desired. Place strips, layer on layer, in a large bowl or crock. Put a plate on top of the meat and weight it on top. Let stand overnight or at least 6 hours. Remove meat strips from bowl and dry.

Remove oven racks. Stretch meat strips across racks, allowing edges to touch but not overlap. Do not cover entire racks—allow for some air circulation in the oven. Arrange racks so that the top rack is no closer than 4 inches from the top source of heat and the bottom rack is no closer than 4 inches from the bottom of the oven.

Set the oven temperature at 150 degrees F. and let the meat dry for 11 hours. Check early in the drying process. If there is excessive drip, catch it on aluminum foil on a rack near the bottom of the oven. Lower the temperature until the oven feels warm but does not cook the meat. Cool the jerky and store it in an airtight container.

—University of Alaska, Cooperative Extension Service

Muktuk

Muktuk is whale blubber. It is enjoyed fresh or rancid. A chunk is taken between the teeth, and while held straight out, the bite is cut off with a knife. This is chewed until all the whale oil is gone, then the stringy fiber is spit out. The flavor is somewhat like a walnut.

Yupik Man With Skin Boat
by Rachel Levine

Watching for whales is an annual spring pastime for Yupik people who live along coastal areas. The boat is always in a position ready for the hunt.

Pickled Whale Muktuk

Pickled *muktuk* (whale skin) is a delicacy still prepared by modern Eskimo housewives. It is eaten as a snack with coffee or tea. The dish is probably from a mixture of Russian and Eskimo cultures.

Take any size of *muktuk* and wash it. Place it on a table and cut off the excess whale blubber with a sharp knife or the ulu (Eskimo women's knife), leaving an inch of blubber next to the skin. Cut it into 3-by-6-inch chunks and boil it until the muktuk is done (15 or 20 minutes). Test it with a wooden toothpick as it boils to make sure it does not overcook and become rubbery. It is done when a toothpick just runs through it easily. Cool muktuk and slice into ¼-inch-thick slices. Pack the strips into quart jars, and fill the jars with a half-and-half solution of water and vinegar, with onion and spices added. Seal jars tightly and store in a cool place. It will be ready to eat after 3 or 4 days.

—University of Alaska, Cooperative Extension Service
Courtesy Emily Ivanoff Brown, Unalakleet

Fish Balls Supreme

1 pound uncooked halibut
1 pound uncooked salmon
4 slices bread
1 cup water
3 eggs

1 medium onion, grated
1 teaspoon salt
¼ teaspoon cayenne pepper
Butter for frying

Put the uncooked fish through a food chopper twice, or finely chop in a food processor. Soak the bread slices in the water and combine with the fish mixture. Add the eggs, one at a time, beating after each addition. Stir in the remaining ingredients. Shape into small balls and fry slowly in butter. Serve with a tartar sauce or a horseradish-sour cream sauce.

Fish Cakes Alaska

Yield: 1 party snack

1 pound cooked halibut
2 tablespoons melted butter
1 cup milk

12 soda crackers, finely crushed
2 tablespoons finely chopped parsley
1 teaspoon salt

2 egg yolks
1 large boiled potato

¼ teaspoon pepper
Butter for frying

Put cold halibut through a food chopper, or finely chop in a food processor. Mix with the butter, milk, and egg yolks. Put the potato through a sieve, or finely rice it, and blend well with the fish mixture. Add remaining ingredients. In a pan, warm the mixture through but do not cook. Cool, shape into small, roundish cakes, and fry in butter. Serve with a sharp tartar or horseradish sauce.

Halibut Spread

Yield: ¾ cup

1/3 cup flaked cooked halibut
3 tablespoons mayonnaise

5 stuffed olives, finely chopped
1 tablespoon grated Parmesan cheese

Combine all ingredients. Spread on crackers or chips just before serving.

—*Alaska Seafood Recipe,* Ketchikan

Dried Halibut

To make dried halibut: Fillet the fish with a sharp knife and cut it in strips, lengthwise. The strips should be about one-inch wide and one-half-inch thick. Hang the strips outside on a drying rack. Sometimes it only takes three days for very thin ones to dry, but it may take a week for thicker ones to dry. Of course, if it rains, they will take longer to dry.

You can smoke the strips for flavor, if you wish. Hang them outside for 1 day to drip dry, then put them in the smokehouse for one day to smoke. Then hang them back outside again to dry completely.

To store dried halibut, place it in a plastic bag and freeze it.

To eat as a snack: Dip it in seal oil or salad oil with a little soy sauce. You may put some salt on it.

—Fedora Hedrick, Port Graham

Sardine Canapes

Yield: 36 small canapes

½ cup mashed sardines
½ cup grated hard-boiled egg yolk
1 tablespoon lemon juice
⅛ teaspoon Worcestershire sauce

4 tablespoons mayonnaise
Pimiento
Parsley

Blend ingredients together to make a paste. Spread on bread; cut into desired shapes. Garnish with strips of pimiento and parsley.

—University of Alaska, Cooperative Extension Service

Musk Oxen Herd
Fairbanks Daily News-Miner

The musk ox industry is limited to Nunivak Island where they are managed very successfully. The musk ox industry is also significant and successful.

Pickled Fish

Salted salmon
Onions, sliced
Garlic, chopped
Carrots, sliced
1 Apple, sliced

1 Orange, sliced
1 Lemon, sliced
Pickling spices
Vinegar
Brown sugar

Soak out the salt salmon for two days in fresh water. Cut into bite-sized chunks. In a large jar, put layers of the salmon and the remaining ingredients, except vinegar and brown sugar, until jar is full. Dilute vinegar by half with water; add some brown sugar, and pour over all. Let stand covered for 3 days. Keep in a cool place.

—Sanna LeVan, Seward

At the turn of the century, Yupik families would go off in the winter to frozen lakes. There they fished for trout through the ice with hooks. Frozen trout, stacked like cordwood, were brought back to the villages by dog team, and distributed to villagers for subsistence.

Herring Salad

Yield: 4 servings

1 salt herring
4 medium boiled potatoes
5 boiled beets
1½ tablespoons finely chopped onion
4 tablespoons mild vinegar

2 tablespoons sugar
¼ teaspoon pepper
2 hard-boiled eggs
½ cup heavy cream

Soak herring in water overnight; clean, and remove bones. Dice herring, potatoes, and beets very small; season with other ingredients—except cream—and mix well. Serve in a mound, garnished with hard-boiled egg slices. Add cream just before serving.

Golden Heart Cookbook, Fairbanks

Spiced Pickled Herring

2 dozen small herring
Salt
Boiling water
2 medium-sized onions
2 small lemons
Paprika

1 quart vinegar
1/2 cup whole mixed pickling spices
Salt to taste
1/2 cup sugar
1/2 cup vegetable oil

Scale and clean the herring, cutting off the heads and tails. Place them in a steamer 1 layer deep, sprinkle with salt, cover, and steam over boiling water until they are barely cooked but not falling apart (about 5 minutes). Remove to an earthenware dish or a crock, and repeat until all the fish are steamed. Slice the onions and lemons very thin, and lay over the fish. You may add a bay leaf if you wish. Dust with paprika.

Heat together the vinegar, spices, salt, and sugar; cook gently over medium heat for 20 minutes. Strain out the spices, allow to cook, and add the oil. Pour over the fish. The herring will keep in a cool place for two to three weeks.

Kayaks, made from seal or walrus skins that are stretched over driftwood frames, are light for portaging any distance. They are also sturdy enough to withstand the sometime heavy maritime storms, which plague the coastal areas at certain times of the year during food quest activities.

Alaskan Herring Salad

6 herring, salted
Pickled Cucumbers
Mustard Pickles
Pickled beans
Capers
Alaskan smoked salmon

6 large apples, finely chopped
1 onion, grated
Mayonnaise
Hard-boiled eggs, sliced
Nuts

Soak herring in water for 24 hours; skin, bone, and cut into small pieces. Cut into very small lengths the pickled cucumbers, mustard pickles, pickled beans, and capers. Add 1/2 pound Alaskan smoked salmon, cut in pieces; add the apples, and onion. Mix thoroughly with a rich mayonnaise. Chill overnight, then serve garnished with sliced hard-boiled eggs, nuts, and capers.

—U.S. Bureau of Fisheries

During the winter lingcod, grayling, whitefish, sheefish, pike, black-fish, and needlefish are caught for subsistence use, along with beaver, rabbit, ptarmigan, muskrats, seal, caribou, moose, spruce hens, mink, seal, and walrus.

Favorite Pickled Salmon or Herring

Yield: 4 pints

1½ to 2 pounds salmon or 12 medium-sized herring, filleted
1 quart cider vinegar
1 pint white vinegar
3 cups brown sugar

3 ounces whole pickling spice
2 medium white onions, sliced
Bay leaves
Red chili peppers, for color

If salt herring is used, soak it in fresh water until excess salt taste has disappeared. Simmer together the vinegars, sugar, and spices for 2 to 3 hours. Cut the fish into 1-inch lengths or cubes. Using sterilized pint jars, put a layer of sliced onion on the bottom with a bay leaf; add fish to within 1 inch of the top. Cover fish in the jars with the vinegar mixture, and top the filled jars with another layer of onion and a few chill peppers. Screw on lids. Let stand at least 2 days or longer, if possible.

—University of Alaska, Cooperative Extension Service

Seaweed Chips

This "munchie" is made in the Aleutian Islands and the southern coastal areas of Alaska, where fresh seaweed is available.

Rinse your seaweed (preferably in clean ocean water) and hang it up to dry. Cut it into 1½-inch pieces, put up to 2 cups into the basket of a deep-fat fryer, and fry very briefly in very hot oil—1 to 3 seconds. Drain. These may be sprinkled with sesame seeds or sugar.

"Mousenuts," which are bits of root and Eriophorum seedlings that are found in underground mouse caches around tundra lakes and ponds in the fall in southwest coastal lowland regions, are eaten. In past years they were stored in tightly sealed, unlined ground pits. Today they are put in gunny sacks and stored in a cool place. This is a traditional food. In recent times they are not used in the quantities as past years. Also during this time of year moose, mink, ducks, and geese are sought after.

Hrutka Cheese

This is an unusual Russian-Alaskan dish from Kenai, Alaska.

1 dozen eggs
1 quart milk
1 teaspoon salt

3 tablespoons sugar
½ teaspoon vanilla

Combine all ingredients well and cook slowly until the eggs coagulate. Drain through a large piece of cheesecloth and hang up so it may drip for about 3 hours. Form a ball and remove from cloth. If desired, rub with butter; brown in a 400 degree F. oven for 10 minutes. Serve in thin slices.

Fish caught by Nushagak area residents were dried on racks. Traditionally, the heads were sometimes buried in the ground and allowed to ripen slightly before being eaten. Fish eggs were put up in seal oil and were considered, traditionally, a delicacy to be eaten during festivals in long winter months.

Crispy Seaweed

Gather black seaweed. Dry it outside in the sun, turning it often so it dries thoroughly. Before it is completely dry, flavor it with sugar, salt water, clam juice, or gum boot eggs which have been soaked overnight. Then put it into the oven to roast. It will be done when it's crispy. Store it in jars and nibble on it all year long.

Tsimshian recipe, Metlakatla

Wild Mushrooms Tempura

Edible wild Alaskan mushrooms, such as "Orange Delicious," are favorites of many pioneer families. Frying them in butter, salt, and pepper to make a gravy has been a favorite treat each fall when these mushrooms are abundantly growing in black spruce forests. Cooking them oriental style is a mouth-watering treat!

Yield: 1 quart

1 cup flour
1 cup cornstarch
1/3 cup baking powder
Beer

1 quart cleaned mushrooms
Oil or fat for deep frying
Garlic powder
Dried herbs

Sift together the flour, cornstarch, and baking powder. To 2 heaping table-spoons of this mixture, add enough beer to make the thickness of pancake batter. Dip mushrooms in batter and deep fry, at 375 degrees F., until golden brown. This same batter may be used for fish or seafood. You may add some dried herbs and a little garlic powder to the batter when frying mushrooms, for even more flavor.

—Phelpsie Sirlin, Fairbanks

Boletus Species Mushroom
by Rachel Levine

Danish Buttermilk Soup

Yield: 6 servings

½ cup raisins
4 ounces ground rice
2 quarts buttermilk
½ teaspoon grated lemon peel
1 stick cinnamon

2 egg yolks
1 tablespoon sugar
Almonds for garnish, chopped
Unsweetened whipped cream for
   garnish

Let raisins soak in boiling water, to cover, until they are plump. In a saucepan, gradually stir buttermilk into ground rice. Add lemon peel, cinnamon stick, and the raisins. Heat mixture, stirring constantly, just until hot—do not let it boil. Whisk egg yolks and sugar together in a cup and add some of the hot mixture, whisking to blend. Return yolk mixture to the saucepan and whisk just until blended. Serve immediately, garnished with the chopped almonds and unsweetened whipped cream.

THE TSIMSHIAN

The Tsimshian Indians, who have a different language from the Tlingits and

Weaving Baskets
by April Kelley

Southeastern linguistic cultures are well known for their lovely baskets.

Haidas, migrated to Annette Island from Fort Simpson, British Columbia fairly recently in comparison to the Yupik and Aleuts who populated western Alaska about nine thousand years ago.

In the mid-1800s William Duncan, a Scottish lay preacher, established at Old

Metlakatla, British Columbia a Christian community of Tsimshian Indians. The community prospered. The Indians built homes and practiced arts and crafts, and the community established its own stores and industries. This tiny village became a trading rival of the well known Hudson Bay Company. After about twenty-five years, Duncan encountered ecclesiastical as well as governmental difficulties while in British Columbia. He was replaced. So Duncan visited Washington, D.C. in 1887, seeking a home in southeastern Alaska for his devoted followers. He sought to purchase an area of land for his ministry, and eventually obtained "squatter's rights" to the land by encouraging government officials. The Old Metlakatla Tsimshians emigrated from British Columbia and settled on one of the group of Annette Islands in the southern part of southeastern Alaska. They numbered about eight hundred and came under the guidance of Duncan and his missionary staff. Their new village was called "New Metlakatla," and by 1890 had a well-equipped store, a salmon-canning plant, a sawmill, a trade school, and a mission church. On March 3, 1891 a government act set apart the Annette Islands as a reservation for the Metlakatla Tsimshian Indians. Duncan remained at Metlakatla until his death in 1918. Afterwards the federal government took over the salmon cannery and the school.

Ketchikan Spruce Mill leased the sawmill at Metlakatla and named it the Annette Hemlock Mill. It produces cants made of hemlock for export. Since ninety-two percent of southeastern Alaska is covered with lush forested land, it is the most productive timberland in the state. The forests are composed of fifty-eight per-cent hemlock, thirty-seven percent Sitka spruce, and five percent of other softwoods—mainly cedar. In southeastern Alaska the selects, peelers, and No. 1 logs comprise about nine percent of the saw timber volume. The earliest use of the timber was for shelter and fuel. Lumber production along with local consump-tion, such as fish-trap logs and material for fish boxes, accounted for most of the commercial use prior to World War II.

The spruce-root hats made by the Tsimshians in years past, when they lived in British Columbia, were subtle in their painted decorations. Some people believe that the woven crest hat with attached basketry may have been Tsimshian, originally. Beautiful twined basketry has been traditionally made by the Tsimshians for centuries using split spruce roots.

Fish are caught for use individually or for the cold storage plant and cannery. There are three or four floating fish traps in use in the Metlakatla area. All other fish traps in the state of Alaska have been abolished. Subsistence utilization of fish and game resources are important to the modern-day Tsimshian.

VEGETABLES AND SALADS

In Alaskan cooking, vegetable recipes are hard to find. All this means is that Alaskans like their vegetables and salads plain and simple. There is no lack of delicious vegetables grown in the state, commercially or by enthusiastic home gardeners, and certainly no lack of vegetables and salads on the dinner plate. In addition, greens and other wild vegetables grow in virtually every part of Alaska. The wild greens are especially important and valued in the diets of many Alaskan native peoples, whose diets traditionally would be mostly fish and meat.

The simplest methods of cooking, such as boiling, steaming, or even microwaving, are perfectly suited to Alaskan vegetables. Some vegetables, such as cabbage, cauliflower, and broccoli—which can be strong-flavored or tough when grown in warmer climates—grow unusually sweet and tender in Alaska. In the Interior, vegetables such as cabbage and squash can grow very large, even to giant proportions, due to the long daylight hours and relatively warm summer climate. Often a home gardener will be surprised that a very large vegetable, such as that "forgotten" zucchini, can still be tender and tasty.

Although Alaskans now enjoy a variety of vegetables, the staple and "winter" vegetables—potatoes, carrots, and cabbage—played the biggest role in older Alaskan recipes. These are easily grown in most parts of the state and are easy to store. They form a practical beginning to vegetable recipes which we consider truly Alaskan.

Tomato Aspic

1 can tomato sauce, diluted with 1 can water
1 box lemon-flavored gelatine
1 envelope unflavored gelatine, softened in small amount of cold water
1 can tomato soup
1 tablespoon Worcestershire sauce
1/4 teaspon hot sauce
1/4 teaspoon garlic powder

Heat the tomato sauce and water to the boiling point; add the lemon-flavored gelatine. Stir the plain, softened gelatine into the tomato soup, and add to the mixture. Stir in seasonings. Pour into a mold and chill to set for several hours. Crab, shrimp, or tuna may be added to this basic aspic.

—Dorothy Wilbur, Fairbanks

The baskets made by the Tlingits, Haidas, and Tsimshians were used for food storage and cooking in years past. They were quite large in comparison to the ones we see today. Hot rocks were tossed into the baskets to make water boil within them. The people dug underground pits or cellars for storing foods, the bottom or sides of which were lined with bark. A bark roof was placed over the pit as well, and covered with dirt. Many vegetables were stored in barrels made of bark, then buried in the pits. Dried meat was stored in bark barrels lined with deerskin. The southeastern Indians ate many roots. The root they liked the best was the wild sweet potato or "silverweed." Sometimes they boiled them, and sometimes they baked them on hot stones and then dried them. When the dried roots were to be eaten, they were soaked in water or added to a meat stew. Leaves and softened stalks were often eaten—boiled, like spinach.

Atkan Plants

During the summers, plants such as wild parsnip, cow parsnip and petruskies (prestuskies) are gathered. The parsnips are peeled and eaten with seal oil. Petruskies, sometimes called wild parsley, are used with all fish soups and with boiled sea mammal meats.

Berries are gathered up on the hills and made into jelly, which is eaten with bread. Berries are also eaten mixed with mashed, cooked fish.

—Atka, Aleutian Islands

Sarana (wild rice) is gathered in July and cooked in the following way:

Wild Rice

After gathering wild rice, wash it and take the bulbs off. Then fill a pot with cold water, add the rice, and cook it. When the water begins to boil, drain and refill with cold water. When it boils, drain and refill the water again. Bring to a boil and cook until done. Drain, and remove the lid from the pot. Place the pot into an oven and let it dry there. It is delicious served with boiled fish.

The wild crab apple, Malus rivularis, was used only sparingly by the natives of southeastern Alaska. A jam was made of wild crab apples in traditional times.

Cranberry Salad

Yield: 12 servings

2 packages of any red gelatine
2 cups boiling water
1 cup sugar
2 cups cranberries

1 whole orange, ground
1 can crushed pineapple
1 cup chopped walnuts
1 cup chopped celery

Dissolve the gelatine in boiling water; add sugar. When cool, add all other ingredients. Let set.

DRESSING

1 orange, juice and grated rind
1 lemon, juice and grated rind
1 heaping teaspoon of flour

1 egg, well beaten
$1/2$ cup of sugar
$1/2$ cup whipped cream

Cook over hot water until thick. When cool, add whipped cream.

—Gwen Weston, Fairbanks

69

Old Style Cabbage

Yield: 6 servings

Local cabbage, chopped
Meat drippings
Salt to taste
1 tablespoon sugar

1 tablespoon flour
1 tablespoon vinegar
1 egg
Cream

    Cook cabbage in meat drippings. Add water, cover, and cook until tender. Add salt to taste, sugar, flour, and vinegar. Break the egg into a cup and beat; fill cup with cream. Add to cabbage just before serving.

—From the *Nome Cookbook,* Nome

*Cabbage
by April Kelley*

German Hot Cabbage

Yield: 4 to 6 servings

1 medium cabbage, sliced
1/4 cup butter
2 medium onions, chopped
1 large apple, chopped

1 bay leaf
2 tablespoons vinegar
1 tablespoon brown sugar

Simmer cabbage with remaining ingredients in a covered pan until thoroughly tender.

—From the *Golden Heart Cookbook*, Fairbanks

Sweet and Sour Cabbage

Yield: 4 to 6 servings

5 cups shredded cabbage
6 slices bacon
2 tablespoons brown sugar
2 tablespoons flour

1/2 cup water
1/3 cup vinegar
1 small onion, sliced
Salt and pepper

Cook the cabbage in boiling, salted water for 7 minutes. Fry bacon, remove from the pan, and chop; set aside. Add sugar and flour to the bacon fat (some of the bacon fat may be removed if desired). Blend. Add water, vinegar, and seasonings. Cook until thick; add onion, bacon, and cabbage. Heat through.

—Mike Dalton, Fairbanks

Cabbage Soup

Yield: 2 to 4 servings

½ head of new, green cabbage
1 large potato, pared
1 large onion
4 tablespoons water

1 cup milk
Salt and pepper
¼ cup butter

Shred the cabbage; cut the potato and onion into thin slices and add to the cabbage. Place in a heavy container with the water, cover tightly, and simmer slowly until very tender. Mash very well or put through a sieve. Add the milk, salt, pepper, and butter; reheat until hot, but do not boil.

—From the *Golden Heart Cookbook,* Fairbanks

Batter Fried Cauliflower

Yield: 6 large servings

1 large cauliflower head broken down into flowerettes, boiled in salt water for 10 minutes and drained.

BATTER

2 eggs, lightly beaten
2 tablespoons of flour
Salt to taste.

Mix and dip the cauliflower into the batter. Fry in olive oil until nicely browned and tender when tested with a fork.

—Eleanor Contento, Fairbanks

The Tsimshian totem carvers were well noted for bold, simple figures and flowing lines that were often repeated the length of tall columns. Their figures are relaxed and seldom crowded for space. There are six general types of totem poles carved by the Tlingits, Haidas, and Tsimshians. The heraldic pole proclaimed the social standing of the chief or head of the house. It bore the family crests and was attached to the front of the building and often had an egg-shaped entrance large enough for a person to enter. The memorial poles were generally erected for deceased chiefs. A shame or ridicule pole was a method of psychological warfare among different chiefs. It would depict a dishonorable act, like breaking one's word. The potlatch pole was the largest when raised and was one over which much rivalry developed. It was erected on occasions of important ritualistic or festive observances. Wealthy chiefs always wanted to outdo rivals in wealth and power by carving the "best" pole, filled with many figures—a declaration of their own strong ingenuity. Mortuary poles were used to deposit the coffin of the dead. The pole had a section removed to receive the entombed body. Often, the body was cremated and the ashes deposited into the crypt. House pillars—inside house pillars, or posts, and false house pillars—were important in traditional houses. Many had crests of the individual owners.

Homemade Sauerkraut

Yield: 100 8-ounce servings

Stone crock of 5 gallon capacity
40 to 50 pounds cabbage
1 pound plain salt

Remove outside leaves of cabbage; quarter and core. Shred about 5 pounds of cabbage at a time, using a scale to carefully measure. Add 3 tablespoons of salt. Measure the salt carefully, as too much salt will prevent proper fermentation.

Pack the cabbage carefully and evenly into a 5-gallon stone crock and pack or tamp with a wooden tamper until the juice comes. A baseball bat works wonders! Add 5 pounds of shredded cabbage each time and tamp down each time as you go.

Cover the cabbage with 2 or 3 layers of cheesecloth. You can tuck the cheesecloth down along the sides. Place a large plate over the cheesecloth and weigh it down with a stone heavy enough to cover the plate with juice.

Remove the scum every few days, and wash the plate, cheesecloth and stone before replacing it over the kraut.

Let the kraut stand for 2 or 3 weeks in a 70 degree F. room. Freeze the kraut in plastic bags or set the crock in a cool (40 degree F.) dark place, and take out the kraut as you need it. You can also preserve sauerkraut by canning.

—Pat Babcock, Fairbanks

Bald Eagle
by April Kelley

The bald eagle is often seen perched on trees along the southeastern coast.

New Green Salad

Yield: 6 servings

1 pound fresh spinach
3 slices bacon, chopped
1 tablespoon chopped onion
6 tablespoons vinegar

1¼ teaspoons salt
⅛ teaspoon pepper
1 tablespoon sugar
½ cup canned milk

Wash spinach and remove stems. Drain spinach thoroughly and cut into thin strips with scissors. Cook the bacon until crisp; add onions, and cook slowly for 5 minutes. Remove from the heat and add vinegar, salt, pepper, and sugar. Stir in the milk slowly. Pour over the spinach and mix well. Serve at once.

—Meredith Eide, *The Petersburg Cookbook*

Traditionally, the Tlingits, Haidas, and Tsimshians loved to dance. They danced for many reasons. Their dance was often a prayer to the god of rain, sun, or almost anything in nature, which had a high spiritual value. Shamans tried to heal the sick while performing unusual dances. They danced when someone died, or for a wedding, or before a hunting trip, or just to entertain one another. A dance was always a big occasion. Dancers wore costumes and masks. The drummer was very important, for he was both the orchestra and the conductor, beating out a steady rhythm while he watched the dancers feet. They often sang too or made noises with rattles or clappers.

Shrimp Potato Salad #1

Yield: 6 servings

6 cups cooked cubed potatoes
6 hard-boiled eggs, chopped
1½ cups chopped celery
1 medium onion, finely chopped
2 teaspoons salt
½ teaspoon celery seed

1 large dill pickle or 2 sweet pickles, chopped
½ cucumber, chopped
2 cups tiny cooked shrimp
Mayonnaise to moisten well

Mix all ingredients. Check to see if more salt is needed. Serve. This may also be broiled briefly on halved buttered buns and topped with grated cheese.

—Mrs. Vern E. Smith, Wrangell

Traditionally, the Indian fisherman of southeastern Alaska wore shirts, robes, and blankets made of bearskin or the fine, soft skin of the sea otter. A few tribes wove blankets out of mountain goat or sheep hair. Others made clothing out of cedar bark.

Winter Salad

Yield: 6 servings

2 cups grated carrot
2 cups unpeeled and diced apple

$\frac{1}{2}$ cup finely chopped onion
Mayonnaise or oil and vinegar dressing

Mix carrots with apple and onion. Let stand about 15 minutes, then mix with mayonnaise or oil and vinegar dressing.

—St. Matthew's Guild, Fairbanks

Among many others, some of the flora traditionally used by the Indians of Southeastern Alaska included: wild celery, silverweed, wintercress, beach greens, blueberry, blackberry, American red currant, trailing black currant, nagoonberry, trailing raspberry and black lily. For emergency use only commandra, buckbean, yellow pond lilies, red berried elder, soapberry and hemlock, were gathered.

Carrot Souffle

1 cup cooked, mashed carrots
1 cup medium white sauce
$\frac{1}{2}$ cup grated cheese
1 tablespoon finely ground onions

Salt
Paprika
2 egg yolks
2 egg whites

Preheat oven to 350 degrees F. Mix all ingredients except egg whites. Stiffly beat the whites and fold into the vegetable mixture. Turn into a buttered baking dish. Set in hot water and bake for 30 minutes at 350 degrees F. Any vegetable, especially spinach, can be used in this recipe.

—From the *Nome Cookbook,* Nome

The Indians of southeastern Alaska in traditional times used the western red cedar for building material. They burned through the trunks to fell the trees and then split them into planks with wedges of horn or wood. The cross planks were tied with roots to the upright planks. Some of the homes were more than fifty feet long and would hold eight to ten families. They were divided into compartments by hanging mats.

Bunchberry Dogwood
by April Kelley

Bunchberry dogwood, a low-growing plant, is often seen covering the ground in spruce and birch forests.

Green Tomato Stew

1 apple, chopped
2 small onions, sliced
3 green tomatoes, sliced

1 teaspoon sugar
¼ teaspoon salt
1 cup water

Simmer all ingredients together over low heat until tender. Serve as a vegetable.

—From the *Nome Cookbook,* Nome

*Garden Vegetables
by April Kelley*

Turnip Slaw

1 cup sour cream
1 tablespoon sugar
1 tablespoon vinegar

1 teaspoon salt
4 cups shredded turnips

Whisk together the sour cream, sugar, vinegar, and salt; pour over turnips and mix well.

—From the *Nome Cookbook,* Nome

Copper Pennies

This marinated carrot recipe is widely found among Alaskan cooks. Since Alaskan carrots grow so sweet, the tangy sauce makes a good contrast of flavors.

2 pounds carrots, sliced ½-inch thick
1 small onion, thinly sliced
1 can condensed tomato soup
½ cup salad oil

1 teaspoon prepared mustard
Salt and pepper to taste
¾ cup vinegar
1 small green pepper, thinly sliced

Steam the carrot slices until tender. Meanwhile, heat the remaining ingredients, simmer for about 5 minutes, and pour over the carrots. When cool, refrigerate overnight. Serve cold.

Cold Pea Salad

1 20-ounce package frozen peas
1/2 teaspoon sugar
1 cup sour cream
1 teaspoon garlic salt
1/2 teaspoon freshly ground pepper

1 tablespoon lemon juice
2 tablespoons cream-style horseradish
Bacon bits
Tomato wedges
Deviled eggs

Cook peas very briefly with the sugar and drain well in a colander. Refrigerate for at least 2 hours. Add sour cream, garlic salt, pepper, lemon juice, and horseradish; chill for at least another hour before serving. Serve on chilled plates. Sprinkle with bacon bits, and serve with tomato wedges and deviled eggs.

—From *Alaska Airlines is Cookin,* Anchorage

Potato Pancakes 1

Potatoes grow abundantly in Alaskan gardens, and potato pancakes are perfect served with a dinner of fried moose sausage and lingonberries.

Yield: 12 or more pancakes

2 large-sized raw potatoes, grated
1 teaspoon salt
1/4 teaspoon pepper

1/4 cup flour
1/4 teaspoon baking powder
2 eggs, well beaten

Add to potatoes salt, pepper, flour, and baking powder; mix in the eggs. Drop by tablespoons on a hot, well-greased griddle. Pat out flat and fry about three minutes on each side or until golden brown.

—Ruth Olson, Fairbanks

Potato Pancakes 2

Yield: 18 or more pancakes

6 raw potatoes, grated
¼ teaspoon baking powder
1 tablespoon flour (or more if potatoes
   are very watery

1 teaspoon salt
1 egg
1 small onion, grated

Mix all ingredients together, drop by tablespoons on a hot, greased skillet, and fry on both sides until golden brown, and insides are tender.

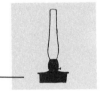

Potato Pancakes 3

Yield: 1 serving

1 medium raw potato, medium-finely grated
2 eggs

Salt and pepper
Bacon fat

Mix grated potato, eggs, and salt and pepper. Fry tablespoons of the mixture in bacon fat in a cast-iron skillet.

—Phelpsie Sirlin, Fairbanks

Hot Potato Salad

Yield: 4 to 6 servings

6 medium-cooked potatoes, chopped
¼ cup finely chopped onion
4 slices bacon
1¾ teaspoons salt

4 tablespoons vinegar
1 beaten egg
2 hard-boiled eggs, sliced

Mix potatoes and onion. Chop bacon and fry until crisp. Add salt and vinegar, and stir into beaten egg while hot. Pour over potatoes and onion. Place in top of double boiler and heat until warmed through. Serve topped with hard-boiled egg slices.

—*Golden Heart Cookbook,* Fairbanks

Basket of Potatoes
by April Kelley

Northern Cranberry Salad

Yield: 6 to 8 servings

2 cups sugar
¹/₂ cup water
4 cups (1 pound) Alaskan lingonberries
1¹/₂ envelopes unflavored gelatine

4 tablespoons cold water
1 tablespoon lemon juice
1 cup chopped nuts
1 cup chopped celery

Boil sugar and ¹/₂ cup water together until sugar is dissolved. Add cranberries and boil until they pop. Soften the gelatine in the 4 tablespoons cold water and add to the hot cranberries, stirring until gelatine is dissolved. Let cool and add remaining ingredients. Pour into molds (if desired) and chill until set.

— *Golden Heart Cookbook*, Fairbanks

Pioneer Salad Dressing

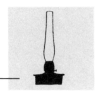

Yield: 1 pint

2 tablespoons flour
1/2 cup sugar
1 teaspoon dry mustard
1 egg

1/2 cup vinegar
1 1/2 cups hot water
2 tablespoons butter
Cream or canned milk

In a saucepan stir together the flour, sugar, and mustard. Add the egg and vinegar, and gradually whisk in the hot water. Add the butter and bring to a boil, stirring constantly. Cool completely and stir in cream or canned milk until dressing is of desired consistency.

—Golden Heart Cookbook, Fairbanks

THE PIONEERS

The original pioneers, new settlers coming into Alaska for the first time, were

Dogmushing
Jeff Studdert Collection

hardy trail blazing men and women. These people helped to make Alaska the powerful state it is today. Many men and women blazed trails throughout the

S. S. YUKON

J. S. McCANN, Master

DINNER

Tanana Radishes	Green Onions		Leaf Lettuce
Dawson Tomatoes		Queen Olives	

SOUPS

Consomme Clear   Cream of Oyster

FISH

Baked Yukon Salmon Maitre d'Hotel

ENTREES

Boiled Brisket of Alaska Beef, Spanish Sauce

Macaroni au Gratin   Pineapple Fritters au Jus

ROASTS

Stuffed Haunch of Native Veal
Roast Chicken with Alaska Currant Jelly

VEGETABLES

Mashed Potatoes   Yukon Spinach   Garden Peas

DESSERT

Bonanza Plum Pudding, Hard Rock Sauce
Sourdough Blueberry Pie   Cheechaco Apple Pie
Assorted '98 Cakes   Golden Fruit
Nuggets of Cheese   Christie's Crackers

Tea   Coffee   Cocoa

Made in U. S. A.

Menu: S.S. Yukon
University of Alaska Archives
Edby Davis Collection

Arcade Cafe

Harry Gleaves, Prop.
Dawson, Yukon Territory, Canada
DISCOVERY DAY, AUGUST 17, 1935

MENU

SOUP

Rice Tomato   Chicken Consomme, a la Pinska

FISH

Fresh-Caught King Salmon, Fishwheel Fry ....$ .75

BOILED

Pelly River Chicken, Bonanza Nuggets 1.00

ENTREES

Baby Moose Steak, Wiley Post's Delight.. .75

Eldorado Caribou Cutlets, Will Rogers' Special .... .75

Pork Sausage and Mashed Potatoes, Nigger Jim's Favorite .... .75

Combination Cold Lunch, Iceworm Salad .... .75

Sirloin Steak, Chechaco's Delight 1.00

T-Bone Steak, Fairbanks Special 1.25

Lamb Chops, a la Bob Service Grill 1.00

ROASTS

Stuffed Young Tom Turkey, Trail of '98 .... 1.50

Leg of Pork, Diamond Tooth Gertie Apple Sauce.................... 1.00

Prime Ribs of Beef, Klondike Kate's Delight 1.00

Milk-Fed Chicken, Husky Dressing, Lone Star Roast 1.25

COLD MEATS

Young Chicken and Pure Gold Salad 1.00

VEGETABLES

Yukon-Grown Steamed and Mashed Potatoes

Garden Island Combination Vegetables

SALADS

Combination Salad, Goldstream Dressing 1.00

Sliced Tomatoes and Cucumbers, Frank Cleary Dressing .... .75

DESSERT

Ridgetop Pumpkin Pie............. .25   Fresh Glacier Apple Pie.......... .25

Frozen North Five-Egg Custard Pie, .25

EXTRAS

Chicken Tamales .... .75   Chili Con Carne .... .75

Tomato Soup .... .550   Fresh Cows' Milk .... .25

Asparagus Tips, with Skookum Jim Mayonnaise, 1.00

Northern Lights Tea—Bear Creek Ice Water—Midnight Dome Coffee

THE LAND OF SUNSHINE AND PURE GOLD

state in areas untouched by any other people. They drifted down turbulent streams and made their camps in remote areas during spring, summer, and fall. Many of them endured the long, silent, cold, and snowy winters and became strong by their experience. The pioneers coming into Alaska also had their dreams. Alaska's charm filled their spirit, and they realized the closeness of man with nature through many wilderness experiences.

Russian seafarers, Vitus Bering and Alexei Chirikov, both from Siberian Kamchatka, came to Alaska in 1741. Vitus was the first to sight Mount Saint Elias in southeastern Alaska on July 16, 1741 and landed ashore on Kayak Island the same day. As the years progressed, Russian fur traders quested for soft and luxurious sea otter pelts. Their fur trading companies were set up, and a settlement was established at Three Saints Bay on Kodiak Island, in the Gulf of Alaska, in 1784. A Russian trading post was established along the Yukon River at Nulato in 1830. On March 30, 1867 Alaska was purchased by the United States from the Russians for $7.2 million.

The whaling industry in the Beaufort Sea north of Point Barrow was a big business. Many of the whalers had San Francisco, California as their base. In the late 1800s, commercial fishing for salmon spread from southeastern Alaska into the Gulf of Alaska bringing Japanese, Chinese, Filipino, and Mexican fishing fleets. Many canneries were established. Many Norwegians settled in the fjords of southeastern Alaska. Consequently, Petersburg is often called "Little Norway." Fur and timber industries continued to strengthen as the years went by.

Throughout the years, the pioneer spirit lingers on. In some areas we experience ice, fog, recalcitrant automobiles in sub-zero winter, frozen water pipes, dismal cold of winter, and mosquitoes of summer as part of the Alaskan lifestyle. We all join the trail blazer of bygone days in strong spirit.

ℬREADS

Alaskan breads seem almost synonymous with sourdough, that tangy mixture with the wild flavor. There are many Alaskan recipes for sourdough breads, and those who keep and "feed" a sourdough starter also may use it to flavor and leaven hotcakes, muffins, and even cakes. Much folklore surrounds sourdough, and every Alaskan seems to claim that his sourdough starter is over one hundred years old, or travelled over the Chilkoot Pass, or was kept for fifty years by a native woman in Sleetmute, *etcetera*. It does not matter if the stories are true—they somehow make the breads seem tastier! Alaskan sourdough has a different flavor than sourdough starters kept elsewhere because each region will have its own strains of wild yeast which populate the sourdough.

Alaskans enjoy many other traditional breads, such as Scandinavian specialties brought by early settlers, and delicious quick breads and muffins using wild berries. Fried bread dough is popular among some native peoples and sometimes fish roe is added to the dough to make it tastier.

Breads are a perfect complement to the simple, hearty, and homey cooking that is widely regarded as "Alaskan." The tasty jams, pickles, and condiments which go well with Alaskan meats are delicious with the bread as well, and you would not have an Alaskan breakfast without sourdough hotcakes or blueberry muffins. It is natural that bread baking seems more popular here than in other states.

Traditionally, in back of the wood stove was the favorite spot for rising bread dough, and this remains true today. However, as modern life has caught up with Alaskans, there is more and more dough being raised in another warm spot—on top of the television set! So bake and enjoy some of these typical Alaskan breads. And if you are given a cup of sourdough starter, we hope that it comes with a bit of Alaskan history and folklore.

Sternwheeler
by April Kelley

Stern-wheelers brought supplies to many pioneer families along the Yukon River and its tributaries.

Blueberry Loaf

This loaf is lower in calories than most sweet breads since it contains no fat or oil.

2 cups sifted flour
1 teaspoon baking powder
1/2 teaspoon salt
3/4 cup sugar

1 egg
1 tablespoon grated orange rind
3/4 cup orange juice
1 cup blueberries

Preheat oven to 350 degrees F. Sift together the dry ingredients. In a separate bowl beat the egg and orange rind; add the orange juice and stir into dry ingredients. Mix lightly. Stir in blueberries. Turn into a greased loaf pan. Bake at 350 degrees F. for 50 minutes. Store in a tightly covered container for several hours or overnight before serving.

—From *Alaska Airlines is Cookin,* Anchorage

The first steamboat came up the Yukon River in 1869, bringing with it people from many culinary backgrounds. Practical pioneer ways of cooking evolved: some food items were stored in root cellars, dug into the permanently frozen ground; shelves of food were lowered into deep cellars and brought up again by hand-cranked pulleys; some food was pickled or smoked for preservation; some pioneers kept their food cool by submerging watertight containers in small streams; and others had screened-in shelves near the coolness of the streams.

Beer Bread

Yield: 3 small loaves

3 cups self-rising flour or add 1 tablespoon *each* salt, soda, and baking
powder to all-purpose flour

3 tablespoons sugar
12 ounces beer
1/2 cup melted butter or margarine

Preheat oven to 350 degrees F. Mix the flour and sugar with a wooden spoon and gradually stir in the beer. Turn batter into three foil loaf pans (6-by-3-inch size), and drizzle the melted butter over the tops. Bake at 350 degrees F. for 50 minutes.

—From *Alaska Airlines is Cookin,* Anchorage

Alaska Beer Rolls

Yield: 3 to 4 dozen

12 ounces light or dark beer—
    preferably Alaskan home brew
2 packages active dry yeast
1 13-ounce can evaporated milk,
    lukewarm
6 tablespoons soft shortening

1 tablespoon salt
3 tablespoons sugar
7½ cups (approximately) unbleached
    white flour
Butter or margarine, melted

Warm the beer in a saucepan or microwave oven until warm (not hot). Transfer to a large bowl and sprinkle on the yeast to soften; stir to dissolve the yeast. Add the evaporated milk, shortening, salt, sugar, and half the flour. Beat with a wooden spoon until very smooth; add enough remaining flour to make a soft dough. Knead for 5 to 10 minutes, until dough is smooth and elastic. Shape into a ball and place in a greased bowl. Cover with plastic wrap or a kitchen towel and let rise in a warm place for about 1 hour, or until doubled in size. Punch dough down and cut into 3 or 4 dozen equal pieces. Shape each into a ball by flattening and rolling under with your hand. Pinch to seal the underside of each roll. Place 1 inch apart in greased pans (such as muffin tins or shallow cake pans). Let rise until light, about 30 minutes. Preheat oven to 425 degrees F. Brush tops of rolls with melted butter or margarine. Bake at 425 degrees F. for 10 to 12 minutes. Remove from pans to cool if not serving immediately. May be packaged when cool, and frozen. The beer gives these rolls a very light, soft, texture and a wonderful malty flavor.

Jack McQuesten, Arthur Harper, and Al Mayo, well known traders, arrived on the Yukon River in 1873. Gold was discovered in southeastern Alaska in Juneau in 1880, bringing to Alaska many pioneers. Some of the adventurous men and women found gold in other areas, such as near the Fortymile River, a tributary of the Yukon, in 1886.

Blueberry Buckle

½ cup sugar
2 cups flour
2½ teaspoons baking powder
¼ teaspoon salt
1 egg

¼ cup melted fat
½ cup milk
1 pint blueberries
Crumb topping (recipe follows)

Preheat oven to 350 degrees F. Sift sugar, flour, baking powder, and salt into a bowl. Make a well in this mixture and add the egg, melted fat, and milk. Beat the liquid ingredients, then slowly stir just enough to mix with the flour. Pour into a greased 13-by-9 inch shallow, glass baking dish. Cover with the blueberries, top with crumb topping and bake at 350 degrees F. for 40 to 50 minutes.

CRUMB TOPPING

$^1/_2$ cup sugar
$^1/_3$ cup flour

$^1/_2$ teaspoon cinnamon
$^1/_4$ cup butter, at room temperature

Mix ingredients together until crumbly.

—University of Alaska, Cooperative Extension Service

Blueberry Kuchen

1 cup firmly packed brown sugar
4 teaspoons cinnamon
1 teaspoon salt
$^1/_3$ cup butter or margarine, at room temperature
1$^1/_3$ cups crumbled shredded wheat biscuit or 1$^1/_3$ cups packaged corn flake crumbs
$^1/_2$ cup chopped nutmeats
1 1-pound, 4-ounce package white cake mix, prepared according to package directions
1$^1/_4$ cups fresh or frozen blueberries

Combine sugar, cinnamon, salt, and butter; mix well with a pastry blender. Add shredded wheat or cornflake crumbs and nutmeats; blend thoroughly. Sprinkle 1$^1/_2$ cups of crumb mixture over bottom of a greased 13-by-9-inch baking pan. Preheat oven to 350 degrees F. Prepare cake mix and spread evenly over crumbs. Sprinkle drained blueberries and remaining crumb mixture onto cake batter. Bake at 350 degrees F. for about 40 minutes, or until done. Serve warm or cold.

—University of Alaska, Cooperative Extension Service

Blueberry Muffins

2½ cups flour
½ cup sugar
3 teaspoons baking powder
½ teaspoon salt

1½ cups blueberries
2 eggs, well beaten
3 tablespoons butter, melted
1 cup milk

Preheat oven to 450 degrees F. Sift together the flour, sugar, baking powder, and salt. Mix berries with ¼ of this mixture, and set aside. Beat eggs and melted butter together. Add flour mixture alternately with the milk. Do not overmix. Lightly stir in blueberries. Bake in greased muffin tins at 450 degrees F. for 25 minutes.

—St. Matthew's Guild, Fairbanks

Gold Dredge at Nome
Watercolor by Rachel Levine

Gold dredges mined the streams for millions-of-dollars worth of gold.

Blueberry Pancakes

Yield: 10 pancakes

This recipe uses no shortening or oil.

1 egg
1 cup milk
1/4 teaspoon salt

1 cup flour
2 teaspoons baking powder
1/2 cup blueberries

Beat egg; add milk and salt. Stir together the flour and baking powder, then add to the egg mixture; beat until smooth. Stir in blueberries, and drop spoonfuls on to a hot griddle. Brown both sides.

—From *Alaska Airlines is Cookin*, Anchorage

By 1893 gold was discovered on another tributary of the Yukon River called Birch Creek. Circle City, the then "largest log cabin city in the world," was founded in 1893. Pat Babcock's great grandfather, Joseph Dahl, was a merchant in Circle City, prior to the Canadian gold strikes in the Klondike, near Dawson, by George Carmack in 1896. It was mostly the gold discoveries that brought people into the Interior of Alaska and on to other gold prospects at Anvil Creek near Nome in western Alaska in 1898.

Blueberry Pudding #1

Yield: 6 servings

2 cups blueberries
4 tablespoons sugar
1 cup flour
1 teaspoon baking powder
1/2 teaspoon salt

1/2 cup sugar
1 egg, well beaten
1/4 cup milk
1/2 teaspoon vanilla
2 tablespoons butter, melted

Preheat oven to 350 degrees F. Cover the bottom of an 8-or 9-inch baking dish with blueberries, and sprinkle with the 4 tablespoons sugar. Sift the dry ingredients. Mix the egg separately with the milk, vanilla, and melted butter, and stir into the dry ingredients—only enough to moisten. Spread the batter over the blueberries and bake at 350 degrees F. for about 40 minutes. Invert on a platter and serve either hot or cold with cream.

—St. Matthew's Guild, Fairbanks

Buckwheat Cakes

2 cups flour
2 cups buckwheat flour
1 tablespoon salt

1 tablespoon sugar
1/2 package dry yeast
1 cup warm water

Mix the dry ingredients. Dissolve the yeast in the warm water and gradually add to the dry ingredients. Add enough additional water to make the batter the consistency of pancakes. Let this stand overnight. Bake like pancakes on a lightly greased griddle.

—St. Matthew's Guild, Fairbanks

Circle City Kitchen photograph
by University of Alaska Archives, Circle Collection

The wood-burning stove was the center of activity in many pioneer cabins.

Code of the North

by Joe Ulmer
Past Grand President Pioneers of Alaska

Take a drink with a friend or friends when you have a chance.

When using a man's cabin and before leaving wash the dishes, leave shavings and kindling and as much wood cut as you used. Also, close the door of the cabin. If barricaded against bears, put the barricade back.

Never ask a man what religion he has for the great outdoors is his place of worship.

Never speak of women disrespectfully; we all had mothers.

Always give a fellow a lift if the going is tough.

Don't abuse a dog. He is the best friend you have on the trail. Be kind to dumb animals, they remember you.

Don't kill any game wantonly . . . only what you have to kill for your need or for someone who is out of meat.

Call the musher in and offer him a mug up or feed and if he is tired give him a shakedown.

Don't waste any animal by shooting at them for targets. The last cartridge may save your life.

Keep your matches and footgear dry on the trail and never drink whisky or other spirits on the trail; it may be fatal to you.

Don't wander around when the fog comes in, and you can't see where you're going; wait till it clears up.

Don't leave any lights or candles burning or heavy fire in the stove when you are going away from the cabin.

Don't set fire to the woods. It will destroy the wildlife and game.

Parboil your bacon before frying; it will not cause you so much rheumatism. Also, be sanitary about the camp so not to pollute the water and atmosphere.

Don't tell the other fellow your troubles, especially love or matrimonial affairs. He may have a lot of his own.

Keep off the other fellows trapline, both literally and categorically speaking.

Lingonberry Coffee Cake

2 cups sifted flour
3 teaspoons baking powder
¾ teaspoon salt
½ cup sugar
5 tablespoons butter

1 egg, beaten
½ cup milk
2½ cups lingonberries or low bush
　cranberries
Topping (recipe follows)

Preheat oven to 375 degrees F. Sift flour, baking powder, salt, and sugar into a bowl. Cut in the butter with a pastry blender until crumbly. Separately mix beaten egg and milk; add to the flour mixture, stirring slowly to mix. Beat until well blended. Spread batter evenly into a greased 8-by-8-by-2-inch baking pan. Sprinkle lingonberries evenly over the top. Sprinkle with topping and bake at 375 degrees F. for 30 to 35 minutes.

TOPPING

¼ cup flour
½ cup sugar
3 tablespoons butter

Mix flour and sugar; cut in the butter until crumbly.

—University of Alaska, Cooperative Extension Service

Christmas Swedish Limpa

Yield: 2 loaves

1½ cups warm water
½ cup molasses
⅓ cup sugar
1 tablespoon salt
Finely grated rind of 2 oranges

2 packages active dry yeast
2 tablespoons shortening
2½ cups rye flour
2½ to 3 cups unbleached white flour
1½ cups raisins

Mix warm water, molasses, sugar, salt, and grated orange rind together. Add yeast and shortening, and stir until yeast is dissolved. Add rye flour, then half the white flour and the raisins. Add remaining white flour to make a soft dough that is no longer sticky when kneaded. Knead well and let rise, covered, in a greased bowl. Punch down and let rise again, until doubled in bulk. Shape dough into two round loaves. Place on a lightly greased baking sheet or in greased layer cake pans. Let rise until almost double in bulk (45 to 60 minutes). Preheat oven to 375 degrees F., and bake loaves for 30 to 40 minutes.

—Ruth Olson, Fairbanks

The pioneer prospectors were of various worldwide nationalities, such as Slavic, German, Irish, English, Swedish, and Norwegian. They came from all walks of life, trades, professions, and religions. Some of them only had enough money to get to Alaska. Pat Babcock's great uncle Louie Golden, who was a gambler in Dawson and Nome, made two million-dollar fortunes and lost them again gambling.

Swedish Orange Rolls

Yield: 2 dozen rolls

3 eggs
¹/₂ cup sugar
1 cup milk
3 tablespoons butter

1 package active dry yeast
¹/₂ teaspoon salt
4 cups unbleached white flour

FILLING

¹/₂ cup butter, at room temperature
¹/₂ cup sugar
Grated rind of 1 large orange

Beat eggs slightly and add sugar. Scald the milk and add butter. When milk is lukewarm, add yeast and salt; stir to dissolve. Add to egg and sugar mixture, and mix well. Add 1 cup of the flour and beat thoroughly. Set aside in a warm place to rise until light. Add 3 cups flour; stir but do not knead. Let rise again until light when lifted. Roll out on floured board and spread with mixture of the butter, sugar, and orange rind. Roll up as for jelly roll and cut into 1-inch lengths. Place, cut side down, in greased muffin pans, and let rise again until light. Preheat oven to 400 degrees F. Bake for 15 to 20 minutes.

—Ruth Olson, Fairbanks

Christmas Bread (Stollen)

Yield: 4 loaves

4 cups milk
4 packages active dry yeast
1 tablespoon salt
3 cups sugar
12 cups flour
1 pound butter

5 eggs
1 pound raisins
½ pound citron
Grated rind of 2 lemons
½ pound blanched almonds

Scald 3 cups of the milk, and cool to lukewarm. Dissolve the yeast in the lukewarm milk. Add the salt, sugar, and 4 cups of the flour. Let this mixture rise overnight in a warm place. Scald the other cup of milk, add the butter and stir until melted. Add this mixture plus the eggs to the sponge; add the remaining flour, kneading until dough is no longer sticky. Combine the fruits, rind, and nuts with a little flour and add to the dough before all the flour is used. Shape into 4 loaves, each looking like a flattened round folded in half (like a Parker House roll). Place in greased 8-by-11-inch pans. Let rise for 2 hours, then bake at 375 degrees F. for 40 minutes.

—St. Matthew's Guild, Fairbanks

Norwegian Lefse

This classic Norwegian flat bread was easily baked on Alaskan woodstoves, but a dry skillet placed over medium-low heat can be used.

4 eggs
1 cup granulated sugar
1 cup brown sugar
2 cups buttermilk or sour milk

2 teaspoons baking soda
Pinch of salt
Enough flour to make a soft dough

Blend all ingredients together to make dough. Take a piece of the dough the size of an apple and roll with rolling pin to about the thickness of pie crust. Bake on top of stove on both sides. These can be stacked one on top of the other and stored indefinitely. When ready for use, dip in warm water and lay between dry towels for about 10 minutes or until soft. Spread with butter, sugar, and cinnamon. Fold double with buttered side in, and cut into any desired shape.

—*Golden Heart Cookbook*, Fairbanks

Prospector and Dog
by Rachel Levine

Ready to "hit the trail," a man and his dog.

Norwegian Spritz Cookies

1 cup butter
1¼ cups sugar
2 eggs
3 tablespoons orange juice

Grated rind of 1 orange
¾ cup cornstarch
2½ cups flour

Cream butter and sugar. Beat eggs slightly and add. Add orange juice and grated rind. Sift cornstarch and flour, and add to the mixture. Press through a cookie press and bake at 375 degrees F. for about 10 minutes.

—*Nome Cookbook,* Nome

Norwegian Horns (Crescents)
Yield: 16 cookies

1 stick butter
½ cup sugar
1 egg
4 tablespoons milk or cream
2 cups flour

2½ teaspoons baking powder
Jelly
Egg white
Sugar
Chopped almonds

Cream the butter and sugar; add the egg and milk, and beat well. Add flour and baking powder to make a smooth dough. Divide into 2 parts. Roll each piece into a circle, and cut the circle like a pie in eight wedges. Put a little jelly on each piece, and roll from the outside toward the point. Pull ends to form a horn or crescent shape. Brush each with egg white, and sprinkle with sugar and chopped almonds. Bake at 350 degrees F. for 12 to 15 minutes.

—St. Matthew's Guild, Fairbanks

Finnish Cardamon Braids
Yield: 2 loaves

2 packages active dry yeast
2 cups warm water
1 teaspoon ground cardamon
2 eggs, at room temperature
1/3 cup sugar

1 teaspoon salt
½ cup butter or margarine, at room
    temperature
6 to 6½ cups unbleached white flour
1 tablespoon milk

Sprinkle yeast into the warm water and let set 3 to 5 minutes, then stir to dissolve. Stir in the cardamon, 1 egg, sugar, salt, and butter or margarine. Add about one-half the flour, and beat with a wooden spoon until smooth and elastic. Gradually add enough remaining flour to make a soft dough. Knead for 5 to 10 minutes, until dough is smooth and elastic. Put into a greased bowl, cover, and let rise in a warm place until double, about one hour. Punch down, turn out, and knead until free of bubbles. Cut dough in half, and divide each half into three pieces. Roll each piece into a rope and loosely braid three pieces together for each loaf, pinching ends well to seal. Place loaves onto two greased baking sheets, cover loosely, and let rise about 30 minutes. Preheat oven to 375 degrees F. Mix together the remaining egg and the 1 tablespoon milk; brush over loaves and sprinkle with extra sugar. Bake at 375 degrees F. for 20 to 25 minutes. Reverse upper and lower baking sheets in oven half way through baking so loaves will brown evenly.

—Bonnie Barber, Fairbanks

Prior to the turn of the century, Alaska was a harsh and cruel place to live. People were lured here by dreams of sudden wealth. Many people were unskilled in the ways of the wilderness and not accustomed to the rigors of wintertime in Alaska. Many of the people were unskilled in mining methods and found out the hard way the difficult work needed for gold extraction. These pioneer men and women established little towns along the way, built bridges across many turbulent streams, and endured the long days of summer sunshine, rain, and muddy trails that hummed with the buzz of mosquitoes. It was a tremendous feeling of accomplishment for those pioneers who "stuck it out."

Just Reminiscing
by Pat Babcock

Goldmining Camp
Watercolor by Rachel Levine

Sourdough Griddle Cakes

SOURDOUGH STARTER

Soak ½ yeast cake in ½ cup warm water (preferably in the morning). When dissolved, add 1 cup of warm water and ⅔ cup flour. Beat thoroughly, and let stand until the next morning. This is the starter for the sourdough and by saving a portion of the mixture each time you use it, it will last indefinitely.

GRIDDLE CAKES

The night before you wish to have hotcakes, add the following to the above mixture.

3 cups milk
1 teaspoon salt

4 tablespoons sugar
2 cups flour

Mix thoroughly and keep in a moderately warm place overnight. When you are ready to serve the hotcakes, pour all but a teacupful or so of the mixture into a mixing bowl. The teacup which is saved serves as the starter for the next batch of cakes. Into the mixing bowl add ¹/₂ teaspoon baking soda which has been dissolved in a little hot water. This will cause the mixture to foam and become very light. While the mixture is foaming, add 2 eggs, folding rather than stirring them in. Cook as pancakes on a lightly greased griddle.

Two tablespoons of cornmeal added to the batter will improve the cakes. Do not cover the sourdough crock tightly at any time as it is constantly working. To retard the action of the sourdough, keep in a cool place and sprinkle dry flour over the surface. (You want to do this if you will not be making hotcakes for several days, as the sourdough would continue to work and become rancid.)

The use of milk and eggs in the above recipe make a luxury out of sourdough cakes as compared with those ordinarily used on the trail. The oldtimers who made sourdough cakes famous used nothing but flour, water, salt, and sugar.

—*Golden Heart Cookbook,* Fairbanks

Government came to Alaska in 1900. James Wickersham was appointed as the District Judge at Eagle, which is located on the mighty Yukon River. Felix Pedro made gold strikes on creeks near the present city of Fairbanks, which was founded in 1902—after Pedro's gold strike—by E.T. Barnette on the Chena River, a tributary of the Tanana River, which is a tributary of the Yukon River. Valdez, a southcentral Alaskan coastal town, served as a gateway to gold deposits in the Interior of Alaska. The Valdez Trail and the Yukon River brought many people into the great Interior. The first auto trip between Fairbanks and Valdez was in 1913.

Hot Cakes

1 cup flour
2 teaspoons baking powder
¹/₂ teaspoon salt
2 tablespoons sugar

2 tablespoons melted fat or bacon
  grease
1 egg
1 cup canned evaporated milk

Sift the dry ingredients into a bowl, then add the melted fat, egg, and milk. Beat well and add some cold water, if necessary, to make the proper consistency. Fry on a hot, greased skillet, using as little fat as possible. Serve with Homemade Syrup (recipe follows).

Homemade Syrup

8 cups sugar
Water
2 teaspoons vanilla

Place sugar in a large pot and add enough water to cover the sugar. Boil for 5 minutes, or until clear. Cool and add the vanilla. Store in a covered jar in a cool place.

—Virginia Doyle "Bunny" Heiner, Fairbanks

Fried Dough

2 cups warm water
1 package active dry yeast
4 tablespoons shortening or lard
4 tablespoons sugar

2 teaspoons salt
Seagull eggs (optional)
4 cups flour, approximately
Fat for deep frying

Soften the yeast in the warm water and stir to dissolve. Add the shortening, sugar, salt, and seagull eggs, if used. Mix in enough flour to make a soft dough which is not sticky. Knead until smooth. Spread oil on top of the dough, cover, and set in a warm place until it doubles in size.

Heat the fat for deep frying in a skillet or pot. Cut off pieces of dough the size for making rolls. Roll each piece into a flattened shape and cook in the hot fat until golden brown, or about 3 minutes on each side.

Baked Flour

2 cups flour
2 tablespoons lard
Boiling water

Sugar
Milk (optional)

Put the flour into a bread pan and shake the pan to spread it evenly. Place in a hot oven and bake until all the flour is golden brown, stirring occasionally. Remove from oven, add the lard, and stir until it is mixed in thoroughly. Store the mixture in a jar and serve as follows: add 2 to 3 tablespoons of baked flour to a glass and add boiling water to fill the glass; stir until smooth. Sugar and/or milk can be added.

Pasque Flower
by Rachel Levine

The pasque flower, known by some Alaskans as the crocus, is the first blooming flower that comes up through the spring thawing snow. A welcome bouquet of these lavender- and gold-centered flowers graced the tables of many pioneers after enduring a long cold winter.

By 1923 a railroad connected Anchorage, a southcentral town, with Nenana in the Interior. The development of aviation in the 1920s was an important factor in changing the lifestyle of the pioneer people. They didn't feel so isolated. Bush pilots pioneered the airway to bring communication to many remote areas of Alaska that in previous times could only be reached by dogteam.

Graham Crackers

1 cup sugar
4 tablespoons butter
1/2 cup sour milk

Graham (whole wheat) flour
1/4 teaspoon baking soda

Mix stiff with Graham flour, to which has been added the soda. Roll thin, cut, and bake.

—Golden Heart Cookbook, Fairbanks

Man's Cake

This cake has been made in several generations of Virginia Doyle "Bunny" Heiner's pioneer family from Nome, Alaska.

1 cup granulated sugar
1 cup brown sugar
1 cup shortening
1 teaspoon vanilla
2 eggs
3 1/2 cups flour
4 teaspoons baking powder
1/2 teaspoon salt

2 teaspoons cinnamon
1 teaspoon nutmeg
1 teaspoon pepper
1 teaspoon ginger
2 cups milk
2 cups raisins
1 cup chopped nuts

Preheat oven to 375 degrees F. Cream the sugars and the shortening well, then add the vanilla and eggs. Sift dry ingredients separately, then add them, alternating with the milk. Beat well; add the raisins and nuts. Place in a greased and floured 9-by-13-inch cake pan, and bake at 375 degrees F. for 45 minutes. Tip upside down on a wire rack to cool. Remove pan. This cake is better on the third or fourth day. It is delicious served hot with canned milk.

—Virginia Doyle "Bunny" Heiner, Fairbanks

In the 1930s airfields, roads, and radio beacons pioneered the ways for many people in remote Alaska. Construction of Ladd Air Force Base—which is presently called Fort Wainwright—as a cold weather testing site, began in 1938.

Sourdough Corn Bread

1 cup sourdough starter (see recipe
   page 102)
1½ cups corn meal
1½ cups canned evaporated milk
2 eggs

2 tablespoons sugar
¼ cup butter, melted
½ teaspoon salt
¾ teaspoon baking soda

Preheat oven to 350 degrees F. Mix together the starter, corn meal, milk, eggs, and sugar thoroughly in a large bowl. Stir in the butter, salt, and baking soda. Turn into a greased, heavy 10-inch skillet, or a greased 9-by-13-inch baking pan, and bake at 350 degrees F. for 25 to 30 minutes.

—From *Alaska Airlines is Cookin,* Anchorage

Whole Wheat Walnut Bread

Yield: 1 loaf

1 cup whole wheat flour
1¼ cups all purpose flour
2½ teaspoons baking powder
¾ teaspoon salt
1 teaspoon baking soda

½ cup firmly packed brown sugar
1½ cups sour milk or buttermilk
2 tablespoons salad oil
¾ cup chopped walnuts

Preheat oven to 350 degrees F. Stir together the dry ingredients. Stir in the brown sugar, sour milk, and salad oil, and continue stirring until smooth. Add walnuts, and mix. Pour into a greased and floured 9-by-5-by-3-inch loaf pan and bake at 350 degrees F. for about 1 hour and 20 minutes.

—St. Matthew's Guild, Fairbanks

Buttermilk Rye Bread with Caraway

Yield: 4 loaves

2 medium potatoes
1 pint potato water
2 tablespoons active dry yeast
1 quart buttermilk
4 cups rye flour
12 cups (approximately) unbleached
   white flour

2 tablespoons salt
1 cup sugar
1 cup molasses
1/2 cup shortening
1 tablespoon caraway seeds
1/2 cup orange peel, finely minced or
   grated

Cook and drain potatoes, saving 1 pint potato water, cooled to lukewarm. Dissolve yeast in 1/2 cup of the lukewarm potato water. Mash the potatoes and add the rest of the potato water and the buttermilk. Mix in dissolved yeast, rye flour, 1 cup of the white flour, and the salt. Let rise in a warm place until doubled in bulk. Heat together the sugar, molasses, shortening, caraway seeds, and orange peel until shortening is melted. Cool and add to the first mixture. Add enough remaining white flour to make a soft dough that is no longer sticky. Knead well and let rise in a greased, covered bowl until doubled. Punch down and shape into four loaves. Place in greased loaf pans and let rise again. Preheat oven to 350 degrees F. Bake loaves for 40 to 50 minutes. Remove from pans when baked and let cool on wire racks.

Potato Dinner Rolls

Yield: 3 dozen rolls

1 package active dry yeast
1/2 cup warm water
1 teaspoon sugar
1 cup canned evaporated milk,
   warmed
2/3 cup margarine, melted

2/3 cup sugar
1 teaspoon salt
1 cup mashed potato (1 large potato,
   chopped, cooked, and mashed)
2 eggs
6 to 7 cups unbleached white flour

Soften yeast in the warm water and stir to dissolve. Stir in the sugar and leave to "proof" while preparing the next mixture. Stir together the milk, margarine, sugar, salt, and mashed potato. Add the yeast mixture and the eggs. Beat in approximately half the flour, cover bowl, and let the "sponge" rise until double. Add enough remaining flour to make a soft dough. Knead for 5 to 10 minutes; place in a greased bowl, cover, and let rise until double again. Shape into rolls and place 2 inches apart on greased baking sheets. Brush rolls with melted butter; let rise until double again, about 45 minutes. Preheat over to 425 degrees F., and bake for 8 to 12 minutes.

—From *Alaska Airlines is Cookin,* Anchorage

Fireweed
by Rachel Levine

The fireweed blazed along many pioneer trails.

THE ATHABASKANS

The Athabaskan Indians are a varied lot of people. They speak eleven separate languages in Alaska, and approximately twenty other groups of Athabaskans live in Canada. Other Athabaskans, the Navajo and Apache, live in the southwestern portion of our United States, and still other groups are located in Washington, Oregon, and northern California. In recent years anthropologists and linguists have developed names like Koyukon, Ingalik, Holikachuk, Tanana, Tanacross, Upper Tanana, Upper Kuskokwim, Tanaina, Han, Ahtna, and Kutchin as ways of distinguising the various people.

Boreal forest environments are typical for the Athabaskans. All over the Interior of Alaska are lowlands that are forested with spruce, aspen, birch, willow, and alder. Here live the major game animals that the Athabaskan people subsist upon traditionally: moose, black and brown bear, snowshoe hares, grouse, ptarmigan, caribou, and Dall sheep. The people trap wolf, wolverine, lynx, otter, marten, and mink for a cash economy.

All subsistence is dependent upon where the different Athabaskans live. Their subsistence is traditionally based on hunting, fishing, and trapping. In modern days, goods that are purchased from stores are added to the subsistence of fish and game.

Most of the fishing is done in the summer, when the rivers are heavily laden with king salmon, chum salmon, silver salmon, and different species of whitefish. Most families who live along the many different rivers do their hunting from boats in the fall, when moose in search of mates are seen more often, caribou begin their migrations, and summer-fattened bears prepare to enter their dens. The winter months are devoted to trapping along traplines which run many miles from the various village settlements. Moose, snowshoe hares, grouse, and ptarmigan are hunted for food. In the spring, fish nets are set in the river after the ice goes out. Geese migrating from the south are awaited by hungry people.

Although the Interior of Alaska provides well at times, there are some years when game is scarce. For the Athabaskans that live on the rivers, reliable runs of fish make life more secure.

The Tanaina Athabaskan, who live along the coast in the Cook Inlet region, have access to salt water fish, shellfish, waterfowl, and sea mammals for subsistence. Perhaps this drew them to the coast from the Interior and gave them the strength of mind to displace the Eskimos who lived there before they came, and to adopt some of their technology.

The Athabaskans are skilled in living with the extreme and harsh conditions that exist in the Interior. Temperatures, for instance, can be above ninety degrees Fahrenheit in the summer and minus sixty degrees Fahrenheit or more in the long, dark winters. Snow covers the frozen ground for about six months of the year. Many traditional tools for hunting and fishing are still used despite the modernization of some of the villages.

Athabaskan children are a vital link between the past and future. They are welcomed as an enrichment of family lives, carrying on family traditions and pride. The elders are respected for their wisdom, experience, and knowledge, and they contribute to the children by sharing their ideals with them.

Sharing a Moment
by April Kelley

The elders of any Athabaskan community are well respected for their wisdom.

Village Life
Photo
Fairbanks Daily News-Miner

The riverboats are a must for Athabaskan families who live along the Interior rivers.

M EAT MAIN DISHES

Meats are at the heart of Alaskan cooking. In a state where game animals are relatively abundant and people relatively few, "living off the land" has always meant hunting animals for food. Also, agriculture is fairly new to Alaska and somewhat experimental, despite the tremendous potential in many parts of the state. As a result, Alaska grows very little of its own food and heavily depends on both imports and harvesting of our own wild game resources. Many parts of Alaska, such as the entire Arctic region, are both unsuited to agriculture and still abundant in wild marine and land mammals. Alaskans living in these regions are particularly likely to have a diet rich in meats, mostly wild game meats.

The recipes in this chapter show the tremendous variety of ways, both traditional and modern, that Alaskan meats are prepared and enjoyed. Even amongst city dwellers, meats such as moose, caribou, sheep, and bear are often a big part of family menus. These meats are lean, tasty and nutritious, and are free of feed chemicals and hormones, so many Alaskan families feel very good about having game meats in their diets. In addition, the fat from animals living in cold climates tends to be more unsaturated than fat from beef or pork. Game meats, by the way, cannot be bought in grocery stores: they are brought home by the many sport hunters throughout the state.

Traditionally, almost none of the Alaskan meat harvested was wasted. In the food literature of the state, recipes and descriptions for preparing nearly every part of an animal are always found. For example, in a paper describing the use and preparation of moose and caribou by the Koyukon Athabaskan Indians, sections are devoted to preparing the head, nose, eyes, ears, tongue, lips, brain, foot, tail, lungs, *etcetera*. And of course, inedible parts, such as antlers and hide, have been tremendously important in making implements and clothing.

Each region of Alaska has its own meat specialties, depending upon the kinds of animals available, facilities for preserving or storing meat, and availability of other ingredients, such as vegetables, herbs and spices, canned goods, and dairy products. Most "typical" Alaskan meat recipes, however, tend to be simple and flavorful, making use of easy-to-store staples and locally grown or wild vegetables. Berries, or tart sauces and jellies made from berries, are a popular accompaniment to game meats. In the northwest and northern coastal regions of the state, marine mammals such as walrus, whale, and seal are the meats which are eaten and enjoyed. Traditionally, these meats made up a huge portion of the diet of the Eskimos inhabiting these regions, since relatively little plant material was available. Today, with grocery stores in all but the smallest villages, the diet is broader, and

Ready For The North American Dog Race
Fairbanks Daily News-Miner

newer cooking methods—with Cooperative Extension Service recipes— are widely used. In the Interior and other regions of the state, the meat from large game animals such as moose, reindeer, caribou, deer, bear, Dall sheep, and mountain goat are used. Vegetables and berries are easier to find or to grow, but people living in the villages or the "bush," still rely on canned and dried staples and a few simple seasonings to prepare their main dishes. City dwellers, however, have all the usual (and unusual) range of groceries found anywhere in the United States, so many of our meat recipes can be as varied and "international" as people desire!

In this chapter, you will find a broad range of meat recipes from around the state, from traditional to modern, and from both village and city environments. They all use the ingredients and styles of cooking which are popularly "Alaskan," however. Many popular American meat recipes such as chili, stroganoff, spaghetti sauce, *etcetera* are often made in Alaska with moose, caribou, or other meats substituting for beef; however, we tried to avoid including too many recipes like this, which are "Alaskan" only by virtue of the kind of meat used. Rather, more interesting recipes that show a particular Alaskan cooking style, and the use of other widely used Alaskan ingredients, were, to us, more meaningful for this cookbook.

Hopefully you will find many truly unique meat recipes which will give you the real flavor of Alaskan cooking. For the cook who does not have access to Alaskan or other game meats, feel free to substitute (usually with excellent results) other meats: very lean beef substitutes for moose, reindeer, caribou or venison; pork for bear meat; and lamb or mutton for Dall sheep or mountain goat. But whatever you use, try a meat dish for a really Alaskan meal!

Bunny Sausage

Yield: approximately 6 pounds

6 pounds rabbit meat
2 small onions, minced
2 tablespoons salt
2 teaspoons pepper
1/4 teaspoon paprika
1 bay leaf, crushed

1/2 teaspoon ground sage
1/2 cup ground cracker or bread crumbs
1 or 2 eggs, well beaten
3/4 cup milk

Mix all ingredients. Shape into small cakes and fry in some fat. Sausage meat may be kept frozen.

—From the *Golden Heart Cookbook*, Fairbanks

117

Reindeer Chili

Yield: 8 servings

2½ pounds reindeer, ground
2 onions, finely chopped
1 large clove garlic
3 tablespoons vinegar

2 teaspoons salt
3 tablespoons chili powder
Dash of cayenne pepper
1 can or 1 pound tomatoes, crushed

Combine all ingredients except tomatoes. Let simmer about 30 minutes, then add tomatoes and simmer another 20 minutes. Remove from heat. You may cook ½ pound of beans and add to the chili if you wish. Reindeer is far superior to any other meat for making chili.

—From the *Nome Cook Book*, Nome

Reindeer Cutlets

Yield: 4 to 6 servings

2 to 3 pounds reindeer steak
Salt and pepper
Dry bread crumbs

½ cup fat
¼ cup currant jelly or Alaskan cranberry relish

Rub the meat with salt and pepper, and roll in the bread crumbs. Melt the fat in a skillet and fry the meat until well browned on both sides and done. Place on a hot platter. Stir currant jelly or cranberry relish into the pan drippings to make a gravy, and pour over the steaks.

—University of Alaska, Cooperative Extension Service

In the last one hundred years, many of the traditional ways of life of the Athabaskan have changed. The band groups, seasonal nomadism, and local group identity are a part of history. The Athabaskan continue to hunt, fish, and trap much as they did in traditional times; however, now there are permanent villages, often centered around the sites of missions, schools, or trading posts, where hunters and fishermen bring home their catch by dog team, riverboat, or snow mobile, depending upon the season. Many Athabaskan families still go to fish camps in the summer months, traveling in flat-bottomed riverboats, which they either buy or make themselves from spruce-wood planks, powered by outboard engines.

Reindeer Sausage

10 pounds lean reindeer meat, finely ground
2½ pounds fat bacon, finely ground
3 tablespoons pepper

3 ounces salt
1 ounce (or less) ground or crushed sage
2 teaspoons dry mustard

Mix ingredients thoroughly. Mixture may be kept frozen. To can sausage: pack in cans to within ¼ inch of top; exhaust 10 minutes at 5 pounds pressure. Seal and cook 45 minutes at 15 pounds pressure. The meat may also be pressed into patties, ½-inch thick and placed in the can with waxed paper between the patties.

—University of Alaska, Cooperative Extension Service

Reindeer Pimiento Steak

Yield: 1 serving

1 reindeer steak or tough steak
Flour
Salt and pepper

Pimientos, halved
Ketchup

This is an old pioneer recipe from Point Barrow, on the Arctic Coast.

Chop or pound flour, salt, and pepper into the steak. Fry in hot drippings until nice and brown. Place halves of pimiento over the steak. Shake a liberal amount of ketchup over it, and add enough water to the skillet so that steak can simmer for a couple of hours, or until tender.

—From the *Nome Cookbook*, Nome

Reindeer or Moosemeat Stew

Yield: 4 servings

1 pound reindeer or moose meat,
  cubed
Water to cover
Salt to taste

Onion to taste, chopped
1 cup rice
1 can vegetable soup

Wash meat and let it simmer in water to cover, along with salt and onion. When meat is soft, add rice and vegetable soup, and cook very slowly so the rice gets fluffy and is ready to eat.

—Sophie Nickolie, Healy

Reindeer Stew

1 pound reindeer meat, with or without
  fat
2 quarts water
1 tablespoon salt

2 or 3 fresh potatoes
2 carrots
1½ cups flour
1 quart water

Cut meat into ¾-inch cubes and boil until tender in the 2 quarts water and the salt. Cut all the vegetables and add to the boiling meat; cook until they are tender. Stir the flour and the 1 quart water together until smooth; stir into the boiling stew and cook until thickened. Serve hot with bread.

—From the *Community Education Program Cookbook*, Gambell

The Kutchin are called a "nation" because they are the most cohesive. In the middle of the nineteenth century the Kutchin were divided into nine regional bands each corresponding to a major river drainage.

Mukluk Burger

½ pound ground mukluk seal meat
  (rinse meat before grinding)
1½ tablespoons dried onion flakes, or
  ¼ cup chopped fresh onion

½ cup oats
¼ cup flour
1 teaspoon salt
¼ teaspoon pepper

Mix all ingredients well. Make burgers and fry them in fat in a skillet for 10 to 15 minutes. You may use walrus meat but fry the burgers for 15 to 20 minutes.

—From the *Community Education Program Cookbook*, Gambell

Seal Liver

There are two traditional Eskimo ways of eating seal liver:

The liver from a freshly killed seal is put on a platter and taken outdoors to freeze. The frozen liver is eaten with seal oil.

In summer, "soured" seal liver is made by placing the liver in an enamel pot or dish and covering it with blubber. It is put in a warm place for a few days until sour.

—From the *Eskimo Cookbook*, Shishmaref

Fried Seal Liver

The Aleuts like to use soy sauce as a seasoning for this favorite delicacy:

Cut up 1 pound of seal liver in any size you wish. Soak it overnight in plain water. Fry it in hot butter, with onions if you wish. Make a flour and water paste to use for thickening.

—From the *Cuttlefish*, Unalaska

Eskimo Seal Meat

Yield: 4 to 6 servings

1 pound seal meat
Salt to taste
1 handful willow leaves
1 small onion, chopped

3 cups macaroni noodles
1 medium onion, chopped
1 cup seal oil

Add salt, willow leaves and chopped onion to seal meat. Cover with water so you have a broth; simmer until meat is almost done. Add macaroni and finish cooking until macaroni is tender. Serve with raw onions and seal oil, if you wish.

—From the *Nome Cookbook,* Nome

The Tanana River Athabaskans are separated into two cultural units and three languages. The two units were separated because of the availability of salmon. The Goodpaster River is the approximate limit of salmon migration on the Tanana River. So, above the Goodpaster the people rely more on caribou hunting. The Upper Tanana people had to fish for whitefish in the late spring and early summer in years gone by. The Upper Tanana people used long snare fences, some of which were six miles long to lead caribou into corrals over five hundred feet long. The caribou were killed through the fences in special "pockets" which were built into the corral fences. The caribou were killed with a knife fastened to a pole. Every part of the animal was used: the meat was cut into strips and dried, the intestines were filled with fat, to be used later, and the skins were used for clothing. Even the foreleg and hoof were hung up and dried for later use. After the hunting was finished, blueberries, cranberries, rosehips, and roots were mixed with grease and stored in birch-bark containers. Snowshoe rabbit snaring was handled by driving the rabbits into a line of snares. The meat and skins were utilized. Dall sheep snared were used for dried meat and clothing.

Seal Meatballs with Macaroni

Yield: 38 meatballs

2 pounds well-rinsed seal meat,
  ground

1/3 cup flour
3 tablespoons margarine, at room

1 large onion, finely chopped
2 eggs
1 cup dried gravy mix
½ cup "bake & fry" mix

temperature
Fat for frying
2 cups cooked macaroni

Hand mix the meat, onion, eggs, gravy mix, and "bake & fry" mix. Shape into 38 meatballs. Roll meatballs in flour and fry in fat for 5 or 10 minutes, turning balls frequently. Cook macaroni while preparing the meatballs—it will be done by the time meatballs are cooked. Add the meatballs to the macaroni and serve hot.

—From the *Community Education Program Cookbook,* Gambell

Lady with Birch Bark Basket
by Rachel Levine

How to Make Seal Oil

Seal oil may be made by melting out the oil at room temperature or by cooking out the oil from the blubber:

Put slices of seal fat or sea lion fat into a large jar until the jar is full. Cover the jar loosely with a lid. Put the jar in a warm place until the seal oil is separated. This separation process depends on the room temperature. When all the oil is drained out of the fat, pour it into a clean jar, tighten the lid of the jar, and store it. Save the seal fat to cook with fresh or partially dried codfish. If the oil is kept with the fat too long, it will become rancid. This seal oil is very good to eat with dried fish.

To make cooked seal oil, cut the blubber from a freshly killed seal into slices and put them in a pot. Cook and stir the slices until the seal blubber looks burned. Remove the pot from the stove and discard the burned blubber. Allow the cooked seal oil to cool and store it in a jar. Cooked seal oil is very good with fried dough, fish, or sea mammal meat.

Cooked and Dried Oogruk in a Seal Poke

Cook some lightly dried *oogruk* meat while the rest of the meat continues to dry on a rack. Cook it in boiling, salted water for only a short time, and cut it in large pieces.

Remove blubber from the seal poke*. Cut the dried meat into chunks the size of the cooked meat. Fill the poke completely with dried meat, cooked meat, and blubber, and store in a cold place. Eat the meat with seal oil.

*A seal poke is a whole seal skin (head and insides removed) which is turned, cleaned, and blown up for drying. It is a traditional winter storage vessel for all Eskimo meats, greens, berries, etc. Seal oil is often used in the poke to preserve the food better.

—From the *Eskimo Cookbook*, Shishmaref

124

Seal Meat Pie

Yield: 1 meat pie

3 cups chopped, well-rinsed seal meat
Salt and pepper
3 tablespoons flour
2 tablespoons butter
½ onion, finely chopped

1 egg
1.87-ounce package chicken gravy
 mix
Pastry for a large 2-crust pie

Rinse seal meat well before grinding: use 1 gallon water and 2 tablespoons salt and rinse the meat for 30 minutes. Line a 10-inch pie plate or shallow casserole with pie crust. Combine ground seal meat and remaining ingredients and put into the pie plate. Top with crust. Bake in a 400 degree F. oven for about 1 hour.

—From the *Community Education Program Cookbook*, Gambell

Long ago Athabaskan people identified themselves as members of small local bands. In each band there were from twenty-five to one hundred or more people, depending upon where the richer subsistence areas were. The coastal Tanaina and the Lower Yukon Ingalik lived in areas where the food supply is more abundant in comparison to some bands who lived in areas where they had to keep moving around in search of food. During lean periods, in the less abundant food areas, the bands split into smaller groups and moved from place to place regularly in hopes of finding game for survival. Each band had its own leader, who was known for his intelligence or hunting skills. People from different bands often got together to hunt, fish, make raids on common enemies, or give potlatches, which are feasts held to celebrate the game or fish harvest, and to honor the dead.

Roasted Seal Meat

Remove all fat from the meat. Rinse the meat thoroughly in 1 gallon of water with 2 tablespoons salt for 30 minutes. Remove from water and let the meat drip for a few minutes. Cut the meat into pieces with bones, and roll every piece in flour to coat thoroughly. Put the meat into a roasting pan and season with 1 chopped onion (or use dried onion flakes), dried gravy mix, or salt and pepper. Put some fresh potatoes among the meat. Cover the pan with a lid or foil. Roast 1 1/2 hours in a 450 degrees F. oven.

—From the *Community Education Program Cookbook,* Gambell

Sea Lion Soup

1 pound sea lion meat, chopped
6 cups water
Salt and pepper
Petruskies

1 onion, chopped
1/2 cup rice
2 potatoes, chopped

Boil meat in water for at least 40 minutes. Add other ingredients and let cook for at least 45 minutes longer, until the meat is tender. You may add a flour and water paste to thicken the boiling soup, if you wish.

—Platonida Gromoff, Sophie Pletnikoff, and Sophie Sherebernikoff
From the *CUTTLEFISH,* Unalaska

Braised Venison

Yield: 6 servings

3 pounds venison (use the less tender
   cuts)
3 slices salt pork
Salt, pepper, flour
1/4 cup fat
1/4 cup hot water

1/2 tablespoon vinegar
1/2 cup chopped celery
1 carrot, chopped
1 tart apple, chopped
1/2 tablespoon lemon juice

Lard the venison with strips of the salt pork, and rub the meat with salt, pepper, and flour. Sauté in hot fat until well browned, turning frequently. Add the hot water and vinegar, cover the pan, and simmer until tender—about 2 hours, adding more water as needed. One-half hour before meat is done, add remaining ingredients. Cook until the vegetables are tender, and serve with a tart homemade jelly.

The use of animals illustrates how tightly Athabaskan people have been traditionally bound to an area in which they live. Long ago, Athabaskan hunters might be clad in moosehide clothing while trying to snare a moose. The snare was made from moose skin that had been made into rawhide line or babiche. If his hunting were successful, he could make a moose skin boat and transport the meat home. At home the hide was scraped with a sharpened moose bone and tanned in a moose-brain solution. The tanned moose hide could then be sewn with a moose-bone awl and moose sinew for another set of moose-hide clothes.

Corned Venison

5 pounds sugar
5 pounds salt
1½ ounces saltpeter

½ cup mixed whole pickling spice
2½ to 3 gallons warm water
25 pounds of meat

Add all ingredients, except the meat, to the warm water and stir to dissolve the sugar and salts. Let the solution cool. Put meat into the liquid and let stand for two or three weeks in a cold place (make sure meat is completely submerged). The meat is then ready to use. If the meat stands longer than two or three weeks, pour off the brine, boil it, strain and let it cool, and pour it back over the meat.

—From the *PTA Cookbook,* Petersburg

Braised Venison in Sour Cream

Yield: 4 to 6 servings

2 pounds venison, cut into 2-inch
   pieces
1/4 cup bacon fat
1 clove garlic, minced
1 cup chopped celery
1 cup chopped carrots
1/2 cup chopped onion
2 cups water
1 cup tart fruit juice

1 bay leaf
8 peppercorns
1 teaspoon salt
4 tablespoons butter
4 tablespoons flour
1 cup sour cream
Cooked and buttered noodles
Plum or currant jelly

Sauté the meat and garlic in the bacon fat in a heavy skillet until the meat is browned on all sides. Arrange meat in a 2-quart casserole. Sauté the celery, carrots, and onion briefly in the skillet. Add the water, juice, bay leaf, peppercorns, and salt; pour the mixture over the venison. Cover casserole and bake at 325 degrees F. for 30 to 60 minutes, until meat is tender.

Melt the butter in a saucepan, stir in the flour, and when well blended, add the liquid from the casserole in which the meat was cooked, stirring constantly until the mixture thickens and boils. Add the sour cream and more salt, if necessary. Reheat sauce, but do not boil; pour over meat and vegetables in the casserole. Serve immediately with cooked buttered noodles and tart plum or currant jelly.

—University of Alaska, Cooperative Extension Service

Venison Hache

Yield: 3 servings

1/3 cup flour
1/4 cup butter
1 onion, chopped
2 cups beef stock or bouillon
1 bay leaf

5 whole cloves
2/3 teaspoon salt
2 teaspoons vinegar
1 pound chopped and cooked venison

Brown flour in the butter, add the onion and cook until softened. Add the beef stock, bay leaf, cloves, and salt; cook for 5 minutes. Add the vinegar and the meat, and simmer slowly for 1 hour, stirring occasionally.

—From the PTA Cookbook, Petersburg

The Ahtna live south of the Tanana River from Cantwell in the Alaska

Range to the Upper Chitna River in the Saint Elias Mountains. Their major resources are the large salmon runs and annual fall caribou migrations.

Oven Venison Hash

Yield: 4 servings

1 cup coarsely ground cooked venison
1 cup coarsely ground cooked potatoes
1/4 cup coarsely ground onion
1/4 cup finely chopped parsley
1 teaspoon salt

Dash pepper
2 teaspoons Worcestershire sauce, or 1 tablespoon steak sauce
1 6-ounce can evaporated milk
1/4 cup fine dry bread crumbs
1 tablespoon melted butter

Lightly mix the venison, potatoes, onion, parsley, salt, pepper, Worcestershire, and milk. Place in a 1-quart casserole. Mix the bread crumbs and butter; sprinkle over the top. Bake at 350 degrees F. for 30 minutes.

Rullespolse (Norwegian Meat Roll)

This specialty is popular in southeast Alaska. It is served thinly sliced for sandwiches.

Venison or mutton flanks
Pieces of meat and fat to fill flanks
2 teaspoons salt
1/4 teaspoon pepper
1/4 teaspoon ground ginger

1/2 teaspoon allspice
1/2 teaspoon thyme
Rock salt
1 tablespoon saltpeter (for each gallon of brine)

Remove bones from the meat. Cut pieces of meat and fat in strips to fill the flanks. Season with the salt, pepper, ginger, allspice, and thyme, using the above amounts *for each flank.* Roll the meat and sew it up with heavy thread, then wrap tightly with twine.

Make enough brine to cover the meat rolls: to the amount of water needed, add enough rock salt to float a peeled raw potato. Bring the brine to a boil to dissolve the salt. Add the saltpeter (1 tablespoon for each gallon of brine) and let it cool. Keep meat rolls preserved in the salt brine until ready to use.

To cook rullespolse: remove meat from the brine and soak overnight in fresh cold water. Simmer in water for two hours, remove meat and let it cool underneath a heavy weight. Serve thinly sliced for sandwiches.

—From the *PTA Cookbook, Petersburg*

Spicy Venison or Beef Short Ribs

Yield: 4 servings

3 pounds venison (or beef) short ribs,
   cut into serving pieces
1 cup ketchup
1 cup water
1 tablespoon sugar
1 tablespoon prepared horseradish
1 bay leaf

1 tablespoon dry mustard
1 tablespoon vinegar
$1/4$ teaspoon pepper
1 teaspoon Worcestershire sauce
Flour
Fat for frying

Place the short ribs in a large bowl. Mix all remaining ingredients, except flour and fat, and pour over the ribs. Cover bowl and refrigerate overnight. When ready to cook, remove ribs from the liquid, drain them, and roll in flour. Brown the floured ribs in hot fat in a heavy skillet, then add the liquid in which the ribs were soaked. Cover and cook slowly until the meat is tender, about $1\frac{1}{2}$ hours.

—From the *PTA Cookbook*, Petersburg

Venison Stew Sauterne

Yield: 6 servings

2 pounds lean venison stew meat
2 onions, sliced
2 cloves garlic, chopped
$1\frac{1}{2}$ cups sauterne

Seasoned flour
2 tablespoons fat
3 cups water
Vegetables, as desired

Cut meat into 2-inch cubes and place in a deep bowl with the sliced onions and the garlic. Add the sauterne, cover, and let the meat stand in a cool place overnight. Remove the meat, roll it in seasoned flour, and brown it in the hot fat. Add the wine-onion-garlic mixture and the water; simmer for $1\frac{1}{2}$ hours. Add vegetables as desired and cook slowly for $1/2$ hour longer.

—From the *Catholic Daughters of America*, Juneau

Venison Zucchini Bake

Yield: 4 to 6 servings

1 pound venison or reindeer sausage,
   ground
1 onion, chopped

1 green pepper, chopped
Oregano, parsley, and basil to taste
1 clove garlic, minced or pressed

1 10½-ounce can tomato soup
4 cups canned whole tomatoes, crushed
1 10-inch zucchini, sliced
2 eggs, beaten
1 part each cornmeal, wheat germ,

grapenut cereal
Salt and pepper to taste
Oil for frying
2 cups shredded Cheddar cheese
½ cup bread crumbs

Brown the venison or reindeer sausage with the onion. Add the green pepper, oregano, parsley, basil, garlic, tomato soup, and canned tomatoes and simmer for ½ hour.

Dip the zucchini slices in beaten egg, then in the combination of cornmeal, wheat germ, and cereal, seasoned with salt and pepper. Fry until brown and crispy.

In a 9-by-13-inch baking pan, place a layer of fried zucchini, then a layer of shredded cheese, then a layer of the meat sauce. Repeat until you reach the top, ending with a layer of cheese. Sprinkle the top with the bread crumbs and bake at 350 degrees F. until bubbling, about 20 to 30 minutes.

—University of Alaska, Cooperative Extension Service

Ingalik *or* deg hetan *means "people from here." They live west and north of Lake Clark. The Anvik-Shageluk people live along the Yukon and Lower Innoko rivers. The Bonasilia Ingalik live in the Bonasilia River drainage. The Holycross-Georgetown people live along the lower part of the Yukon and middle sections of the Kuskokwim River. Their subsistence patterns include fishing for grayling, sheefish, and pike in late May, along with snaring rabbits and hunting for muskrats and waterfowl. Historically, the gill nets were replaced with traps made of willow in June to catch dog salmon. After the first fish was caught, it was cooked and eaten by the men and boys. Young boys were told to throw a piece of fish back into the river to hope for a continuance of this bountiful resource. Throughout the summer, the Ingalik catch and prepare fish, which are dried on racks. In addition, the people hunted ducks, geese, swans, and cranes while women gathered eggs and a variety of vegetable products. Berries, such as rosehips, low-bush cranberries and blueberries, were gathered in late summer and fall and stored for later use in birch-bark baskets. In November fish were caught using traps and gill nets under the ice. Lampreys were also caught. They snared rabbits and ptarmigan in the winter to add to the caribou, which historically were herded into brush-rimmed corrals and shot with bow and arrows or stabbed with spears. Trapping for fur continues all winter.*

Fried Walrus Liver

Yield: 4 servings

1 pound walrus liver, cut into ¾-inch
   slices
1 cup flour

1½ tablespoons salt
1 tablespoon pepper
Fat for pan-frying

Shake the liver slices in a paper bag with the flour, salt, and pepper until all slices are coated. Fry in fat in a skillet for about 15 minutes.

—From the *Community Education Program Cookbook,* Gambell

Walrus Kyusolik

Yield: 4 servings

1 pound walrus meat, cubed
4 cups water
1 tablespoon vinegar
¼ teaspoon salt
¼ teaspoon pepper
1 teaspoon dry mustard
½ teaspoon meat tenderizer (optional)
Flour

2 tablespoons fat
1 tablespoon dried onion flakes
1 cup water
½ cup dry milk powder (or ½ cup
   canned evaporated milk)
2 tablespoons ketchup
Cooked rice

Soak the meat chunks in a mixture of the 4 cups water and the vinegar for 10 minutes. Pour off the water, and sprinkle the meat with the salt, pepper, mustard, and meat tenderizer. Let it stand for 2 hours with the seasonings.

Roll the meat in flour. Heat the fat in a frying pan and brown the meat, along with the dried onion flakes. Remove the meat and add a little more flour to the frying pan and stir. Then stir in the 1 cup water, and the milk, and heat until the gravy is smooth. Return the meat to the pan. Add the ketchup, cover with a lid, and let cook very slowly until the meat is tender. Check it once in a while and if it begins to get dry, add a little more water. Serve over hot cooked rice.

—University of Alaska, Cooperative Extension Service

Fish Wheel
by Rachel Levine

Fish wheels are important to the Athabaskan subsistence lifestyles along many of the Interior Alaskan rivers.

Mukluk or Walrus Meat Loaf

Yield: 4 servings

1 pound mukluk seal or walrus meat,
    rinsed in water with 2 tablespoons
    salt
1 egg or 3 tablespoons dry powdered
    egg

1 cup oats
¼ cup flour
1 cup canned peas with juice
½ teaspoon salt
¼ teaspoon pepper

Grind the meat or chop it finely, and mix with remaining ingredients. Bake in a greased loaf pan at 450 degrees F. for 20 to 30 minutes (if using mukluk), or for 30 to 45 minutes (if using walrus).

—From the *Community Education Cookbook*, Gambell

> *The Tanaina inhabit the area around Cook Inlet and the areas imme-diately west and north. The Kachemak Bay Tanaina live in a marine environment and have access to many kinds of sea mammals and fish, as well as large and small game. Subsistence patterns of the Kenai and Tyonek people emphasize salmon fishing over marine mammals since their environment changes. The Kenai and Tyonek people also hunt for caribou, moose, Dall sheep, and small game. The Susitna River people hunt no sea mammals and depend on summer runs of salmon and fall caribou hunts for their subsistence base. The Iliamna people depend on sockeye salmon migrating into the lakes. Caribou, moose, rabbits, and other mammals are hunted in this area.*

Four-Day Spiced Walrus

6- to 8-pound chunk of cleanly
    trimmed walrus meat
1 gallon water
¼ cup vinegar
1 tablespoon garlic salt

1 tablespoon saltpeter
4 tablespoons salt
5 tablespoons allspice
5 tablespoons sugar
½ teaspoon cinnamon

Soak the meat in a solution of the water and vinegar, in a container large enough to hold it all, for about 10 minutes. Take the meat out and wipe it dry. Combine all the spices. With an *ulu* (Eskimo women's knife), make a few cuts into the meat and put some of the spice mixture down into the cuts. Rub the rest of the spice mixture over the outside of the meat.

Wrap the spiced meat well in aluminum foil, or put it into a heavy, clean, plastic bag, folding the bag closely around the meat. Store the meat in a cold (but not freezing) place for 4 days.

If the meat has been wrapped in foil, leave it in the foil (make sure the foil is tight) and cook it in an uncovered pan at 300 degrees F. for about 4 hours. If the meat was stored in plastic, remove it and wrap it well in foil before cooking. When the meat is done, let it cool before slicing.

—University of Alaska, Cooperative Extension Service

Walrus Steak with Gravy

Yield: 4 servings

4 walrus steaks, cut ¾-inch thick
Flour, salt, and pepper
2 tablespoons fat

2 tablespoons dried onion flakes or
   1 medium onion, finely chopped
¼ cup ketchup
1 cup water

Pound seasoned flour into the walrus steaks. Melt the fat in a heavy skillet and brown the steaks on both sides. Cover steaks with a mixture of the onion, ketchup, and water. Cover pan tightly with a lid, and cook slowly over low heat for 1 to 2 hours, depending on the tenderness of the meat. Add water as needed to the pan.

—University of Alaska, Cooperative Extension Service

Nome Walrus Stew

Yield: 4 servings

2 pounds walrus meat, cut in pieces
4 whole hot red peppers
1 teaspoon allspice
6 bay leaves

4 large potatoes, chopped
2 carrots, sliced
2 onions, chopped or sliced
¼ raw rice
Salt

Place walrus meat in a large pot and cover with cold water. Bring to a boil; change the water and bring to a boil again. Drain, cover with water a third time, add the spices, and boil for 1 hour. Add the vegetables and rice and let cook slowly until the potatoes are done. Salt to taste.

—From the *Nome Cookbook,* Nome

Norwegian-Style Whale Meat Cutlets

Yield: 6 servings

4 pounds whale meat, cut into six
　³⁄₄-inch-thick cutlets
1 teaspoon salt
1 pinch pepper
1 egg white
Zwieback crumbs

6 tablespoons butter
1 lemon, thinly sliced
6 rolled anchovy fillets
¹⁄₂ tablespoon capers
1 cup meat stock

Pound the whale cutlets lightly. Season with salt and pepper. Dip into egg white and coat with zwieback crumbs. Melt the butter in a skillet and fry the meat until it is light brown. Remove meat to a serving platter. Place a slice of lemon on each cutlet and top each with a rolled anchovy surrounded by 4 capers. Add the stock to the pan and simmer for 5 minutes. Pour over the meat and serve.

—University of Alaska, Cooperative Extension Service

In traditional times, Athabaskan people hauled their sleds by hand while wearing snowshoes. There were two types of snowshoes, made for either deep powder, or for well-packed or shallow snow. The frames were made of birch wood and the webbings were made from caribou or moose rawhide babiche. Without snowshoes winter travelers would be stranded in deep snow. The importance can not be emphasized enough for the Athabaskan traditional winter survival.

White Whale

Cut the whale meat into pieces and let it boil in a cooking pot with water and salt. Add the blubber found inside the small intestine and cook.

Winter Hunting
by Rachel Levine

Gray Whale Steak

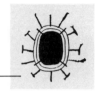

Yield: 4 to 6 servings

2 pounds gray whale meat, in ³/₄-inch-thick slices
1½ cups flour

3 tablespoons salt
1 tablespoon pepper

Shake meat slices in a paper bag with the flour, salt, and pepper. Keep them in the bag for 5 to 10 minutes before frying. Shake again and fry the slices to your preference in fat in a skillet.

—From the *Community Education Program Cookbook,* Gambell

Alaska Goulash

Yield: 4 servings

1 large onion, chopped
¼ cup butter or shortening
3 cups cold roast reindeer
1 1-pound can tomatoes

1 cup sliced celery
½ cup sweet pickle juice
2 cups prepared gravy

Sauté onion in the melted butter or shortening until soft. Add remaining ingredients and simmer for 1 hour.

—From the *Nome Cookbook,* Nome

Aleutian Beef Stew

Yield: 4 to 6 servings

2 pounds beef stew meat
Flour
2 tablespoons fat
1 onion, sliced

4 cups chopped and rinsed seaweed
2 carrots, sliced
1 cup rice
Salt and pepper

Coat meat with flour and brown slowly in the fat in a heavy Dutch oven. Add onions; cover meat with water and simmer until meat is tender. Add remaining ingredients and cook until the rice and carrots are tender. Season to taste with salt and pepper.

Barbecue Sauce

This sauce is delicious on any Alaskan game meat or fish.

1 stick butter
¼ cup brown sugar
2 tablespoons Worcestershire sauce
3 tablespoons lemon juice

4 tablespoons prepared mustard
2 teaspoons garlic powder
Salt, pepper, and horseradish to taste

Boil all ingredients together for 5 minutes.

—Virginia Doyle "Bunny" Heiner, Fairbanks

Barbecued Alaskan Meat

This recipe works equally well with reindeer, moose, ptarmigan, beef, or veal.

3 pounds meat, sliced ¼-inch-thick,
   lightly salted
2 tablespoons shortening
1 medium green pepper, chopped

1 medium onion, chopped
1 large can tomato puree
Salt

Brown meat well in a heavy skillet, using no fat. Remove meat from pan, and melt the shortening in the skillet. Sauté green pepper and onion until soft. Return meat to the pan and add the tomato puree and salt. If meat is not covered by the puree, you may add a can of tomatoes. Let the meat simmer slowly, covered, until it is tender enough to cut with a fork. Stir occasionally during cooking, adding a little water if necessary.

—From the *Nome Cookbook,* Nome

Mrs. Lear's Barbecue Sauce

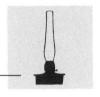

For any Alaskan meat or fish.

1½ cups honey
1 cup ketchup
½ cup soy sauce
2 tablespoons cider vinegar
1 teaspoon Worcestershire sauce
2 teaspoons ground cloves

1 teaspoon poultry seasoning
1 teaspoon dry mustard
½ teaspoon MSG (optional)
1 clove garlic, minced or pressed
Salt and pepper to taste

Combine all ingredients.

—Gladys Parker, Fairbanks

The Holikachuk people live north of the Ingalik and share a similar culture, even though their language is different. They utilize the upper Innoko, lower Iditarod and lower Dishna rivers. Since the salmon do not migrate up the Innoko, these people have to go to the Yukon River for fishing.

Cabbage Rolls

Yield: 4 to 6 servings

1 large firm cabbage head
½ cup rice
1½ cups milk
1 pound boneless meat (beef or any Alaskan game meat)
3 ounces boneless fat pork or other meat

Salt and pepper
1 to 1¾ cups milk
1 egg
2 tablespoons butter
2 tablespoons brown sugar
1 tablespoon flour
Generous ½ cup cream

Discard outer leaves of cabbage. Remove the large leaves one by one, immersing them in boiling salted water until leaves are partially transparent. Remove them from the water and drain.

Cook rice in milk until tender. Grind meat and pork finely, and add rice, milk, salt and pepper, and egg. Stir with a wooden spoon; the consistency should be like thick mush.

Trim center veins from cabbage leaves; lay a large spoonful of meat mixture on each leaf. Roll and tie with string or fasten with toothpick.

Brown the rolls in the butter; sprinkle with brown sugar, and baste with a little stock or water. Cover and cook very slowly for 1 to 2 hours. When done, remove string or toothpicks from cabbage rolls. Mix flour and cream; add to pan juices and cook until smooth. Return rolls to gravy and reheat, then serve.

—From the *Golden Heart Cookbook*, Fairbanks

Collups—A Pioneer Breakfast Dish

Yield: Depends on appetite!

Take a piece of the round of beef, moose, or caribou that is frozen until very firm, and shave into thin slices like dried beef. Put into a frying pan and add water sufficient for gravy. When it comes to a boil, add thickening. Season with salt, pepper, and butter. Do not boil too long, or the meat will be tough.

—From the *Fairbanks Cookbook*, circa 1910, Fairbanks

Corned Beef Hash

Yield: 4 servings

3 or 4 medium potatoes, peeled and chopped
½ to 1 onion, chopped

1 can corned beef
Pepper
Bacon fat

Barely cover potatoes with water in a saucepan and simmer until they are just tender. Drain, and mix potatoes with the onion. Chop the mixture up a bit with a potato masher—don't get it too mushy. Flake the corned beef and add to the mixture. Season with pepper; turn mixture into a hot skillet in which you have melted bacon fat. Cook on one side and turn over to brown the other side.

—Millie Terwilliger, Tok

Kaklukax

1½ pounds sea lion meat
1 large onion, chopped
3 carrots
½ cup milk
½ teaspoon salt
½ teaspoon pepper
1 tablespoon Worcestershire sauce

½ teaspoon petruskies
1 egg
2 tablespoons flour
2 tablespoons butter
1 8-ounce can tomato sauce
½ cup water

Soak meat overnight in plain water. Trim off fat. Grind meat, onion, and carrots. Add the milk, seasonings, and egg; mix well. Form meat into balls and roll in the flour. Place a piece of butter on top of each meat ball. Bake at 350 degrees F. for 1 hour. Pour tomato sauce and water over the meat balls as they are cooking. This is good served with rice or potatoes.

—Platonida Gromoff, Sophie Pletnikoff, and Sophie Sherebernikoff
From *Cuttlefish*, Unalaska

"Old Standby"

When Bunny Heiner was growing up in Nome, this was her family's "old standby."

1 pound pinto beans
¼ cup bacon fat or other fat
1 cup canned tomatoes or tomato juice
2 teaspoons salt
½ teaspoon pepper

1 tablespoon pickle juice
¼ cup molasses or brown sugar
¼ teaspoon dry mustard
1 can applesauce
1 teaspoon cinnamon

At 9:00 A.M., cover rinsed and picked-over pinto beans with cold water. Bring to a boil and drain; repeat this 3 times, never boiling the beans hard. Leave the beans to soak in the hot water when simmered for the third time.

At 1:00 P.M., drain the beans and add enough fresh water to cover. Add remaining ingredients, except applesauce and cinnamon, and bake at 350 degrees F., uncovered, for 4 or 5 hours, adding boiling water when needed to keep the beans covered. Serve the beans with the applesauce mixed with the cinnamon.

—Virginia Doyle "Bunny" Heiner, Fairbanks

The Koyukon inhabited the largest area of any of the Alaskan Athabaskans. There are three major dialects and several subdialects among these people. Their subsistence patterns emphasize salmon fishing during the summer with moose, caribou, and an assortment of small game being hunted in the fall and winter.

Danish Winter Pea Soup

Yield: 6 servings

1 pound dried yellow peas	2 leeks
2 pounds lightly salted pork	2 stalks celery
Herbs (green top of celery and thyme)	Boiled potatoes for 6 people, chopped

Let peas soak overnight. Drain them and simmer in 3 pints unsalted water. Simmer the pork separately with the herbs, leeks, and celery. When peas are tender, remove the pork from its broth, skim fat from the broth, and cut the vegetables into pieces. Drain the peas and press them through a sieve. Mix peas with the pork broth and vegetables. Add boiled potatoes and serve hot.

—From the *Golden Heart Cookbook,* Fairbanks

Pioneer Fricassee

Yield: 4 to 6 servings

2 pounds ground beef or other meat
1 large onion, finely chopped
³/₄ cup canned evaporated milk
¹/₂ cup flour
2 tablespoons baking powder
1 egg

¹/₂ teaspoon salt
¹/₄ teaspoon pepper
1 can or 1 pound peas
1 can or 1 pound carrots
Parsley and celery leaves, chopped
1 teaspoon cornstarch

Mix ground meat with the onion, milk, flour, baking powder, egg, salt, and pepper. Shape into meat balls and drop into 2 cups of boiling, salted water. Add the liquid from the can of peas and the can of carrots; simmer for 20 minutes. Add the vegetables and the parsley and celery leaves. Thicken the mixture with the cornstarch dissolved in a little cold water.

—From the *Nome Cookbook,* Nome

Ground Meat Perok

This recipe is similar to the well-known Russian-Aleut salmon pie, but made with ground meat:

Yield: 10 servings

Enough pastry for a 9-by-13-inch pan,
  2 crusts
3 carrots, chopped
1 onion, chopped
1 stalk celery, chopped
1 green pepper, chopped (optional)

¹/₂ medium cabbage, finely chopped
¹/₄ cup butter or margarine
3 pounds ground meat (moose,
  caribou, or beef)
6 cups cooked rice

Sauté the vegetables in the butter until they are soft. Combine with the raw ground meat and the cooked rice. Put into the pastry-lined pan and cover with a top crust. Bake at 400 degrees F. for about 45 minutes, or until the crust is well-browned.

Pirozhkies

1 medium onion
2 pounds ground meat

2 packages or 2 tablespoons active
  dry yeast

1 teaspoon finely chopped garlic
1 tablespoon petruskies or parsley,
    minced
1 teaspoon salt
1 teaspoon pepper
2 tablespoons flour
4 hard-boiled eggs, chopped

3 cups lukewarm milk
12 cups sifted flour
6 eggs
1 cup butter, melted
4 teaspoons sugar
2 teaspoons salt

Fry the onion, ground meat, seasonings, and flour together in a large skillet until cooked. Remove from heat; add the chopped hardboiled eggs and let the mixture cool.

To prepare the dough, dissolve the yeast in the lukewarm milk. Stir in half the flour. Let stand for at least 1 hour in a warm place. Beat the eggs slightly and add, along with the butter, sugar, and salt, to the yeast mixture. Beat in remaining flour to make a soft dough. Knead thoroughly; form the dough into a ball, and place in a large greased bowl to rise. Cover and let rise in a warm place for several hours.

For each pirozhkie, pinch off a piece of dough (about ¼ cup) and roll or flatten to a ¼-inch-thick oval. Fill with meat mixture and carefully seal the edges. Fry in deep-fat.

—Platonida Gromoff, *Cuttlefish*, Unalaska

The Kolchan inhabit the upper Kushkokwim River and its tributaries. They rely primarily on caribou hunting, rather than fishing, for a living. Historically, they lived in semi-subterranean houses situated near lakes or clear-water streams. Small game, caribou, and fish provide winter subsistence. Brush corrals were used long ago to capture and kill caribou. They also hunted caribou, sheep, and bears in the summer, while women picked berries. Fishing for salmon and whitefish was done in the fall, using nets and weirs.

Pot Roast with Dill Pickles

Yield: 4 servings

Piece of beef for pot roast
Salt and pepper
1 tablespoon flour
1 onion, chopped

1 carrot, chopped
1 bay leaf
$1/2$ cup dill pickles

Salt and pepper the beef, and dust it with flour. Brown it on both sides in hot fat in a pot. Add onion and carrot to brown with the roast. Then add enough water to half-cover the roast. Cover and let simmer for $1^1/_2$ hours. Turn the roast, add bay leaf and dill pickles. Let it cook 1 hour longer.

—From *The Fairbanks Cookbook,* circa 1910, Fairbanks

Potted Meat

Yield: 6 servings

Shank of beef
2 or 3 onions, chopped
Salt and pepper

3 or 4 bay leaves
2 whole cloves or small amount of
sage

Wash beef and boil it until it drops to pieces. Take out and remove the bones, and chop the meat up fine. To the stock add onions, season with salt, pepper, bay leaves, and cloves or sage, and let it simmer until the onions are tender. Return the chopped meat to the pot and let it simmer $1/2$ hour. Turn it into molds and let it cool; it will keep for quite a while.

—From *The Fairbanks Cookbook,* circa 1910

146

Vertical Barbecued Meat, Tlingit Style

This is the old style of barbecueing meat used by the Tlingit Indians of Southeast Alaska. It is a clever way of cooking the meat evenly:

Attach meat to a stick using a pair of thongs so that the meat is hanging. Twist the thongs, and fasten the stick into the ground at an angle over an open fire. The thongs untwist and retwist as the meat hangs over the fire, cooking it evenly without burning in any spot.

Mrs. Wehner's Pork and Sauerkraut

Yield: 4 servings

1 piece (about 1 pound) cooked pork
1 can or 1 pound sauerkraut
1 onion, chopped
1 green pepper, chopped

1 teaspoon caraway seed
1 teaspoon mustard seed
1 tablespoon brown sugar

Combine all ingredients in a saucepan and add enough water to cover. Simmer very slowly for 2 to 3 hours. Serve with boiled potatoes.

—Gladys Parker, Fairbanks

147

Pot Roast Beaver

Yield: 2 servings

Small beaver's hindquarters
Flour
2 small onions

2 bay leaves
Salt and pepper

Cut a beaver's hindquarters in pieces. Dip in flour and brown in a Dutch oven. Add onions, bay leaves, and salt and pepper to taste. Cover and let cook slowly until fork-tender.

—Sophie Nickolie, Healy

In the Goodpaster River area of Delta, "Women would melt down spruce pitch and cool it. This was best for sores, like from cleaning fish, and for boils besides and for canoes and for arrow to stick the feather on. This sap from spruce trees they used for medicine too" says Bessie Barnabus. In the same area, dried wild rhubarb root is evidently brewed into a tea and used in the treatment of heart conditions.

Beaver Tail with Beans

Yield: 6 servings

1 or 2 pounds beans
1 beaver tail

1 large onion, chopped
Salt and pepper

Soak beans overnight. Pour off water, add fresh water, and bring to a boil. Lower heat to a simmer. Singe the beaver tail over an open flame, then remove the skin. Cut into 1- or 2-inch cubes. Add to the beans along with the onion and continue cooking until done. Season to taste with salt and pepper.

—From *A Book of Recipes,* Galena

The term "Athabaskan" designates a language divided into three subfamilies. It can be found spelled Athabascan or Athapaskan. One of these subfamilies is the Northern Athabaskan, which is spoken by at least twenty-eight different peoples residing in the Interior of Alaska, the Yukon Territory, the western district of the Mackenzie, northern and central British Columbia, and northern and central Alberta. Alaskan Athabaskans are divided linguistically into eleven major groups: Tanaina, Ingalik, Holikachuk, Kolchan, Koyukon, Kutchin, Han, Tanana, Ahtna, Upper Kuskokwim, and Upper Tanana.

Beaver Hats
by April Kelley

There is strength in generations of Athabaskans.

Braised Caribou with Vegetables

Yield: 4 servings

2 pounds caribou, cubed
Seasoned salt
Flour
Water or stock
1 large rutabaga, quartered
2 large turnips, cut in half

4 large carrots, cut in half
4 small onions, peeled
1 or 2 bay leaves
1/2 teaspoon seasoned salt
5 medium potatoes

Season the meat with the seasoned salt, then roll in flour. Braise slowly in a heavy pan until nice and brown, then add just enough water or stock to barely cover meat. Let it simmer until it starts to get tender, then add all vegetables (except potatoes) and seasonings. Add potatoes after the mixture has simmered about 15 minutes; cook slowly until all vegetables are tender. Thicken the stock with flour or cornstarch mixed with cold water if you wish to make gravy.

—From the *Nome Cookbook, Nome*

Caribou Hot Pot

Yield: 4 servings

6 white potatoes, sliced
1 pound caribou meat, chopped
1 onion, sliced
3/4 teaspoon salt

1 teaspoon paprika
1 can or 1 pound stewed tomatoes
1/3 cup sour cream or yogurt

Fill a 1-quart casserole almost to the top with: a layer of white potatoes, sliced 1/4-inch-thick; a layer of tough, lean caribou meat; and a layer of onions. Sprinkle with the salt, paprika, and pour over all the stewed tomatoes. Cover and bake at 350 degrees F. for about 2 hours. About 1/2 hour before it is done, stir in the cup sour cream or yogurt.

—From the *Nome Cookbook*, Nome

Meat and Cheese Loaf

Yield: 10 servings

2 pounds ground caribou (you may
   substitute moose or beef, but
   caribou is most flavorful)

2 teaspoons salt
1 teaspoon pepper
1 teaspoon celery salt

2 cups cubed cheese
3 eggs
1 large onion, chopped
1 large green pepper, chopped

$\frac{1}{2}$ teaspoon paprika
$1\frac{1}{2}$ cups dry bread crumbs
$\frac{1}{2}$ teaspoon garlic salt

Combine ingredients in the order given; mix well. Press into 2 greased loaf pans, and bake at 350 degrees F. for about $1\frac{1}{2}$ hours.

—From *Cooking Favorites of Fairbanks, Alaska,* Fairbanks

Caribou
by Rachel Levine

Northwest Caribou Soup

Yield: any amount you choose

Caribou
Macaroni
Rice
Salt and pepper

Vegetables (potatoes, carrots, celery,
onion, and any others you prefer)
Stewed tomatoes

Boil caribou in water until cooked. Add remaining ingredients to taste and simmer until vegetables and meat are tender.

—Northwest Arctic School District Home Economist, Selawik

Caribou Wild Rice Casserole

Yield: 3 to 4 servings

1/2 pound caribou, chopped
1/2 pound pork, chopped
1 medium onion, chopped
1 cup chopped celery
3 tablespoons salad oil or butter

4 cups boiling water
1/2 cup raw wild rice
1/2 cup raw white rice
4 tablespoons soy sauce

Sauté the meats, onion, and celery in the salad oil or butter until lightly brown. Add remaining ingredients. Bake in a large covered casserole at 350 degrees F. for 1 1/2 hours.

—From *Alaska's Cooking,* Anchorage

Burgundy Moose

Yield: 6 servings

2 tablespoons vegetable oil
2 onions, quartered
2 pounds moose, cut into 2-inch cubes
Salt and pepper
2 cups Burgundy wine
1/2 teaspoon nutmeg

1/4 teaspoon garlic powder
1/2 teaspoon grated orange peel
1/2 teaspoon poultry seasoning
1 cup sliced mushrooms
1 tablespoon dried parsley flakes

Heat the oil in a Dutch oven and brown the onions. Remove from pan. Brown the meat and season it with salt and pepper. Return onions to the pan and add the wine, nutmeg, garlic powder, orange peel, and poultry seasoning. Cover and bake at 300 degrees F. for 3 hours. Add the mushrooms and parsley. Cover and bake 15 minutes longer. Serve hot on cooked rice or noodles.

—From *Cooking up a Storm,* Homer

Moose Feeding On River Vegetation
by Rachel Levine

Russian Moose-Cabbage Soup

Yield: 4 servings

¹/₂ pound lean moose meat, chopped	1 onion, sliced
¹/₂ pound fat pork, chopped	1 bay leaf
5 cups water	2 teaspoons salt
1 large head cabbage, shredded	¹/₄ teaspoon pepper
1 large tomato, chopped	Sour cream

Simmer the meat in the water until almost tender. Add the vegetables and seasonings, and simmer until the vegetables are done. Garnish each serving of soup with sour cream.

Moose and Cabbage Casserole

Yield: 6 servings

1 tablespoon vegetable oil
1 pound ground moose meat
1 cup chopped celery
¼ cup chopped onion
2½ cups canned tomatoes

2 teaspoons salt
¼ teaspoon pepper
4 cups coarsely shredded cabbage
1 cup bread crumbs

Brown the moose meat in the oil; add the onion and celery and cook for 5 minutes. Add the tomatoes, salt, and pepper. Bring to a boil and remove from heat. In a 13-by-9-inch baking pan, make two alternate layers of cabbage and meat mixture. Top with the bread crumbs and bake at 375 degrees F. for 45 minutes.

The Tanaina Indians near Anchorage have used several kinds of plants as herbal remedies. Such plants as nettle, coltsfoot, sage bush, and spruce gum have been used in treatment of diseases from rheumatism to tuberculosis.

Corned Moose

1 pound pickling salt
12½ pounds boneless moose meat
Pepper, freshly ground
Bay leaves
1 cup sugar

3 teaspoons baking soda
1 tablespoon saltpeter
1 pint warm water
½ cup mixed pickling spices

Sprinkle some of the salt in the bottom of a stone crock or stainless steel container. Put in a layer of meat, then more salt, then a generous amount of pepper and bay leaves. Continue the layering until all the meat and salt are used. Let stand overnight. Make a brine from the sugar, baking soda, saltpeter, and warm water; let cool and add enough water so it will cover the meat completely. Place the pickling spices in cheesecloth and put into the crock with the meat. Place a plate on top of the meat and weigh the plate down, so meat stays under the brine. Let stand 28 to 40 days in a cool place. To cook; wash meat and soak all day in fresh water. Remove meat and place in a pressure cooker with 2 cups water. Add garlic and freshly ground pepper and pressure-cook for 45 minutes.

—Phelpsie Sirlin, Fairbanks

Jellied Moose Nose

Jellied moose nose is a sourdough specialty known and enjoyed only in moose country. It is not easy to prepare, but, like head cheese, is worthwhile as a delicacy, and a way of saving a fair amount of meat.

Cut the upper jawbone of the moose just below the eyes. Put it into a large kettle of scalding water and boil it for 45 minutes. Remove it and put it into cold water to cool. Pick the hairs from the nose as you would the feathers from a duck (the boiling loosens them), and wash it thoroughly.

Put the nose in a kettle and cover it with fresh water. Add a sliced onion, a little garlic, and some pickling spices, and boil it gently until the meat is tender. Let it cool overnight in the broth.

In the morning, take the meat out of the broth and remove the bones and cartilage. You will have two kinds of meat—the bulb of the nose is white and the thin strips along the bone and jowls are dark. For immediate use, slice the meat thinly and pack it into a loaf pan. Cover it with the cooking broth, seasoned as desired with salt, pepper, other spices, and vinegar. This mixture will jell when chilled. Serve cold in slices.

—University of Alaska, Cooperative Extension Service

Alaska Kabob

Yield: enough for two hungry men

1 pound moose, caribou, or mountain sheep
2 small onions, cut thinly across the grain
½ pound thinly sliced bacon, cut in 2-inch pieces
Salt and pepper

Slice meat about ½-inch thick and cut into 2-inch circles. For each person find a straight, green sweetwood stick, such as cottonwood, birch, or willow—about 5 feet long—and sharpen at the small end. Skewer on the stick first a piece of meat, then onion, and bacon, and repeat until there is enough for one person. Broil over a good bed or coals, turning constantly to prevent burning. An easy way to handle the kabob stick is to rest it on a forked stick set securely in the ground at a comfortable distance from the fire. Remove from the stick as eaten and place between slices of bread or rolls. Note: meat is never eaten freshly killed.

—From the *Golden Heart Cookbook*, Fairbanks

Long ago Athabaskans used the moose bladder and pericardial sac from around the heart to store bear grease. Caribou and moose fat could be stored as chunks, but it was not so with bear grease.

Moose Loaf with Dill in Sour Cream Pastry

This is one of Diane's favorite "real Alaskan" dishes. It can be prepared as individual moose tarts, as well.

Yield: 6 to 8 servings

2¼ cups flour
1½ sticks butter, cut into ¼ inch cubes
1 egg
½ cup sour cream

4 tablespoons butter
¼ pound chopped fresh mushrooms
3 pounds lean moose meat, finely
    ground
2 tablespoons flour
1 onion, finely chopped

¼ cup minced parsley
2 teaspoons dried dill weed
1 cup shredded Swiss cheese
½ cup milk
Salt and pepper to taste
1 egg, beaten with 2 tablespoons milk
Sour cream
Lingonberry-port wine sauce (recipe
    follows)

In a large bowl, combine the flour and butter cubes. Using your fingertips, rub the flour and butter together until they have the appearance of flakes of coarse meal. In a small bowl, mix the egg and sour cream; stir this into the flour mixture, working with your fingers until you can gather the dough into a ball. Wrap in waxed paper and refrigerate while you prepare the filling.

Melt the butter in a large skillet and cook the mushrooms and moose meat over medium-high heat until the meat loses its color and the liquid in the pan evaporates. Stir in the flour. Scrape the mixture into a large mixing bowl, and stir in the onion, parsley, dill weed, cheese, milk, and salt and pepper. Let the filling cool.

Roll out half the dough into a rectangle and place on a greased baking sheet. Spread moose filling onto the dough rectangle, leaving a border of dough all around. Roll out remaining dough into a similar rectangle and drape it over the meat. Trim the rectangle neatly and moisten the edges of the dough with the egg-milk mixture; press the edges of the 2 sheets together. Press with the tines of a fork all around to seal the edges. Preheat oven to 375 degrees F. Brush the loaf with remaining egg-milk mixture and prick the top of the loaf in several places to allow steam to escape. You may decorate the top with cut-outs made from the pastry scraps. Bake at 375 degrees F. for 45 minutes, until the pastry is a golden brown.

Serve the moose loaf in thick slices with sour cream and lingonberry-port wine sauce.

Lingonberry-Port Wine Sauce

2 cups lingonberries (Alsakan low
   bush cranberries)

1½ cups sugar
¼ cup port wine

Place ingredients in a saucepan and bring to a fast rolling boil, stirring well. Cook for about 15 minutes, until the mixture jells in the bowl of a spoon. Serve warm with the moose loaf, or chill to serve like cranberry sauce with meats and poultry.

—Diane Shaw, Fairbanks

Mooseburgers

Because moose meat is much leaner than beef, pork sausage is added to make juicier burgers:

Yield: 4 servings

1 pound ground moose meat
½ pound bulk pork sausage
4 crushed soda crackers

1 egg
Salt and pepper to taste
1 slice bacon

Combine the moose, sausage, crackers, egg, salt, and pepper. Shape into burgers. Fry the bacon in a heavy skillet until crisp. Brown the burgers in the bacon fat, and let cook slowly until they are done. This same mixture makes good meatballs to serve with spaghetti and sauce.

> *"Head cheese is made from the head and leg joints of moose or caribou. It is delicious when spiced with onion and celery. The moose nose is one of the most delicious and tender parts to eat boiled. The only part of the moose stomach used traditionally for eating is the third sac, which is called the 'book' or 'bible,' since it has a leaf-like structure that looks like a book," says Betty Starr, Athabaskan from Fairbanks, Alaska.*

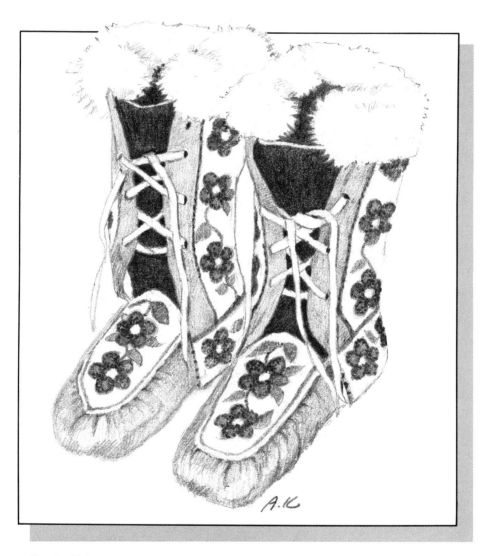

Beaded Moccasins
by April Kelley

The Athabaskan people are well noted for their lovely beadwork.

Glorified Mooseburgers

Yield: 6 servings

2 pounds moose meat or very lean
  beef such as round steak, freshly
  ground
½ stick butter
2 medium onions, chopped
¼ pound fresh mushrooms, sliced

½ teaspoon salt
¼ teaspoon thyme
¼ teaspoon coarse black pepper
⅛ teaspoon crushed rosemary
½ cup sherry wine
½ cup water

Shape the meat into 6 patties. Do not season. Broil the patties (7 or 8 minutes for medium rare).

Meanwhile, make sauce: melt the butter in a small skillet; add the onions, mushrooms, and seasonings, and sauté until they are golden brown. Add the sherry and water; bring to a boil and simmer for 2 or 3 minutes. Pour over the mooseburgers and serve.

—From the *Catholic Daughters of America,* Juneau

Mooseburger Meat Loaf

Yield: 6 servings

2 pounds mooseburger
2 eggs
1 cup ground dry bread crumbs
2 or 3 large onions, ground or finely
  chopped
½ cup chopped celery or 3 tablespoons dried celery tops
2½ cups evaporated milk
1½ teaspoons salt

¼ teaspoon pepper
2 cloves garlic, minced
2 teaspoons celery salt
1 teaspoon dry mustard
¼ teaspoon sage or thyme or ½ teaspoon cumin and 1 tablespoon chili
  powder for a Spanish flavor
3 or 4 slices bacon

Combine mooseburger with other ingredients, except bacon, using enough milk so that the mixture is very soft. Place in a large, deep pan, pressing down well. Do not attempt to shape meat into a loaf. Lay strips of bacon across the top, cover, and bake at 350 degrees F. for 2 to 2½ hours. This loaf is delicious hot or cold and makes great sandwiches.

—From *Out of Alaska's Kitchens,* Anchorage

Italian Pot Roast of Moose

Use moose, reindeer, caribou, or beef in this recipe.

Yield: 8 servings

1 cup chopped mushrooms
½ cup fat
2 large onions, chopped
4 cloves garlic, minced

4 pounds roast
Salt, pepper, ginger
1 8-ounce can tomato sauce
1 cupful pitted ripe olives, sliced

Sauté the onion and garlic in the fat until they are softened. Add the meat, seasoned with salt, pepper, and ginger, and brown on all sides. Cover meat and simmer slowly for 2 hours. Add the mushrooms, tomato sauce and olives, and cook for 1 hour longer. Serve with rice or mashed potatoes.

—Wynola Possenti, Fairbanks

Moose Pot Roast

4- to 5-pound moose roast
Fat for browning
½ cup sherry
2 large onions, sliced
1 can beef consommé
2 bay leaves

⅓ cup vinegar
3 tablespoons ketchup
½ cup raisins
Potatoes, carrots, and other
    vegetables as desired

Brown the roast on all sides in hot fat in a heavy Dutch oven. Remove, and pour sherry over the meat. Brown the onions in the Dutch oven, return meat and sherry to the pan, and add the consommé, bay leaves, vinegar, ketchup, and raisins. Cover and bake at 300 degrees F. for about 45 minutes per pound of roast. During the last hour of cooking, add the potatoes, carrots, and other vegetables used.

—From the *Headstart Cookbook,* Fairbanks

Marinated Moose, Caribou, Venison, or Beef

5- or 6-pound rump or round roast
1½ cups vinegar
3 cups water
3 bay leaves
3 onions, chopped

2 tablespoons fat or oil
½ cup chopped onion
1 teaspoon ginger
1 cup tomato puree
⅔ cup red wine

1 teaspoon cinnamon
1 teaspoon pepper
1 teaspoon ginger

1½ cups meat broth
Salt and pepper to taste
Flour for thickening

Let the meat marinate, refrigerated, in a mixture of the vinegar, water, bay leaves, onions, cinnamon, pepper, and ginger for at least 24 hours, turning the meat several times a day.

Remove meat, wipe it dry and brown it quickly all over in the hot fat or oil in a heavy Dutch oven. Add the chopped onion and let it sauté with the meat for a few minutes. Boil the marinade for 10 minutes and strain 1½ cups of it over the meat. Add the ginger, tomato puree, red wine, meat broth, and salt and pepper; cover and let simmer very slowly for 2 to 3 hours, until meat is tender. Thicken the gravy with a flour and water mixture if desired, and serve with noodles or potatoes.

—From the *Catholic Daughters of America*, Juneau

Marinated Moose Salad

Yield: 4 main dish servings

1 pound cooked moose steak,
  (leftovers)
1 medium onion, thinly sliced
Salt and pepper to taste

2 tablespoons lemon juice
1 cup sour cream
Lettuce

Slice cooked steak into julienne strips. Add the sliced onion, and salt and pepper. Sprinkle lemon juice over meat mixture, and blend in sour cream. Mix well and serve on lettuce leaves.

—From the *Catholic Daughters of America Cookbook*, Juneau

Meat with Cranberries

Yield: 6 servings

2 pounds lean meat (moose or beef), cut in 2-inch cubes
1/2 teaspoon salt
1/4 teaspoon pepper
3 tablespoons flour
2 tablespoons shortening

2 cups Alaskan lingonberries, fresh, frozen, or canned
1 tablespoon sugar
2 sticks cinnamon
1/2 teaspoon ground cloves
3/4 cup water
1 tablespoon flour

Trim all fat from meat and dredge in a mixture of the salt, pepper, and flour. Melt shortening in a Dutch oven and brown the meat over high heat; drain off any fat. Mix lingonberries, sugar, cinnamon, cloves, and water, and pour over the meat. Cover and cook at 300 degrees F. for about 1 1/2 hours. When done, thicken the sauce with the 1 tablespoon flour.

—From *Northern Nuggets,* Fairbanks

Fairbanks Skillet Meal

Yield: 4 servings

1 pound lean ground beef or mooseburger
1 can or 1 pound tomatoes, crushed
1 teaspoon salt
1 teaspoon Worcestershire sauce

1 1/2 cups chopped cabbage
2 tablespoons chopped parsley
1 cup uncooked elbow macaroni or noodles
1/2 cup shredded Cheddar cheese

Cook ground beef or mooseburger over medium heat until browned. If using beef, drain off any excess fat. Blend in tomatoes, salt, and Worcestershire sauce. Bring mixture to a boil, and add the cabbage, parsley, and macaroni; cover. Reduce heat and simmer about 15 minutes or until macaroni is cooked. Sprinkle cheese on top and serve immediately.

—From *Cooking Favorites of Fairbanks, Alaska,* Fairbanks

Moose Meat Soup

Yield: 4 servings

2 cups chopped moose meat
3 potatoes, chopped

2 cups water
1/2 cup raw rice

162

5 carrots, sliced	¼ cup macaroni
2 onions, chopped	Salt and pepper
1 can or 1 pound tomatoes	Fresh turnip or beet greens (optional)

Brown the meat and add the remaining ingredients, cooking until the meat and vegetables are tender. You may add chopped fresh greens toward the end of the cooking, if you wish.

> *"Before the freezers of modern days, lingonberries, (low-bush cranberries) were stored in the ground in birch-bark baskets. They could be used for long periods of time, since much of the ground is layered with many feet of permafrost. Wild rhubarb and fiddlehead fern, when young, are delicious eating. When there was no refrigeration, jerky was made of moose, caribou, and duck. Muskrat and beaver can be used dried, although the fat gets rancid quickly. Lynx has a white meat the consistency of snowshoe hare. Lynx is not a favorite, only a survival food. Porcupine is used only when the menu gets tiresome or as a survival food," says Effie Kokrine, an Athabaskan from Fairbanks, Alaska.*

Moose or Caribou Soup

Yield: 6 servings

If you want to make soup from moose meat or any other kind of meat, just put water in the pot, and boil all your cut up vegetables together—carrots, celery, onion, green peppers. Boil them until they cook.

Put lots of garlic on top of a moose or caribou roast, and cook in the oven for 1 hour, or until half cooked. Then cut it up and put everything into your cooking vegetables, even the juice of your roast. Cook all together. Thicken soup with flour mixed with cold water. Stir the soup while pouring in the flour mixture slowly. Season to taste.

—Sophie Nickolie, Healy

Yukon Moose or Caribou

Yield: 4 to 6 servings

2 pounds moose or caribou, cut into
   stew meat
2 tablespoons lemon juice
1 teaspoon salt
1 teaspoon chili powder

$^1/_3$ cup flour
2 tablespoons fat
$^1/_2$ cup chopped olives or $^1/_4$ cup
   chopped pimiento

Sprinkle meat with lemon juice. Season with salt and chili powder; roll in flour. Brown well on all sides in the fat. Add water to cover and let simmer, covered, about 2 hours. Twenty minutes before serving, remove the lid and let the liquid cook down to a rich gravy. Add olives or pimiento, and serve with noodles, hominy, or rice.

—From *Out of Alaska's Kitchens,* Anchorage

Alaska Hunter's Stew

Yield: 8 servings

4 slices bacon, cut into 1-inch pieces
1 tablespoon butter
1 pound moose meat, cut into 1-inch
   cubes
2 large onions, chopped
3 medium apples, peeled and
   chopped

1 can condensed beef broth
2 cups water
1 teaspoon salt
2 cups chopped carrots
1 pound Polish sausage, cut into 1-inch
   pieces
4 cups shredded cabbage

Cook the bacon until crisp; drain and reserve. Add butter to drippings, and brown the pieces of moose. Add onions and apples; cook for 5 minutes. Add the beef broth, water and salt. Simmer for 1 hour and 20 minutes. Add the carrots and sausage; simmer for 30 minutes. Add the cabbage and reserved bacon; cook for 10 minutes, or until cabbage is tender.

—Irene Peyton, Fairbanks

Moose Sukiyaki

Yield: 4 to 6 servings

1$^1/_2$ pounds moose steak, thinly sliced
   and cut in strips
Beef suet

$^1/_4$ cup water (if needed)
1 can or 1 pound chow mein
   vegetables, drained

½ cup sugar
½ cup sherry
¾ cup soy sauce

½ cup sliced scallions (green onions)
Cooked rice

Heat the suet, and sauté the meat in a large skillet. Add the sugar, sherry, and soy sauce; cook 5 minutes. Add the vegetables and scallions, and heat just until hot. Serve over rice.

—From *Cooking up a Storm,* Homer

Moose Tongue

Yield: 2 to 4 servings depending on size

1 moose tongue
1 teaspoon garlic powder

3 bay leaves
1 tablespoon vinegar

Boil the tongue in water with garlic salt and bay leaves for 3 to 4 hours, depending on size. Remove tongue and peel off outer skin (it should peel off easily if tongue is well cooked). Serve hot, in slices, and sprinkle with vinegar if desired. It is delicious served with boiled potatoes.

Moose tongue may also be served cold, and sliced for sandwiches, *etcetera.*

The Han people live south and near the Canadian border. They rely on the annual run of silver, king, and chum salmon. Historically, the king salmon were caught in dip nets lowered from canoes. The chum salmon were caught in fish traps. All through the summer, salmon fishing activities continue along with its storage and preservation for use during the long winter months. Waterfowl is hunted by men. Traditionally, women used to pick wild rhubarb and gather bird eggs. The winter subsistence for the Han is much like the Ingalik. Historically, the Han used caribou-catching corrals.

Sweet and Sour Moose

Yield: 4 servings

2 pounds boneless moose or beef
1 tablespoon shortening
1 onion, chopped
4 tablespoons flour, browned in the oven
1/2 cup vinegar

1 cup meat stock (liquid from simmering moose)
8 whole cloves
8 whole allspice
1 stick cinnamon, broken
2 teaspoons salt
2 tablespoons sugar

Wipe meat and simmer slowly in water until tender. In another pan, sauté onion in melted shortening until tender. Stir in flour, then remaining ingredients (tie spices in cheesecloth). Cook until thickened. Cut meat into pieces and simmer in the sauce about 30 minutes.

—From the *Golden Heart Cookbook,* Fairbanks

Tender Moose

Yield: 3 servings

1 pound moose stew meat
1 package dried onion soup mix
1 cup water

Place ingredients in a covered casserole dish. Bake at 325 degrees F., covered, for 4 hours.

—Jean Kurtz, Anchorage

Roast Mountain Goat

Yield: 6 to 8 servings

1 5- or 6-pound roast of mountain goat
2 cloves garlic
Salt and pepper

Water
High bushcranberry catsup
(see page 289)

Clean the meat thoroughly, then make small slits in the meat with a sharp knife and insert small pieces of garlic. Rub meat with salt and pepper. Put the roast in a pan with a small amount of water, and bake at 325 degrees F. until tender. Turn up *oven heat, and brown the roast quickly, if desired. Serve with high bushcranberry ketchup for a real Alaskan meal.*

Wild Rabbit with Potato Dressing

Yield: 4 servings

1 wild rabbit (snowshoe hare, Arctic hare), chopped
Salt, pepper, and flour
Bacon fat for frying
2 cups mashed potatoes, unseasoned

2 teaspoons butter
1 teaspoon salt
½ teaspoon pepper
1 teaspoon thyme or ½ teaspoon sage
1 cup chopped celery

Season pieces of rabbit with salt and pepper. Roll in flour, and brown in hot bacon fat. Cover and set aside. Mix remaining ingredients to make a dressing and place in a well-greased Dutch oven or casserole. Place rabbit on dressing. Cover, and bake at 350 degrees F. for about 1 hour, or until rabbit is tender. Add water if dressing seems to be drying out during cooking.

—From *Cooking Up A Storm,* Homer

Because the early-day Athabaskans were great nomadic wanderers, they made contact with people who lived beyond the Interior region of Alaska. The Kutchin, who did a lot of trading, acquired many items that had travelled many miles from their source. Dentalium shells came from the Pacific Northwest. Iron pots, which originally came from Siberia or from early-day ships that reached the Arctic Ocean, were trade items obtained from the northern slope region Eskimos.

Rabbit Pot Roast

Yield: 4 servings

1 wild rabbit, cleaned and cut into serving pieces
Flour
Salt, pepper, and thyme
Butter or fat for browning

2 or 3 onions, sliced
2 teaspoons prepared mustard
1½ to 2 cups boiling water
1 bay leaf

Shake pieces of rabbit in a paper bag with a mixture of the flour, salt, pepper, and thyme. Brown in hot butter in a Dutch oven. Add onions while you are browning the rabbit. Add remaining ingredients to the Dutch oven and let simmer, covered, for about 2½ hours, until rabbit is tender.

—From the *Nome Cookbook,* Nome

Pioneer Roast Rabbit

Chop the rabbit liver fine, and mix it with bread crumbs and a chopped slice of salt pork. Season this with salt, pepper, and onion juice. Stuff the rabbit with this, sew up, and annoint well with salad oil and lemon juice. Leave it for 1 hour. Lay slices of bacon over the rabbit, then put into a roaster, and pour a cup of boiling water over it; cover, and cook for 1 hour. Take off the bacon, spread melted butter over rabbit, and let it brown. Thicken the gravy with browned flour.

—From *The Fairbanks Cookbook,* circa 1910, Fairbanks

Bear Steaks

Cut steaks or chops into 1-inch-thick serving size pieces. Mix ½ cup flour, ½ teaspoon cloves and 1 teaspoon ground ginger. Pound the mixture into the meat on both sides. Brown in fat in a moderately hot skillet. Salt and pepper after browning. Cover the skillet, lower heat and simmer the meat for 10 to 15 minutes. Always cook bear until well done.

—University of Alaska, Cooperative Extension Service

Corned Bear Meat

100 pounds bear meat
8 pounds salt
4 pounds sugar

2 ounces baking soda
2 ounces saltpeter

Salt the meat down in layers in a keg, alternating the salt. Let it stand overnight. At the same time the meat is put down, make a solution of the sugar, baking soda, and saltpeter in 1 gallon of warm water, and let it stand overnight. Next day, pour the solution over the meat. After a few days, drain off the solution and bring it to a boil, straining off the blood. Cool the liquid and pour it back over the meat, keeping meat completely covered by inverting a large plate on the meat, weighing it down if necessary. This is ready to use as corned meat within 4 to 6 weeks, but it may be used at intermediate stages as well.

Soak or parboil the meat before cooking, if too salty. Always cook bear meat very well.

In order to survive in the Interior of Alaska, in older times, the Athabaskan people needed a place to keep out of the deep cold of the winter and the chilly rains and mosquitoes of the summer. In the summer, people would often sit around inside bark-walled houses filled with smoke from smudge fires to fight the hordes of mosquitoes. Even when people went outside the houses, they carried with them a little smoke from a portable smudge-pot. In colder seasons, substantial log dwellings with thick insulation roof covers of dirt were made. Modern day villages are made up of log or frame homes, which are well-built and insulated. They are kept warm with woodburning stoves. Small log cabins are often built along permanent traplines. Temporary encampments are usually canvas-wall tents.

Roast Bear Meat No. 1

Use about one 8-pound roast off of the rump of a young bear. Put it in cold water, along with 3 or 4 sliced onions, and let it soak for about 4 hours. Remove meat from water and wipe dry. Force small pieces of garlic deep into the meat, using a sharp knife to make holes. Put pieces as near to the bone as possible. Season meat with salt and pepper, and brown slowly all over in hot bacon drippings. Bake in an open roasting pan for 3 hours at 350 degrees F., turning the meat several times during cooking.

—From the *PTA Cookbook*, Petersburg

"A black bear killed in the fall is very good to eat, and usually is very fat. The fat can be rendered useful in baking products like pastries, doughnuts, or fry-bread. Bear meat is oily, because of intra-muscular fat. It should be cooked like pork to avoid trichinosis," says Effie Kokrine, Athabaskan from Fairbanks, Alaska.

Cache
Photo
Fairbanks Daily News-Miner

Roast Bear Meat No. 2

3- or 4-pound young bear roast
Vinegar
Red wine

Salt, pepper, allspice, garlic, thyme,
and marjoram
2 tablespoons fat

Wipe the meat and place in a large bowl. Cover with a mixture of half vinegar and half red wine. Let soak at least 3 hours or overnight. Remove meat and save the liquid. Season meat with the seasonings; brown on all sides in the hot fat in a Dutch oven. When very brown, add about 1½ cups of the wine-vinegar mixture. Cover and cook very slowly until tender, about 30 minutes per pound of meat.

—From *Alaska's Cooking,* Anchorage

Orange Glazed Bear Roast

4 pound bear roast
1 small onion, chopped
1 tablespoon butter
2 tablespoons brown sugar

1½ teaspoons cornstarch
½ teaspoon ground ginger
1 cup orange juice
1 tablespoon bottled steak sauce

Place roast, fat side up, on a rack in a roasting pan. Roast at 325 degrees F. for 1½ hours. Meanwhile, sauté onion in butter in a small pan; stir in the remaining ingredients. Cook, stirring constantly, until thick. Brush part of mixture over the meat. Continue roasting, brushing meat every 15 minutes, for 1 hour longer, until meat is richly glazed.

—From Sugardoe Homemakers, *The Northern Lights,* Nenana

THE ALUTIIQ

Alutiiq is the name given to a linguistic variety of Central Yupik that is spoken in the Gulf of Alaska, from the Alaska Peninsula to Prince William Sound, including Kodiak and nearby islands. These people are distinguished from the Aleut.

The Alutiiq-speaking Eskimos occupied their region when it was discovered by Europeans. Archaeologists have found signs of human habitation as far back as 3500 B.C. on Kodiak Island. Mountainous areas of the Kenai-Chugach Range in the lower, south-central part of Alaska are from seven thousand to thirteen thousand feet in height. All high parts of this range are buried in ice fields. The separate Saint Elias Mountains of the same area are fourteen to nineteen thousand foot masses, which have glaciers from four to fifteen miles wide and eighty miles long.

The islands of the Kodiak Island group are drained mostly by swift, clear streams that are less than ten miles long. Two rivers, each about twenty-five miles long, drain much of southwestern Kodiak Island.

Two natural catastrophes have hit the Alutiiq's region during historic times. The eruption of Mount Katmai in 1912 and the great earthquake of 1964. The Katmai eruption dumped ash eighteen inches deep over the region; its effects on the people, flora, and fauna were not overcome for many years. The 1964 earthquake generated tsunami waves that caused great devastation to the fishing fleet, shore facilities, and towns throughout the region.

Parts of some of the Kodiak Islands support a lot of spruce timber. Willow and alder are also common, along with shrubs and grasses. The Kodiak Island area is suitable for agriculture because of its maritime environment.

The mountainous areas along the Prince William Sound of lower, south-central Alaska serve as a barrier to the flow of cold air from wintertime Interior Alaska. Precipitation is heavy. Snow accumulations in the Prince William Sound sometimes exceed ten feet. Forests here are predominantly Sitka spruce and western hemlock with dense patches of alder occurring near timberline, on slide areas, and on steeper exposures. Cottonwood, birch, willow, and other woody plants are scattered. Berries are found in great variety and seasonal abundance. Grasses dominate the deltas of rivers.

The original livelihood patterns of the Alutiiqs, called *Koniags* on Kodiak Island, were altered by the Russians. Hundreds of men with their bidarkas, which are skin boats, were organized into fleets and sent on long sea otter hunting expeditions lasting sometimes a year or more. The traditional ways of life were altered with the activities and developments of the Russians. Iron foundries were built and operated, ships were built, and agriculture practiced. The sea otter stocks were nearly extinct after the turn of the century. After Alaska was purchased by the United States, gardening and other Russian endeavors were abandoned, and commercial salmon fisheries developed rapidly. Many Alutiiqs are commercial fisherman today. Substantial crab and shrimp fisheries have developed in recent years, and bottom fish fisheries have great potential to add to their economy.

Village sites for the Alutiiqs, called *Chugach,* along the Prince William Sound, were near protected waters, since travel here traditionally was by boat. Nearby, rich salmon streams and shellfish beds were important. Vitus Bering saw their hunting camps in 1741. The most important sources of food were sea mammals and salmon. With the building of salmon canneries in the late 1800s, the Alutiiq were employed as fishermen and cannery workers.

Many other early Russian influences, including the Russian Orthodox Church, are apparent today.

Russian Orthodox Church
by Rachel Levine

Clearly the Alutiiq people are an industrious and genuine people closely attached to the places in which they live.

$\mathcal{S}$ EAFOOD AND FISH

Fish and seafood are as popular and prized in Alaska as they are in the rest of the world. What we have that other lands often lack, is a tremendous variety of fresh-water fish and ocean seafoods which inhabit the vast and relatively clean waterways and coastline of our enormous state. Because every village and city in Alaska is close to water, these foods have been an extremely important part of our diet.

From the cook's point of view, fish and shellfish are tender, quick-cooking, mildly flavored and take well to a tremendous variety of seasonings, sauces, and cooking methods. They are literally a playground for the creative cook! In addition, seafoods are delicious and nutritious, and many are prized (and priced) as delicacies. So Alaskans from all regions are very fortunate to have an abundance of fish and other seafoods sharing the center, along with meats, of Alaskan meals.

Salmon has been the true staple of Alaskan seafoods. Various kinds are found, usually in great abundance, both in the oceans and Interior waterways of nearly the entire state. Historically it has been of great importance as a staple food for nearly all Alaskans. Beside the many ways of preparing fresh or frozen salmon, it is popular smoked, dried, salted, and pickled, showing the great use of and need to preserve such an important food.

Halibut and sheefish are two absolutely delicious firm, and pure white fish, which are greatly used and prized in Alaska, although they often do not find their way out of the state. And of course, Alaskan king and snow crab meat are prized everywhere, and are usually available canned or frozen. Many other seafoods and fresh water fish are abundant in Alaska, and they usually have their counterparts found elsewhere: shrimp, clams, octopus, cod, snapper, trout, whitefish, tomcod, and grayling are only a few of the many kinds. Hopefully, it will not be difficult to enjoy the uniquely Alaskan seafood recipes in this chapter, no matter where you live.

The armchair travelers amongst you will note some of the strong Japanese and Russian influences in the regional seafood dishes of the Aleutians, from the salmon-vegetable pies, to seafoods cooked with seaweed, seasoned with soy sauce, and served with rice. Similarly, Norwegian influences are seen in seafood dishes principally from Southeast Alaska. We are sure that you will enjoy a journey through all the regions of Alaska, and all the varied groups of people inhabiting our state, by trying some of these Alaskan fish and seafood specialties.

Smoked Abalone

Using an oven rack on an open fire, place abalone on top of the rack, shell side down. Keep on the fire until tender when poked with a fork. Remove from the fire and cool. Cut abalone from the shell to eat.

—Tsimshian, Metlakatla

The Koniag-and Chugach-Alutiiq-speaking people eat many species of fish found in their different areas, particularly salmon, halibut, herring, crabs, and clams. Prominent marine mammals used are the sea otter, harbor seal, and sea lion. Whales and porpoise also frequent the coastal waters. Historically, the culture and economy were centered on these resources. Fish and marine invertebrates were a source of food, as were the birds and their eggs, along with marine mammals.

Abalone (or Octopus) Goma Zu

Yield: 4 to 8 servings

1 tablespoon sesame seeds
1 tablespoon sugar
¼ teaspoon salt
1 teaspoon cornstarch
2 tablespoons water

½ cup rice-wine vinegar or white vinegar
2 small cucumbers
Salt
1 pound boiled abalone (or octopus),
    sliced in thin strips, 2-by-½-inches

Toast sesame seeds on a baking sheet in a 350 degree F. oven for 5 minutes. Meanwhile, blend the sugar, salt, cornstarch, water, and vinegar in a saucepan; heat, stirring, until it thickens. Add sesame seeds and allow to cool. Peel the cucumbers, slice them in half lengthwise (remove any large seeds), then cut into thin crosswise slices and sprinkle them with salt. Combine the cucumbers, sliced abalone (or octopus) and cooled vinegar mixture. Chill before serving.

Silianka (Eskimo Clam Soup)

3 medium potatoes, chopped
1 slice salt pork, chopped

4 cups shucked and finely chopped
    clams

Wild onion   Salt to taste

Cook potatoes in water to cover for about 5 minutes. Add salt pork and wild onion. Add the clams and simmer until tender, adding salt to taste.

Gooey Duck Clams

Actually, "geoduck" clams are a large, Southeast Alaska variety. Larger than any other clam in the world, except the giant East Indies clam, the geoducks average about three pounds each. Geoducks have been found that weigh as much as twenty pounds each!

The clam meat is sometimes baked in a slow oven, strung up, and hung to dry. It is then eaten with ooligan grease or plain, like jerky.

Fried Gooey Duck: Shell and clean the clams, slit one side of the neck to open up flat and slice the main part of the gooey duck in half. Dip in beaten egg with grated onion added, then dip in seasoned cornmeal. Fry for 3 minutes on each side and serve with steamed rice.

Scrambled Eggs and Gooey Duck: Clean gooey duck and mince or grind. Fry small pieces of bacon until crisp; add beaten eggs and minced gooey duck, and scramble.

—Tsimshian, Metlakatla

Horse Clams

Drop the clams into boiling water until the clams open and you can get the meat out. Squeeze the clams and mash them into the juice. Mix them with ooligan grease and serve seaweed on the side.

—Tsimshian, Metlakatla

Northern Lights
Photo
Fairbanks Daily News-Miner

Alaska Razor Clam Chowder

Yield: 4 to 6 servings

2 cups chopped razor clam meat
1 cup diced potatoes
½ cup chopped celery
½ green pepper, chopped
1 medium onion, chopped

1 or 2 cloves garlic, finely chopped or
    pressed
3 cups water
Salt and pepper to taste
2 cups milk
4 tablespoons butter

Cook the clams and vegetables in the water with salt and pepper to taste, until the vegetables are tender. Scald the milk and butter and add to the clam mixture. Serve hot, garnished with fresh, minced parsley.

Clam Suey

1 bucket of clams in the shell
4 to 6 slices bacon
1 stalk celery, sliced

1 large onion, sliced
¹/₂ medium-size cabbage, sliced
Soy sauce to taste

Steam the clams open and cut the meat into small pieces. Fry the bacon until crisp and remove from the pan. Fry the clams in the bacon grease and add the vegetables. Add a little water and soy sauce, and simmer briefly until vegetables are cooked, but not mushy. Serve with rice.

—Tsimshian, Metlakatla

Codfish or Halibut Liver Paste

Clean and rinse well the liver of a halibut or codfish. Let the liver cook in water for a short time. Drain it, and mash the liver with a fork. Chop approximately half an onion and add it to the liver, along with salt and pepper. Mix well, and serve the paste as a spread on bread.

Boiled Codfish Stomachs

Take a codfish stomach and clean it on the inside and outside, scraping it well. Clean the liver of the cod and stuff it into the cod stomach, filling it half full. After the stomach is stuffed, hold it in the palm of the hand and squeeze it, mashing up all the liver. Then put it into a pot of cold water, add a dash of salt, and cook it. Let it cool before you serve it. This type of food is good for breakfast.

Crab A La Fannie

Yield: 4 to 6 servings

8 slices bread, crusts removed and cut
   into cubes
2 cans crab meat
1 cup chopped celery
½ cup chopped green pepper
1 cup chopped onion
1 cup sliced mushrooms

4 eggs, beaten
3 cups milk
½ cup mayonnaise
2 cups shredded cheese
Paprika
Parsley, chopped

In a buttered casserole dish spread half the bread cubes. Top with the crabmeat and vegetables. Cover with remaining bread cubes. Whisk together the eggs, milk, and mayonnaise and pour over the casserole. Let the casserole stand, refrigerated, for several hours or overnight to completely absorb the liquid. Top with shredded cheese, paprika, and parsley. Bake at 350 degrees F. for 1 hour.

—Gladys Parker, Fairbanks

Crab Meat Bourbonnaise

Yield: 6 servings

¼ cup butter
2 cups sliced fresh mushrooms
¼ cup diced pimiento
1 tomato, peeled and sliced
1 tablespoon finely chopped onion
4 tablespoons flour
2 cups heavy cream

Salt and pepper
1 pound crab meat or 2 7½-ounce
   cans crabmeat
1 tablespoon minced chives
¼ cup bourbon whisky
Cooked wild rice

Melt the butter in a skillet and sauté the mushrooms for about 5 minutes. Add the pimiento, tomato, and onion, and cook for 1 minute longer. Blend in the flour; add the cream, crab meat, salt, and pepper, and heat until mixture is thickened and bubbly. Add the chives and bourbon, and serve over wild rice.

—Virginia Doyle "Bunny" Heiner, Fairbanks

Crab Casserole Newburg

Yield: 6 servings

3 tablespoons butter
4 tablespoons flour
1½ cups milk
½ teaspoon nutmeg
Salt and pepper
2 teaspoons sherry
1 pound crabmeat
½ cup canned, sliced mushrooms
¼ cup chopped green pepper

½ cup chopped celery
½ cup chopped pimiento
1 teaspoon paprika
Salt and pepper to taste
¼ cup fresh bread crumbs
¼ cup grated Parmesan cheese
3 tablespoons sherry
Lemon wedges

Preheat oven to 350 degrees F. Melt butter; add flour and gradually stir in the milk. Cook, stirring, until sauce is thick and smooth. Remove from heat and add nutmeg, salt, pepper, and sherry. Mix in the crabmeat, mushrooms, green pepper, celery, pimiento, paprika, and salt and pepper. Place in a greased casserole or individual ramekins; top with crumbs and cheese. Bake for about 30 minutes at 350 degrees F., until heated through. Sprinkle with the 3 tablespoons sherry and serve with lemon wedges.

—From the *PTA Cookbook*, Petersburg

Crab Fried Rice

½ cup chopped onion
¼ cup butter or oil
2 cups cooked rice
1 4-ounce can sliced mushrooms,
  drained

1 teaspoon soy sauce
1 cup Alaska king crab meat
2 eggs, well beaten
1 teaspoon butter
1 tablespoon chopped green olives

Sauté onion in the butter or oil until softened. Add the rice and cook over low heat, stirring constantly, until golden brown. Add the mushrooms, and sauté briefly. Add soy sauce and crab meat. Heat through and serve garnished with strips of egg omelette (made from the eggs and 1 teaspoon butter) and green onion.

—From *Cooking Up A Storm*, Homer

Open-Face Crab Louis

Yield: 6 servings

1 pound crab meat or 2 6½-ounce
   cans crab meat
12 slices white bread, toasted, crusts
   trimmed
6 lettuce leaves
3 tomatoes
1 cup mayonnaise

3 tablespoons ketchup
2 tablespoons chopped sweet pickle
   or drained pickle relish
1 tablespoon lemon juice
2 hard-boiled eggs, sliced
Paprika

Pick over the crab meat. On each plate arrange a whole slice and two diagonally cut half slices of toasted bread. Place a lettuce leaf, 3 tomato slices and approximatley ⅓ cup crab meat on the toast. Combine the mayonnaise, ketchup, chopped pickle, and lemon juice; spoon 3 tablespoons of this mixture over each sandwich. Garnish with hard-boiled egg slices and paprika.

—University of Alaska, Cooperative Extension Service

Rice and Crabmeat

Yield: 3 servings

½ onion, finely chopped
2 tablespoons butter
½ cup light cream
1 cup cooked rice

1 cup flaked crab meat
½ cup chili sauce
Toast (if desired)

Sauté onion in the butter for 2 minutes. Add cream, rice, and crabmeat, and heat slowly until almost boiling. Add the chili sauce and serve on toast, if desired.

Kodiak Crab Meat Omelette

Yield: 2 servings

4 tablespoons shortening or butter
1 green onion, chopped
1 teaspoon finely chopped fresh ginger
½ pound crab meat

1 tablespoon dry sherry
2 eggs, well beaten
Salt and pepper to taste

Heat the shortening or butter in a 12-inch skillet and sauté the green onion and ginger briefly. Add the crab meat, sherry, and beaten eggs. Sprinkle with salt and pepper to taste and cook for about 2 minutes, stirring and lifting cooked portions to let uncooked egg run underneath. Cook until just set and serve immediately.

—From *What's Cooking in Kodiak*, Kodiak

Midnight Sun
Photo
Fairbanks Daily News-Miner

Hideaway
Photo
Fairbanks Daily News-Miner

Kodiak Salad

This is a very attractive salad for buffets.

Yield: 4 to 6 servings

2½ cups or 1 pound flaked crab meat,
  or other cooked seafood
½ cup chopped celery
2 cups chopped lettuce
1 tablespoon chopped stuffed green
  olives
1 tablespoon chopped ripe olives

Salt, pepper, and paprika
1 small cucumber, thinly sliced
½ cup bottled French dressing
1 medium head Romaine lettuce
4 sprigs parsley, chopped
1 can asparagus spears, drained
3 tomatoes, quartered

½ cup mayonnaise   1 green pepper, thinly sliced

Toss together the crab meat, celery, lettuce, and olives. Add the mayonnaise, and toss lightly (mayonnaise should just barely coat the ingredients). Season to taste with salt, pepper, and parika. Marinate the sliced cucumber in the French dressing for 5 minutes.

Line a large salad bowl with Romaine leaves. Drain the cucumber slices. Heap the crab mixture into the lined bowl. Garnish with cucumber slices, paprika, parsley, asparagus, tomatoes, and green pepper. Serve immediately.

—From the *Catholic Daughters of America*, Juneau

Cream of Crab Soup

Yield: 6 servings

6 tablespoons butter
3 cups cooked crab meat or
   3 6½-ounce cans crab meat
1½ cups diced carrots
¾ cup minced onion
½ cup chopped celery
1 bay leaf

Pinch of thyme
6 cups water
2½ teaspoons salt
3 tablespoons flour
Paprika
1½ cups light cream

Melt 2 tablespoons of the butter in a skillet; add carrots, onion, celery, bay leaf, and thyme, and cook five minutes. Reserve 6 pieces of firm crab meat; add the rest to the vegetables. Add the water and salt, and simmer gently for 20 minutes. Strain liquid from crab and vegetables, reserving both. Melt the remaining butter in a saucepan, stir in the flour and let bubble for 1 minute. Add the hot crab-vegetable liquid and cook, stirring constantly, until it is thick and smooth. Serve the soup with or without the crab-vegetable mixture, each serving garnished with a piece of firm crabmeat.

During the 1920s it was recognized that the Kodiak bear was the largest carnivorous animal in North America. Since that time, the commercial guiding industry has developed in both the Alaska Peninsula and Kodiak.

Alaskan Crab Pie

Yield: 4 to 6 servings

2 cups flour
1 teaspoon sugar
1 squeeze of lemon juice
Pinch of salt
1/2 cup butter, chopped
1 to 3 tablespoons ice water
1 cup flaked crab meat
2 eggs, beaten

1/2 cup heavy cream
1 tablespoon lemon juice
1 teaspoon chives
3/4 teaspoon garlic salt
1/2 teaspoon salt
1/8 teaspoon pepper
1 1/2 cups shredded Swiss cheese

To make crust: Sift flour and sugar into a bowl. Add lemon juice, salt, and butter. Cover well with flour and rub together lightly with tips of your fingers until it resembles fine bread crumbs. While rubbing, keep lifting the flour into the bowl so air can mix in also and the butter does not become too soft. Make a well in the center of the mixture and very gradually add the ice water, mixing with one hand or a knife. Roll out dough and line a 9-inch pie plate. Preheat oven to 375 degrees F. Place crab meat in unbaked pastry shell. Mix together remaining ingredients, except cheese, and pour over crab; sprinkle with shredded Swiss cheese. Bake at 375 degrees F. for 30 to 40 minutes or until the custard is set and the pie is puffed and golden brown.

—Shirley Dyer, Seward

Crab Salad

Yield: 2 to 3 main dish servings

4 medium potatoes, boiled, peeled,
    and sliced
1/2 pound crab meat
1 large mild onion, chopped
1 cup chopped celery

2 hard-boiled eggs, chopped or
    sliced
1/2 teaspoon paprika
Salt and pepper
Mayonnaise

Mix all ingredients, using enough mayonnaise to moisten. Chill for at least 2 hours. Serve attractively on lettuce as a main dish salad.

—From the *PTA Cookbook*, Petersburg

Hot Crab Salad

Yield: 8 servings

2 cups crab meat
1 1/2 cups soft white bread crumbs
6 hard-boiled eggs, chopped
1 cup evaporated milk
1 1/2 cups mayonnaise
1 tablespoon chopped parsley

1 tablespoon finely chopped onion
1/2 teaspoon salt
1/2 teaspoon pepper
1/4 teaspoon cayenne pepper
Dash of hot sauce
Buttered bread crumbs

Combine all ingredients except buttered bread crumbs, and bake in a small, buttered casserole dish for 20 minutes at 350 degrees F. You may also bake the mixture in buttered scallop or clam shells. Before serving, sprinkle with the buttered bread crumbs.

—Dolores Dodson, Fairbanks

Swiss Pie with Crab Sauce

Yield: 4 to 6 servings

1 unbaked 9-inch pie shell
4 eggs, separated
1 1/2 cups light cream
1/2 teaspoon salt
1/2 teaspoon nutmeg
6 ounces Swiss cheese, shredded
  (1 1/2 cups)

1 cup crab meat or a 7 1/2-ounce can
  crab meat
2 tablespoons butter
2 teaspoons flour
1/2 teaspoon salt
1 cup light cream

Bake the pie shell for 7 minutes at 450 degrees F. Reduce oven heat to 350 degrees F. and remove pie shell. In a large bowl, beat the egg yolks, and combine with the cream, salt, and nutmeg. In another bowl, beat the egg whites until they form stiff peaks. Fold the egg whites into the yolk mixture, and fold this into the cheese. Pour into the pie shell and bake at 350 degrees F. for 40 to 45 minutes.

Meanwhile, prepare crab sauce: drain and flake the crab meat, and heat it with the butter. Blend in the flour, salt, and 1 cup cream. Stir over medium heat until thickened. Slice the pie and top each serving with crab sauce.

Dungeness Crab Stew

Yield: 5 servings

2 or 3 live Dungeness crabs
5 slices bacon
3 onions, chopped
1 green pepper, chopped
3 tablespoons cornstarch

Water
2 tablespoons butter
1 tablespoon soy sauce
Salt and pepper

Boil the crabs for 20 minutes. Remove meat from the claws and bodies. Fry bacon in a large skillet; add the onions and green pepper, and cook until tender. Add the cornstarch and enough water to thicken into a gravy. Add the butter and the crab meat, and simmer briefly. Season with the soy sauce, and salt and pepper to taste.

Baked Halibut No. 1

Halibut, cut into serving-size pieces
Parmesan cheese, grated
1/2 cup salad oil

1 teaspoon garlic salt
Cracker crumbs

Preheat oven to 450 degrees F. Roll halibut in the Parmesan cheese. Dip into a mixture of the oil and garlic salt. Roll fish in cracker crumbs. Bake on a flat pan at 450 degrees F. for 12 minutes.

—Audrey Myers, Wrangell

Baked Halibut No. 2

Bacon slices
Thin onion slices
Halibut cheeks or sections of halibut
    steak (skin and bones removed)
Salt
3 tablespoons butter (per pound of
    fish)

3 tablespoons flour (per pound of fish)
Buttered crumbs
3 tablespoons flour
1 1/2 cups milk or thin cream
Lemon slices, pimiento strips, and
    parsley (garnish)

Line the bottom of a flat baking dish with short slices of bacon and partially cook in the oven or under the broiler. Place a layer of thin onion slices over the bacon, then add a layer of halibut. Salt lightly. Work together the 3 tablespoons each of butter and flour (per pound of fish) and spread over the fish. Cover with buttered crumbs, and bake at 350 degrees F. for 45 minutes.

Drain fat from the baking dish into a saucepan. Add the 3 tablespoons flour and mix well. Whisk in the milk or cream, and let cook, stirring, until sauce boils and thickens. Season to taste, and pour it around the fish. Garnish with lemon slices, pimiento strips, and parsley.

—Susie Swaim, Fairbanks

Lupine
by April Kelley

The lupine is one of the many flowers found in the area populated by the Alutiiq-speaking Eskimos.

Savory Baked Halibut

Yield: 4 servings

2 pounds halibut, skinned, boned, and
  cut in thin slices
Butter or bacon fat
1 medium onion, finely chopped
½ green pepper, chopped

Salt and pepper
2 tablespoons soy sauce
¾ cup water
Butter

Brown the halibut slices on both sides in the butter or bacon fat. Place fish in a casserole dish, and sprinkle with the onion and green pepper. Salt and pepper to taste. Mix the soy sauce and water, and pour over the fish. Dot with butter and bake, uncovered, at 350 degrees F. for 1 hour.

Baked Halibut Supreme

Yield: 4 to 6 servings

2 pounds halibut steaks
2 tablespoons butter
1 4-ounce can sliced mushrooms,
  drained

1 cup sour cream
¼ cup white wine
1 teaspoon salt
Paprika

Preheat oven to 425 degrees F. Place halibut in a buttered shallow baking dish. Bake at 435 degrees F. for 10 minutes.

Meanwhile, sauté the mushrooms in the butter for a few minutes. Remove from heat, and add sour cream, wine, and salt. Remove halibut from oven and pour the sauce over the fish. Sprinkle with paprika. Lower oven heat to 375 degrees F., and return fish to oven; bake for 10 minutes longer.

— Parent-Teachers Organization, Coffman Cove

Sour Cream Baked Halibut

Yield: 6 servings

2 pounds halibut fillets, or other boneless fish fillets about ¾-inch thick
White, semi-sweet wine

Dry bread crumbs, plain or seasoned
  with herbs and Parmesan cheese
1 cup sour cream
½ cup mayonnaise
½ cup sliced green onions

Preheat oven to 425 degrees F. Dip fillets in wine and coat with the dry bread crumbs. Place in a single layer in a buttered baking dish. Mix sour cream, mayonnaise, and green onion and spoon over the fish. Bake, uncovered, at 425 degrees F. for 20 to 25 minutes.

Chef Dieter's Halibut en Papillote

Yield: 6 servings

6 7-ounce halibut filets
3 cucumbers, peeled, seeded, and
 sliced
1 tablespoon fresh dillweed or 1 teaspoon dried
6 tablespoons butter
1/2 teaspoon salt
Pinch of pepper

2 tablespoons parsley
2 tablespoons green onions
1/4 cup chablis
1/4 cup French brandy
1/2 cup butter, at room temperature
1 cup whipping cream
6 sheets oven-proof (parchment)
 paper

Cut pockets in halibut fillets. Sauté cucumbers and dillweed lightly in the 6 tablespoons butter (do not overcook). Add salt and pepper; fill pockets generously with cucumbers. Puree parsley and green onions with chablis; cook in a small saucepan to reduce until slightly thickened. Add the brandy and remove from heat. Add the 1/2 cup softened butter to the sauce, then whisk in the cream. Place each halibut filet on a sheet of oven-proof paper and cover with sauce. Fold and crimp paper to enclose the halibut. Bake in a convection oven at 325 degrees for 15 minutes. (If using a regular oven, bake at 375 degrees F. for 20 or 25 minutes.)

—Dieter Doppelfeld, Anchorage

Deep-Fried Halibut with Sweet-Sour Sauce

Yield: 4 to 6 servings

2 eggs, beaten
1 cup flour
1 teaspoon baking powder
1 teaspoon salt
1 tablespoon vegetable oil

Stale beer
2 pounds halibut fillet, cut into serving
  pieces
Oil for deep frying

Mix eggs, flour, baking powder, salt, and oil with enough beer to make a medium-thick batter. Dip pieces of halibut into the batter, and deep fry in hot oil until golden on both side. Serve with Sweet-Sour Sauce (recipe follows).

—Jennie Wenstrom, Fairbanks

Sweet-Sour Sauce

¹/₄ cup vinegar
¹/₄ cup brown sugar
¹/₄ cup ketchup
2 tablespoons soy sauce

¹/₄ cup water
1 teaspoon cornstarch
¹/₂ teaspoon ground ginger
¹/₄ teaspoon garlic powder

Mix all ingredients in a saucepan until well blended. Cook, stirring, over medium heat until sauce boils and thickens.

—Jennie Wenstrom, Fairbanks

Halibut Delmonico

Yield: 6 servings

6 halibut fillets
1 onion, sliced
1 pint milk
2 tablespoons butter or margarine
2 tablespoons flour
2 tablespoons sherry

1 cup fresh, seedless white grapes or
  2 small cans seedless white grapes
Grated cheese
Bread crumbs
Butter

Place the fish fillets in a large skillet with the onion and milk. Simmer about 8 minutes, covered, until fish is just cooked. Grease a large, flat casserole, and lay the fish fillets in it. Preheat oven to 350 degrees F. Make a sauce by melting the butter, stirring in the flour, and then the milk in which the fish was poached. Cook, stirring, until sauce is thickened. Add the sherry and grapes to the sauce, and pour over the fish. Sprinkle generously with grated cheese, bread crumbs, and bits of butter. Bake at 350 degrees F. for about 25 minutes, until well heated.

—From the *PTA Cookbook*, Petersburg

Janis's Halibut

Marinate halibut, cut into 2-inch strips, in oil and garlic for 2 hours. Roll in an equal mixture of grated Parmesan cheese and cracker crumbs. Bake at 425 degrees F. for 10 to 15 minutes. Or, you may remove the fish from the oil and simply broil it.

Halibut is also delicious dipped in melted butter, then rolled in crushed potato chips and baked at 425 degrees F. for 17 to 25 minutes.

—Janis Meckel, Fairbanks

Liska's Halibut

Halibut fillets
Mayonnaise
¼ cup flour
¼ cup cornmeal

Salt, pepper, and poultry seasoning
Butter or margarine
Lemon juice

Cover halibut with mayonnaise; dip in mixture of the flour, cornmeal, and seasonings. Fry in butter or margarine for 5 to 10 minutes, each side, and serve sprinkled with lemon juice.

Halibut Steak

Yield: 2 or 3 servings

1 1-pound halibut steak
2 tablespoons butter
2 tablespoons lemon juice

Place halibut steak on a small baking pan. Dot with butter, and sprinkle with lemon juice. Bake at 350 degrees F. for about 30 minutes.

—Jean Kurtz, Anchorage

Octopus Chowder

Yield: 4 servings

2 medium octopus tentacles
3 medium potatoes, peeled and diced
1 small onion, chopped
1/4 cup butter

1 cup water
1 quart milk
Salt and pepper to taste
Chives, chopped as a garnish

Cook octopus in boiling, salted water for 10 minutes. Remove from heat, and peel off tough white skin. Put the skinned tentacles through a food chopper until finely chopped (or use a food processor to chop). Sauté potatoes and onion in the butter over low heat. Add the 1 cup water and the chopped octopus; simmer until tender. Add milk, and season to taste. Serve hot, garnished with chopped chives.

—From the *PTA Cookbook*, Petersburg

There are a number of sea bird rookeries in the Kodiak-Afognak Island group. Game birds such as willow and rock ptarmigan abound on these islands, although the area does not produce a lot of waterfowl. It does, however, offer resting sites for migratory waterfowl, which sometime overwinter here. Bird life is also abundant in the gulf of Alaska region. Puffins, petrels, murres, auklets, murrelets, cormorants, guillemots, various species of ducks, gulls, kittiwakes, and Arctic terns are members of the marine environment. In the Copper River delta alone, the dusky Canada goose and trumpeter swan nest. Ducks and many shorebirds breed in this delta area also, and the bald eagle is abundant here.

Baked Alaska King Salmon
(With Bread Dressing and Creole Sauce)

Yield: 3 servings

1 large king salmon, prepared for baking
2 cups dry bread crumbs
2 tablespoons minced parsley
1 cup hot water or stock
4 tablespoons melted shortening
1/2 teaspoon pepper
2 teaspoons salt
1 teaspoon ground sage
3 or 4 strips of bacon

2 tablespoons butter
3 tablespoons flour
1/2 cup water
1/4 cup chopped green pepper
3 tablespoons chopped onion
1 cup tomato puree or crushed tomatoes
Salt and pepper
Olives or canned mushrooms (if desired)

194

Stuff the salmon with a mixture of the bread crumbs, onion, parsley, water or stock, melted shortening, pepper, salt, and sage. Place strips of bacon over the salmon to keep it moist. Bake at 350 degrees F. until done.

Meanwhile, make creole sauce: melt the butter in a saucepan, add the flour, and stir in the water and remaining ingredients. Let cook, stirring, until thickened, and simmer very slowly for about 20 minutes. Serve sauce poured over servings of the baked salmon.

—From the *Nome Cookbook,* Nome

Cutting and Drying Salmon
by Rachel Levine

Cold Baked Salmon

1 whole salmon
Lettuce
1 cup mayonnaise
1 cup sour cream
1 tablespoon crushed tarragon

2 tablespoons lemon juice
1 tablespoon minced onion
¾ teaspoon salt
¼ teaspoon pepper

Bake the salmon on a bed of lettuce at 400 degrees F. for an hour until done. Chill well. Make a sauce by combining remaining ingredients: chill the sauce. Both salmon and sauce can be prepared a day ahead, if desired.

Remove skin from top side of salmon. Place on a bed of fresh lettuce and cover with the sauce.

—Helen Finney, Ketchikan

Florence's Baked Whole Salmon

When Mary Daubersmith came to Southeast Alaska in 1962 as a new teacher, she was "taken in tow" by the local cannery superintendent and his wife, who taught her many things about Alaska life, including how to bake fresh salmon.

Yield: 12 servings

1 6-to-8-pound whole coho salmon
½ cup mayonnaise
2 tablespoons orange juice
Grated onion

Salt and pepper
½ teaspoon celery salt
Parsley

Put salmon in foil wrap and seal tightly. Bake at 450 degrees F. for 20 minutes. Remove from oven, open foil, and with a fork and paring knife remove the skin on the top side. (But along the back with the knife to lift skin easily.) Mix remaining ingredients together, and spread on top of salmon. Wrap foil very loosely, and continue baking at 400 degrees F. for 1 hour.

—Mary Daubersmith, Ward Cove

Baked Salmon with Mushroom Stuffing

Yield: 8 servings

2 pounds salmon roast
Salt

½ cup sliced water chestnuts
¼ cup chopped fresh parsley

4 tablespoons butter
2/3 cup sliced fresh mushrooms
1/3 cup sliced green onion

3/4 teaspoon salt
1/4 teaspoon pepper
1/4 teaspoon dried tarragon

Thaw, rinse, and dry the salmon; cut along the center bone to enlarge the cavity, keeping the roast in one piece. Lightly salt the cavity. Place on a baking pan lined with greased foil.

Melt 3 tablespoons of the butter in a skillet; sauté mushrooms and onion for about 3 minutes, or until tender. Add water chestnuts, parsley, and seasonings.

Spoon stuffing into salmon cavity. Drizzle top of roast with remaining one tablespoon of butter, melted. Measure thickness of salmon at the thickest part of the roast. Bake at 450 degrees F. for 10 minutes per each inch of thickness, or until salmon flakes easily.

—Jeanette Trumbly, Anchorage

Baked Alaska Salmon with Tomato Sauce

Yield: 4 to 6 servings

2 cups canned tomatoes
1 cup water
1 onion, sliced
3 whole cloves
1/2 tablespoon sugar
3/4 teaspoon salt

1/8 teaspoon pepper
3 tablespoons butter
3 tablespoons flour
2 pounds Alaska Salmon steaks, any
    kind

Cook tomatoes, water, onion, and seasonings together in a saucepan for 20 minutes. Melt the butter; add the flour, and stir into the hot mixture. Cook for 10 minutes longer, and strain the sauce. Put fish in a baking dish, and pour half the sauce over the fish. Bake at 350 degrees F. for 35 minutes, or until fish is done. Remove to a hot platter, and pour remaining sauce over fish.

—From the *PTA Cookbook,* Petersburg

Haida Indian Beach Party Salmon

Dig a pit on the beach and collect uncracked stones about twice the size of a fist. Line the pit with rocks, in a double layer, and then build a fire on them to heat the rocks—this takes more than half an hour.

When the rocks are hot, lift the fire to one side with a shovel and take out all but the lining layer of rocks. Line the pit with large skunk cabbage leaves, rinsed in sea water, with the center ribs cut out. (Despite the name, these leaves have no real odor—just don't pick the flower and bring it into the house!) Have the tips above the edge of the pit and the whole inside covered with overlapping leaves.

Put in chunks of salmon, chunks of peeled potatoes and onions, and pieces of bacon. Cover with more skunk cabbage leaves and bend the tips of the bottom leaves over to seal the whole thing. Push a couple of leaves aside and pour in a small saucepan of sea water—this takes care of the seasoning and gives enough water for steaming. Shovel back on top the layer of hot rocks removed earlier. Shovel the fire back on top of the rocks and later set the coffeepot on that. The food will be ready to eat in one to two hours, depending on the size of the pit and the amount of food.

—Alice Kitkun, Hydaburg

Many game species have been introduced to the Kodiak Island group. The Sitka black-tailed deer, elk, beaver, snowshoe hare, and muskrat were introduced at various times during Kodiak's history and have been quite successful for harvest. Other animals, such as mink, marten, mountain goat. Dall sheep, moose, and spruce grouse may reach harvestable numbers during some years. The Alaska brown bear is the outstanding species of this region. Mountain goats; introduced moose; black-tail deer; and brown, black, and glacier bears are located in the Gulf of Alaska region. Fur-bearing animals, including mink, otter, marten, weasel, wolverine, coyote, wolf, and beaver are also found in the Gulf of Alaska region.

Alaskan Barbecued Whole Salmon

1 8-pound whole salmon, cleaned,
   outside scraped well
Sliced lemons and limes

Garlic salt
Hickory barbecue sauce
Margarine or butter

198

1 white onion, sliced

Fill the salmon cavity with sliced lemons and limes, and sliced onion. Sprinkle generously with garlic salt and barbecue sauce. Place salmon on several layers of foil. Sprinkle the top with garlic salt, and pour on more barbecue sauce. Dot with chunks of margarine or butter, and seal fish tightly in the foil. Bake at 400 degrees F. for 15 to 20 minutes; lower oven heat to 300 degrees F. and continue cooking for 1½ hours or longer.

To cook in a covered barbecue use hot coals for 15 to 20 minutes, then cook on each side for 45 minutes.

Remove foil before serving. The meat is easily lifted from the bones.

—From *Alaska Airlines is Cookin,* Anchorage

Barbecue King Salmon, Indian Style
(over an open fire)

Build a fire, not too large, and let it die down to a nice bed of coals. Clean a king salmon well and split it down the center, removing backbone, to make two equal-sized halves. If parts of the salmon are thicker than others, cut lightly into the thicker parts so salmon will broil evenly. Cut two straight boughs or willows of medium size, and split each down one end. (The boughs or willows should be about two feet longer than the side of salmon.) Place a side of salmon between each split willow. Whittle some small sticks and place them crossways on both sides of the salmon between the split willow, which will hold the side of salmon flat. Draw the split end of the willow tight and fasten it to hold the salmon firmly in place. When the fire coals are glowing, stick the end of the willow into the ground alongside the fire with the salmon extending over the coals (not too close). Baste the salmon with melted butter, and a little vinegar, pepper, and salt. Turn the salmon over the fire when necessary, and broil until well done.

—From the *PTA Cookbook,* Petersburg

Salmon-Potato Casserole

1 cup cooked or canned salmon
6 small raw potatoes, diced
2 tablespoons chopped green pepper
2 tablespoons chopped pimiento
2 hard-boiled eggs, sliced
2 tablespoons chopped parsley

2 tablespoons minced chives or onion
1 cup thin white sauce, well seasoned
4 tablespoons bread crumbs
4 tablespoons butter
1/4 cup slivered blanched almonds

Mix all ingredients except for crumbs, butter, and almonds, and place in a shallow buttered baking dish. Melt the butter, stir in the crumbs and almonds, and sprinkle the mixture over the casserole. Bake at 350 degrees F. for 1 hour until potatoes are tender.

—Ada Wien, Fairbanks

Salmon and Potato Casserole

Yield: 4 servings

4 large potatoes, thinly sliced
1 large onion, sliced
Salt and pepper
2 hard-boiled eggs, sliced

2 cups cooked or canned salmon,
    drained and flaked
3 tablespoons butter
3 tablespoons flour
2 cups milk

Line a casserole with a layer of potatoes and onions, salt and pepper, then a layer of salmon and eggs. Repeat the layers, ending with potatoes and onions. Make a white sauce by melting the butter, stirring in the flour, and gradually adding the milk. Cook, stirring, until the sauce is thickened and smooth. Pour over the casserole and bake at 350 degrees F. for 1 1/2 hours.

Salmon Chowder

Yield: 6 servings

1 pound canned salmon, undrained
2 cups water
1 cup tomato juice
1 teaspoon celery salt

4 tablespoons butter
4 tablespoons flour
3 cups milk
1 teaspoon salt

1/2 cup chopped onion
1 cup raw cubed potatoes

1 teaspoon dry mustard
1/2 teaspoon Worcestershire sauce

Combine salmon, water, tomato juice, celery salt, onion, and potato in a large saucepan. Cover, and simmer for 40 minutes. In another saucepan melt the butter; add the flour, salt, and mustard, and mix until smooth. Add the milk, and cook, stirring, until thickened and smooth. Combine with salmon mixture, stir in Worcestershire sauce, and serve hot.

—From the *PTA Cookbook,* Petersburg

Yukon Baked Noodles

Yield: 4 servings

2 tablespoons butter
1 tablespoon flour
1/2 teaspoon salt
1 cup milk
1 1/2 cups grated cheese

1/4 teaspoon hot sauce or 1/8 teaspoon
   cayenne pepper
2 cups cooked salmon
2 cups cooked noodles
1 cup buttered bread crumbs

Preheat oven to 375 degrees F. Melt butter in a saucepan; stir in flour and let bubble 1 minute. Add milk and salt; bring to a boil, stirring constantly. Remove from heat and stir in the grated cheese and the hot sauce until the cheese is melted and the sauce is smooth. Add the salmon. In a buttered shallow casserole, make layers of the noodles and the salmon mixture, sprinkling each layer with buttered crumbs. Bake at 375 degrees F. for 20 to 30 minutes.

Salmon Croquettes

Yield: 4 to 6 servings

1 1-pound can salmon, undrained
1 teaspoon baking powder
1 cup flour
2 eggs

Salt (optional)
1 can vacuum-packed sweet corn,
   drained
Fat for deep frying

Combine undrained salmon, baking powder, flour, eggs, and salt. Beat until well mixed. Stir in corn and drop by tablespoons into hot deep fat, cooking until well browned. Serve with mustard gravy (recipe follows). To serve fewer people you may omit the corn.

—Evelyn Valentine, Ketchikan

Mustard Gravy

2 tablespoons butter
1 tablespoon flour
1 tablespoon dry mustard

Salt
1 cup milk

Melt the butter in a saucepan; stir in the flour, mustard, and salt. Slowly add the milk and cook, until sauce is thickened.

—Evelyn Valentine, Ketchikan

Pirog (Russian-Aleut Salmon Pie)

Yield: 6 servings

Helen Malcolm grew up in Unalaska, in the Aleutian chain, where this recipe is very popular. She freezes her year's supply of salmon by placing chunks in empty milk cartons, filling the cartons with water and freezing. This keeps the salmon very fresh-tasting with no "freezer burn."

Pastry for a 2-crust pie
2 cups cooked rice
2 pounds salmon, cooked and flaked
2 onions, sliced

2 stalks celery, sliced
2 cups cabbage, sliced
2 tablespoons vegetable oil
Salt and pepper

Roll out 2/3 of pie dough to line an 8-inch square baking pan. Spread cooked rice over pie crust, and spread cooked salmon over the rice. Preheat oven to 425 degrees F. Briefly sauté the vegetables in the oil. Using a slotted spoon, spread the vegetables over the salmon. Sprinkle with salt and pepper, and top with remaining pie crust. Bake at 425 degrees F. until crust is nicely browned, about 40 minutes.

—Helen Malcolm, Anchorage

Pirox

Here is another version of the well-known Russian-Aleut salmon pie.

202

1 box of biscuit mix or muffin mix
3 cups water
3 cups cooked rice
1 onion, finely chopped
1 teaspoon salt

1 teaspoon pepper
1 tablespoon petruskies or parsley
1 pound fresh salmon, cooked or
   1 pound canned salmon
6 hard-boiled eggs, sliced

Make a pastry from the biscuit mix and water. Roll out 2 crusts to fit your pan (such as a rectangle casserole). Mix the rice with the onion, salt, pepper, and petruskies, and put half the mixture into the pastry-lined pan. Spread on the cooked salmon, then add a layer of the hard-boiled eggs. Top with remaining rice mixture, then add the top crust. Cut steam vents in the top of the pastry. Bake at 425 degrees F. for 30 to 45 minutes.

—Sophie Sherebernikoff, in the *Cuttlefish,* Unalaska

Dried Salmon or Tomcod in Oil

Dried salmon or tomcod can be kept in oil, seal oil, or oogruk oil, and eaten any time. If the fish is too dry, it can be placed in a pan of water until soft. Then put it into the oil and keep in a cool place.

—From the *Nome Cookbook,* Nome

Salmon Kebabs

Yield: 4 servings

2 pounds salmon steak, cut into 1-inch
   pieces
1 green pepper, cut into 1-inch squares
10 small "boiling" onions
1 cup vegetable oil

$1/2$ tablespoon oregano
$1/2$ tablespoon salt
$1/2$ teaspoon thyme
1 teaspoon pepper
$1/2$ teaspoon garlic powder

Place alternately on skewers the salmon pieces, green pepper, and onions.

In a shallow baking dish combine the oil and seasonings. Let the skewered fish and vegetables marinate for 1 hour in the mixture. Drain, and cook the kebabs over hot coals for 4 to 6 minutes, turning them often. Do not overcook—they are done when the fish just flakes.

Salmon Loaf Juneau

Yield: 4 servings

1 1-pound can salmon, drained
1 cup chopped celery
1/2 cup mayonnaise
1 cup dry bread crumbs

1/3 cup chopped green pepper
1 small onion, finely chopped
Salt and pepper to taste

Flake the salmon. Simmer the celery in unsalted water for 5 to 10 minutes; drain and add to the salmon. Mix in remaining ingredients. Put into a greased loaf pan and bake at 350 degrees F. for about 45 minutes. This is equally good hot or cold.

—From the *PTA Cookbook,* Petersburg

Salmon Mousse

Yield: 4 to 6 servings

1 envelope unflavored gelatine
1/4 cup cold water
1/4 cup vinegar
2 cups cooked or canned salmon,
 flaked

1/4 teaspoon salt
1 teaspoon sweet pickle relish
1 teaspoon prepared mustard
1 cup finely chopped celery
1/2 cup heavy cream or sour cream

Soften the gelatine in the water and vinegar. Dissolve by heating over boiling water. Stir in the salmon, salt, relish, mustard, and celery. Fold in the cream. Turn into a mold and shake well. Chill until set.

—From *Cooking up a Storm,* Homer

Eskimo Salmon Patties

Yield: 4 servings

2 cups cooked, boned salmon
1 cup cooked rice
Wild onion
Flour

Lard
Seal oil
Broiled potatoes

Mix the salmon, rice, and wild onion with enough flour to hold the mixture together. Make into patties and fry in lard until golden brown on each side. Eat with seal oil and boiled potatoes.

Salmon and herring are seasonally the most abundant fish in the

Alutiiq area. However, the cod family, which includes the Pacific cod, tomcod, and pollack, are harvested by Japanese and Russian trawlers. In the future these cod may be harvested like the industry of New England fame.

Salmon Pie

Yield: 4 to 6 servings

1 pound cooked or canned salmon, drained and flaked
1 cup cream, scalded
1 cup fresh bread crumbs
3 eggs, beaten
1 cup chopped onion
1 cup chopped celery
2 tablespoons butter
1 teaspoon dried thyme
$^1/_2$ teaspoon salt
1 tablespoon lemon juice
1 9-inch unbaked pie shell

Preheat oven to 375 degrees F. Combine the cream, bread crumbs, and eggs; mix with the flaked salmon. Sauté the onion and celery in the butter until softened, and add to the salmon mixture along with the seasonings. Pour into the pie shell, and bake at 375 degrees F. for about 40 minutes, or until the salmon mixture is set like a custard.

Whole Poached Salmon, Party Style

1 8-pound whole salmon with head
   and tail
½ gallon dry white wine
5 quarts water
2 medium onions, each stuck with
   2 whole cloves

1 tablespoon salt
12 peppercorns
1 teaspoon whole thyme
1 bay leaf
Parsley sprigs

Decorations: slice hard-boiled eggs, cucumber slices, parsley, and lemon slices. Also cooked, sliced carrots, black or stuffed green olives, celery leaves, chives, pimiento, etc.

Make a hammock of unfolded cheesecloth for the salmon allowing 6 inches at each end for handles. Lay fish on the cloth. Combine all other ingredients (except decorations) in a poacher or roasting pan large enough to contain the fish. Cover the pan tightly with a lid or heavy aluminum foil. Bring the stock to a boil and simmer for 20 minutes. Lower the salmon into the broth, immersing as much of it as possible. Return broth to a simmer. Put lid or foil back on in such a way that it does not touch the fish. Allow 6½ minutes cooking time for each pound of fish. Lift salmon by the cheesecloth handles several times during the cooking to prevent it from sticking to the bottom of the pan. There is no need to do this if you are using a fish poacher with a rack. When fish is done, remove from heat and let fish sit in the liquid for a few minutes. Carefully lift out fish by the cheesecloth handles, drain, and place on a large serving platter. From the sides, gently pull out the cheesecloth—the bottom skin will slide out with it. If you are losing too much juice, let the fish sit a little longer. Cut the skin around the head and above the tail, then remove the top skin. Use a spoon to remove the brown fat (for a prettier salmon color). Decorate with rows of hard-boiled eggs and cucumber slices arranged alternately down the center of the fish. Trim everything with lots of parsley, and add lemon slices and whatever food decorations you wish—use your imagination!

—Emily Marten, Petersburg

Poached Salmon with Shrimp Sauce

Yield: 6 servings

6 individual salmon steaks or fillets
White wine
Lemon slices
1 tablespoon butter
1 tablespoon flour
2 cups light cream

½ cup sliced cooked mushrooms
1 cup small cooked shrimp
2 egg yolks
Juice of 1 lemon or 2 tablespoons fresh
   lemon juice
Salt and white pepper to taste

206

Poach the salmon steaks in white wine with lemon slices added. In a saucepan, melt the butter, stir in the flour, and cook for 1 minute. Stir in the cream, mushrooms, shrimp, egg yolks, and lemon juice; heat until it thickens and just reaches the boiling point. Season to taste with salt and white pepper, and pour over the poached salmon.

—From *Alaska Airlines is Cookin,* Anchorage

Salmon Rice Squares

Yield: 6 servings

1 10-ounce package frozen chopped spinach
2 cups or 1 pound canned salmon, liquid reserved
Milk
3 cups cooked rice
1/4 cup finely chopped onion

1 1/2 cups grated sharp cheddar cheese
2 eggs, slightly beaten
3 tablespoons butter or margarine, melted
1 tablespoon lemon juice
3/4 teaspoon salt

Cook and thoroughly drain spinach. Flake the salmon; add milk to reserved salmon liquid to equal 1 cup. Combine all ingredients and mix well. Preheat oven to 350 degrees F. Spoon the mixture into a greased 8-inch square baking dish. Bake at 350 degrees F. for 40 minutes or until set.

Alaskan Salmon Salad

1 head cabbage, chopped
1 tablespoon finely chopped onion
Salt, pepper, and celery seed to taste

1 or 2 1-pound cans salmon, drained, and broken into large chunks
1 tablespoon lemon juice
Mayonnaise

Combine all ingredients, using enough mayonnaise to moisten. Serve with crackers or bread as a main dish salad.

Scalloped Salmon

Yield: 4 servings

2 tablespoons butter
2 tablespoons chopped onion
1 tablespoon chopped green pepper
½ teaspoon salt
2 tablespoons flour

1 cup canned (evaporated) milk
2 cups flaked, cooked, or canned salmon
¼ cup dry bread crumbs

Simmer the onion and green pepper briefly in the melted butter. Stir in the salt and flour; let bubble 1 minute. Slowly stir in the milk and cook, stirring, until it thickens. Stir in the salmon and put into individual greased shells or ramekins, or a small greased baking dish. Top with crumbs, dot with butter, and bake at 400 degrees F. for 15 minutes, or until browned.

—From the *PTA Cookbook,* Petersburg

*High Bushcranberries
by Rachel Levine*

Salmon Souffle

Yield: 4 to 6 servings

⅓ cup butter

2 tablespoons grated onion

¼ cup flour
1 teaspoon salt
¼ teaspoon pepper
4 eggs, separated
1½ cups milk
7 ounces cooked or canned salmon

1 tablespoon grated onion
1 tablespoon lemon juice
2 cups cooked rice or mashed
  potatoes
2 or 3 slices processed American
  cheese, cut in half diagonally

Make a sauce by melting the butter, adding the flour and seasonings, and stirring in the milk gradually. Bring to a boil, stirring constantly. Beat egg yolks slightly, stir in some of the sauce, then return it to the remaining sauce and cook for 2 minutes longer over low heat. Fold in the salmon, onion, lemon juice, and rice or potatoes. Preheat oven to 350 degrees F. Beat egg whites until stiff. Fold into the salmon mixture. Pour into an ungreased casserole or souffle dish. Arrange the cut cheese slices around the edge of the casserole. Set dish in a pan of hot water and bake at 350 degrees F. for 40 minutes, or until firm. This souffle keeps well and does not collapse if not served immediately.

—From *Cooking Favorites of Fairbanks, Alaska*, Fairbanks

Salmon Cream Soup

Yield: 6 servings

1½ pounds salmon steaks or fillets
2 cups hot water
1 slice onion
1 stalk celery
1 sprig parsley
1-inch piece of green pepper

1 quart milk
5 tablespoons butter or other fat
5 tablespoons flour
2½ teaspoons salt
¼ teaspoon pepper
Chopped parsley

Remove skin and bones from salmon and grind finely. Stir into the hot water; simmer 3 minutes, stirring constantly. In another pan add onion, celery, parsley, and green pepper to milk; scald and strain. Melt the butter in a saucepan, and stir in the flour, salt, and pepper. Add the scalded milk gradually and cook, stirring, until thick and smooth. Add the salmon mixture; heat. Serve garnished with chopped parsley.

—From *Alaska Seafood Recipes*, Ketchikan

Eskimo Salmon Soup

Yield: 4 servings

1/2 cup raw rice
4 cups water
2 medium potatoes, sliced
1/2 medium salmon, cut into pieces

Pinch of rock salt
Wild parsley
Wild onion

Cook the rice in the water for 25 minutes. Add the remaining ingredients and cook until done. Serve with homemade bread.

Super Salmon Steaks

Yield: 4 servings

2 large or 4 small salmon steaks
1/4 cup orange juice
1/4 cup soy sauce
2 tablespoons vegetable oil
2 tablespoons ketchup
2 tablespoons minced parsley

2 tablespoons fresh lemon juice or juice of 1 lemon
1 clove garlic, finely chopped or pressed
1 teaspoon leaf oregano
1/2 teaspoon pepper

Place steaks in a single layer in a shallow pan. Mix remaining ingredients and pour over the fish. Refrigerate for 1 hour, turning the steaks 2 or 3 times in the marinade. Drain the fish and broil it in a shallow pan, basting with the marinade 1 or 2 times on each side, until the salmon flakes.

—Ida Knaebel, Fairbanks

Salmon Steaks with Blue Cheese

Yield: 4 servings

4 salmon steaks
Olive oil or salad oil
Salt and pepper
1/2 cup butter
2 egg yolks, slightly beaten
2 tablespoons lemon juice

1/2 teaspoon horseradish
1/4 cup crumbled blue cheese
2 tablespoons chopped cucumber
1 teaspoon grated onion
1/8 teaspoon pepper

Brush the salmon steaks with oil and sprinkle with salt and pepper. Oil the broiler pan and place steaks on it. Preheat broiler while preparing sauce:
Melt the butter in the top of a double boiler set over hot water. Add the yolks, lemon juice, and horseradish. Cook, stirring constantly, over hot water until

thickened. Add cheese, cucumber, onion, and pepper; mix well.

Broil the steaks to taste and serve immediately with the hot blue cheese sauce.

—From *Alaska's Cooking,* Anchorage

Salmon Steaks Oriental

Yield: 4 servings

4 salmon steaks, 1 to 1½ inches thick
½ cup soy sauce

1 lemon, thinly sliced
½ cup sliced almonds

Line a shallow baking dish with foil. Place fish on foil, and pour soy sauce evenly over fish. Cover with lemon slices, and sprinkle almonds over all. Bring ends of the foil together and seal. Bake at 350 degrees F. for 30 to 40 minutes.

Norwegian Salmon Steaks

Fry floured salmon steaks, seasoned to taste, in hot shortening melted in a skillet. Brown them on both sides, but do not cook through. Pour milk around the salmon just to the tops of the steaks. Cover with a tight lid, turn heat to low, and let simmer slowly until the milk is absorbed. The salmon remains moist and delicious when cooked this way.

—From *Alaska Airlines is Cookin,* Anchorage

Casserole of Sea Scallops

Yield: 6 servings

2 pounds fresh scallops
½ cup light Rhine wine
2 teaspoons lemon juice
2 tablespoons chopped green onions
2 tablespoons chopped parsley
¼ to ½ teaspoon dill seed

½ teaspoon pepper
½ cup light cream
¼ cup bread crumbs
2 tablespoons butter

Preheat oven to 350 degrees F. Place scallops in a large buttered baking dish. Blend the wine, lemon juice, green onions, parsley, dill seed, salt, and pepper; pour this mixture over the scallops. Drizzle the cream over all, sprinkle with the bread crumbs and dot with butter. Bake, uncovered, at 350 degrees F. for 30 minutes. If the top has not been browned, place dish under the broiler.

—From the *Catholic Daughters of America,* Juneau

Sea Cucumber

You need a stick to get a sea cucumber, or go out at low tide when they are drying on the beach. It takes about 20 of them to make a good meal. To prepare, slit the side jacket and pull the white meat out. Fry in hot fat with onions and celery. Make a gravy with a little flour and water added to the pan. Sea cucumber meat is very white and tender.

Kotzebue Sheefish Nuggets

The sheefish is a large, delicious white fish found only in the Arctic—a real local delicacy for the people of Kotzebue.

Cut sheefish into fillets, then into diagonal strips. Dip into a thin pancake or beer batter and deep fry. Serve with tartar sauce or cocktail sauce.

—Rachel Adams, Kotzebue

Sheefish Soup

Cut and wash sheefish. Put them into a pot with water, salt, curry powder, onion, and ketchup. Let boil slowly for 30 minutes. Mix together flour and water to thicken the soup. Cook for 15 minutes longer.

—Cape Espenberg

Nome "Scallops"

Cut sheefish into 1-inch cubes. Dip in egg and cracker crumbs. Fry in deep fat and serve with tartar sauce.

—From the *Nome Cookbook*, Nome

On the Copper River Delta the Chugach Alutiiq speaking people coexisted with the Eyak Indians in hostility. They both were skilled boatmen, living principally on fish and marine mammals. When the fur

212

hunters and traders visited this area in the 1700s, they exchanged their sea otter and seal furs for trade goods. In the Prince William Sound area copper played a role in the lives of the people, who made arrowhead, shields and masks.

Prince William Sound Ice
Photo
Fairbanks Daily News-Miner

Shrimp and Rice Casserole

Yield: 3 or 4 servings

½ cup butter
3 cloves garlic, minced
½ cup chopped onion
1 tablespoon dried chives
2 teaspoons finely chopped parsley
1 teaspoon chervil

½ teaspoon rosemary
1 teaspoon garlic salt
1 tablespoon lemon juice
1 pound cooked shrimp
2 cups cooked rice
½ cup chopped tomatoes

Melt butter in a skillet. Add garlic, onion, and spices, and cook over low heat for 10 minutes, stirring frequently. Remove from heat and stir in lemon juice. Mix this sauce with the shrimp, rice, and tomatoes. Bake in a medium-size casserole dish at 350 degrees F. for 20 minutes. Garnish with chopped parsley or grated Parmesan cheese. Note: If you have large shrimp or prawns, you may prefer to serve individual portions, with the shrimp arranged over the hot rice and the sauce poured over.

—Shirley Dyer, Seward

Shrimp Potato Salad #2

Yield: 4 to 6 main-dish servings

6 cups cubed cooked potatoes
6 hard-boiled eggs, chopped
1½ cups chopped celery
1 medium onion, finely chopped
2 teaspoons salt
½ teaspoon celery seed

1 large dill pickle or 2 sweet pickles, chopped
Pepper to taste
2 cups tiny cooked shrimp
Mayonnaise to moisten well

Mix all ingredients and chill well. Serve on lettuce as a main dish salad.

—From the *PTA Cookbook,* Petersburg

Tomcod Livers

Tomcod livers are always given first to children because of all the vitamins they contain, especially vitamin D. Here is a widely found Eskimo method of preparing them:

Place tomcod livers in a pot and cover them with water. Cook until they are thick and soft, stirring occasionally. Let them cool completely. Add salmonberries—as much as you want—and sugar to taste.

—From the *Eskimo Cookbook*, Shishmaref

Adak Fisherman's Soup

Yield: 4 servings

4 cups water
2 cups finely chopped seaweed
3 to 4 cups cooked shellfish (any kind)

1 tablespoon soy sauce
1/4 teaspoon MSG (optional)
Cooked rice or noodles.

Boil the seaweed in the water for about 15 minutes, until almost tender. Add the shellfish and remaining ingredients and simmer 5 minutes longer.

—Univesity of Alaska, Cooperative Extension Center

Alaskan Style Bouillabaisse

Yield: 8 servings

1/2 cup olive oil
1 large onion, chopped
4 tomatoes, chopped
1 tablespoon chopped parsley
Pinch of saffron

Salt and pepper
4 pounds Alaska red snapper or trout, sliced
Fresh parsley, finely chopped

Heat the olive oil in a large saucepan. Simmer the onion, tomatoes, garlic, and parsley in the olive oil until tender. Season with saffron, and salt and pepper. Add the fish slices to the saucepan; cover with water, and bring to a boil. Cover pan and let the fish cook gently for 10 to 12 minutes. Sprinkle with fresh parsley, and serve over slices of toasted French bread in soup plates.

—From the *PTA Cookbook*, Petersburg

Alaska's Seafood Creole

Yield: 6 servings

2 tablespoons vegetable oil
2 medium onions, chopped
1/2 cup chopped green pepper
4 cloves garlic, finely chopped or
    pressed
1 16-ounce can tomatoes, chopped
1 6-ounce can tomato paste
1/2 cup dry white wine

1 teaspoon dried basil
1/2 teaspoon MSG (optional)
1 bay leaf
1 10-ounce can whole clams, drained
1 pound fresh or frozen halibut fillets,
    cut into 1-inch pieces
1/2 pound fresh, medium, peeled raw
    shrimp

In a saucepan heat the oil. Add the onions, green pepper, and garlic; cook over medium heat for 10 minutes. Stir in tomatoes, tomato paste, wine, basil, MSG, and bay leaf. Cover and simmer over low heat for 1 hour. Add clams, halibut, and shrimp; cook over medium heat for 20 minutes, stirring occasionally. Serve over rice.

—Shirley Dyer, Seward

Baked Seafood Southeastern

1 cup cooked shrimp
1 cup crab meat
1 1/2 cups chopped celery
1/2 cup chopped green pepper
1/4 cup chopped onion
1 cup mayonnaise

1 teaspoon Worcestershire sauce
1 1/2 cups crushed potato chips
1/2 teaspoon paprika
2 tablespoons butter, at room
    temperature

Preheat oven to 400 degrees F. Combine shrimp and crab meat with the vegetables, mayonnaise, and Worcestershire sauce. Spread in a small casserole. Bake for 10 minutes at 400 degrees F. Remove from oven and top with a mixture of the crushed potato chips, paprika, and butter. Bake 10 minutes longer.

Favorite Fish Cakes

Yield: 4 servings

4 tablespoons shortening, melted
4 tablespoons flour
1 teaspoon salt
1/4 teaspoon pepper

1 1/2 cups cooked, canned, or leftover
    fish
1 tablespoon lemon juice
1 onion, grated Dry bread crumbs

1 cup milk
1 egg beaten
1 cup ground fresh bread crumbs

1 egg, beaten with 2 tablespoons water

Make a white sauce by blending the melted shortening, flour, and seasonings. Add the milk and cook, stirring, until thickened. Cool slightly. Stir in the egg, crumbs, fish, lemon juice, and onion. Chill. Form into small patties or sticks; dip in the dry bread crumbs. Dip into the egg-water mixture, and then into the dry crumbs again. Fry in hot fat, $^1/_4$-to $^1/_2$-inch deep. Serve with tartar sauce (recipe follows).

—From the *PTA Cookbook,* Petersburg

Tartar Sauce

2 to 4 tablespoons grated or finely chopped onion
2 tablespoons finely chopped celery
2 tablespoons pickle relish

1 tablespoon lemon juice
$^1/_3$ cup ketchup
$^2/_3$ cup mayonnaise

Mix all ingredients together well.

—From the *PTA Cookbook,* Petersburg

Fish Mousse with Cucumber Sauce

Yield: 6 to 8 servings

2 pounds salmon or other fish
Water, seasonings, and aromatic vegetables for poaching fish
2 envelopes unflavored gelatine
$^1/_2$ cup cool fish stock (from poaching fish)
1 cup boiling fish stock

$^3/_4$ cup mayonnaise
1 tablespoon Worcestershire sauce
1 teaspoon lemon juice
1 tablespoon onion juice or grated onion
$1^1/_2$ cups heavy cream
Shredded lettuce

Poach the salmon in the seasoned water. Let fish cool in the fish stock. Bone and flake the fish; chop it very finely. Soften gelatine in $^1/_2$ cup of the cooled fish stock. Heat 1 cup fish stock to boiling and stir into the gelatine mixture until dissolved. Chill the gelatine mixture until it begins to thicken, then add the mayonnaise and beat until frothy. Add the fish and the seasonings. Whip the cream until stiff and fold into the fish mixture. Turn into a lightly oiled fish mold. Chill until firm, then unmold and serve on shredded lettuce with Cucumber Sauce (recipe follows).

—From the *Alaska's Cooking,* Anchorage

Cucumber Sauce

1 large cucumber, peeled, large seeds
   removed, and grated
¹/₂ cup mayonnaise
¹/₂ cup sour cream

¹/₂ teaspoon prepared mustard
2 teaspoons lemon juice
1 tablespoon minced chives

Combine all ingredients and chill.

—From *Alaska's Cooking,* Anchorage

Samovar
by Marionette Donnell Stock

The brass Russian samovars are vivid reminders of the times when the Russians occupied Alaska. Hot water in the samovars is heated to boiling to make brews of any sort of tea.

Fish Soup With Prestuskies

Prestuskies are a wild green gathered in the summer in the western Aleutians.

Cook a halibut, cod, or a red sculpin in water. Add potatoes, rice, and any other vegetables you want. Cut prestuskies into small slices and add to the pot. When prestuskies are used, you don't need to use onions. When the prestuskies are cooked thoroughly, make a flour paste and add it to the soup to thicken.

Fish Steaks with Herbs

Yield: 4 to 6 servings

2 pounds fish steaks or fillets (salmon or halibut)
6 tablespoons butter
1 large clove garlic, split
1/3 cup chopped onion
1/4 teaspoon tarragon
1 tablespoon chopped parsley

1/4 teaspoon thyme
Dash of nutmeg
Dash of mace
1 teaspoon salt
2 tablespoons lemon juice
3/4 cup fine fresh bread crumbs

Preheat oven to 400 degrees F. Arrange the steaks in a shallow baking dish. Melt butter in a saucepan; add the garlic and cook until tender. Remove garlic; add onion and saute just until soft. Stir in remaining ingredients except bread crumbs. Spoon about half the mixture over the fish. Add the crumbs to the remaining mixture and spread on the steaks. Bake at 400 degrees F. for 25 minutes or more, depending on the thickness of the steaks.

—From *Cooking up a Storm,* Homer

Fish Teriyaki

Yield: 4 to 6 servings

1 cup soy sauce
½ cup sugar
¼ cup vegetable oil
2 teaspoons grated fresh ginger root
1 clove garlic, finely chopped

2 or 3 pounds rockfish (rock cod)
   fillets, red snapper, or salmon
1 tablespoon sesame seed
Shredded lettuce

In a bowl, combine soy sauce, sugar, oil, ginger, and garlic. Marinate the fish fillets in this mixture for several hours (covered and refrigerated). Line a shallow baking pan with aluminum foil. Lift the fillets from the marinade and arrange in the pan. Broil 5 to 7 inches from the heat for about 4 minutes, brushing once or twice with a little additional oil. Turn, brush with more oil and sprinkle with sesame seed. Broil for 3 to 5 minutes longer or until the fish flakes. Serve on a bed of shredded lettuce.

Fish with Seal Fat

If you have a fresh codfish or a partially dried codfish, you can cook it with seal fat (the fat remaining when seal oil is melted out).

Put 2 cups of water with rock salt into a pot and add ¾ cup seal fat. Cook until the fat hardens. Clean the fish, cut into pieces and add to the pot. Boil it until the fish is cooked, and serve.

Fresh Fish or Salted Fish Pie

This dish, from Atka Island in the Aleutians, resembles the well-known Russian dish, coulibiac.

Cook some rice. Boil a halibut, or a fresh water fish, until it is cooked. Pour the water out of the pot and pick the bones from the fish. Now fix some dough and roll it out with a rolling pin. Spread the dough over a long oblong pan, leaving some dough over the edges of the pan.

Put the fish in a large bowl and mash it. Add rice, onions, salt, pepper, hot sauce, and melted butter; stir, and put them into the pan. Put on the top crust and cut some holes in the top to let steam escape. Put the pie into a hot oven and let it cook until the crust is golden brown. Let the fish pie cool before serving.

Kotzebue Baked Fish

Yield: 2 servings

Approximately 1 pound fish, any kind
2½ cups water
1 cup cooked rice
2 teaspoons salt

¾ teaspoon pepper
2 tablespoons chopped onion
White sauce (recipe follows)

Boil fish in the water until done; drain and let cool enough to handle. Remove bones from fish. Grease a casserole dish and add the cooked fish. Add the rice and sprinkle with the salt, pepper and onions. Top with the white sauce, (recipe follows) and bake at 350 degrees F. for 20 to 60 minutes, until brown.

—Elsie Adams, Kotzebue

Medium White Sauce

2 tablespoons butter
2 tablespoons flour

1 cup milk
¼ teaspoon salt

Melt butter in a saucepan over low heat. Stir in the flour thoroughly and let cook for 1 minute. Remove from heat and add milk slowly, stirring well after each addition, until smooth. Add salt and cook over medium heat, stirring constantly, until sauce is thickened and smooth.

—Elsie Adams, Kotzebue

Mashed Fish with Berries

Among the berries gathered in the Aleutians and used in this dish are moss berries, blueberries, and strawberries.

Boil a halibut or pink salmon in water and drain it. Remove fish from the bones and mash it. Mix in clean berries, in any amount greater than the fish. Mix in seal oil, as much as you like, and serve.

Metlakatla Fish Chowder

Yield: 2 servings

1 pound fresh or frozen salmon or
 halibut, cut in 1-inch cubes
1 medium potato, chopped
1 medium onion, chopped

1 tablespoon ooligan grease or
 vegetable oil
½ teaspoon salt
Pepper to taste

Place ingredients in a saucepan. Cover with cold water to 1 inch above the ingredients. Cook until the potatoes are tender.

Molded Salmon and Shrimp

2 pounds fresh salmon, cut into 1-inch
 strips
2 cups water
1 tablespoon vinegar
¾ tablespoon salt
2 or 3 bay leaves

½ teaspoon dill seed
2 envelopes unflavored gelatine
¼ cup cold water
Hard-boiled eggs, quartered
Tomatoes, cut in sections
1 cup small cooked shrimp

Simmer the salmon in a mixture of the 2 cups water, vinegar, salt, bay leaves, and dill seed for about 10 minutes. Remove salmon and strain the stock through a fine strainer or cheesecloth. Reserve 2 cups stock. Soften the gelatine in the ¼ cup cold water and dissolve in the 2 cups of hot fish stock. Let cool.

Make a pattern in the bottom of a ring mold with the hard boiled eggs, tomato sections, and some of the shrimp. Add just enough of the aspic (gelatine and fish stock) to hold them in place. Chill until set. Set cold salmon and shrimps on the jelled mixture and pour the remaining aspic over. Chill until set, then unmold on a platter covered with lettuce.

—From *Alaska Airlines is Cookin,* Anchorage

Swedish Fish Pudding

Yield: 4 servings

2 cups cooked rice
2 cups prepared salt cod fish or

1 teaspoon sugar
½ teaspoon pepper

1 pound canned salmon, drained	1½ cups rich milk, or canned
2 eggs	evaporated milk
¼ cup butter, melted	

Mix ingredients well and pour into a buttered casserole. Bake at 350 degrees F. for 1 hour. Serve with clarified melted butter, or a white sauce with added hard-boiled eggs, chopped chives, or parsley.

—From the *PTA Cookbook,* Petersburg

Norwegian Fiske Pudding

Yield: 12 servings

| 8 to 10 cups raw ground fish | 3 tablespoons salt |
| 1 cup butter, at room temperature | 2 quarts milk |

In a large mixing bowl, beat the fish with the butter and salt until mixture is very smooth. Gradually add the milk, blending well. Pour into a greased baking dish; set in a larger pan of hot water, and bake at 350 degrees F. for 1½ hours.

—From the *PTA Cookbook,* Petersburg

Seafood and Wild Rice Casserole

Yield: 4 to 6 servings

2 cups wild rice	½ teaspoon salt
4 tablespoons butter	¼ teaspoon garlic salt
1 onion, chopped	¼ teaspoon dried tarragon
1 pound mushrooms, sliced	3 tablespoons grated Parmesan
2 tablespoons lemon juice	cheese
1 tablespoon flour	1 pound cooked shrimp
1¼ cups chicken broth	⅓ pound crab meat
½ cup dry white wine	Additional Parmesan cheese

Cook wild rice in 4 cups boiling water for 45 minutes. Melt 2 tablespoons of the butter in a skillet and sauté the onions and mushrooms, adding the lemon juice when nearly done. In another pan, melt the remaining butter, whisk in the flour and let bubble 1 minute. Whisk in the chicken broth, wine, and seasonings and bring to a boil stirring constantly. Stir in the cheese; mix this sauce with the cooked wild rice, sautéed vegetables, and seafood in a 2-quart casserole. Sprinkle with a little additional Parmesan cheese. Bake at 350 degrees F. for 20 to 25 minutes.

—From *Cooking Favorites of Fairbanks, Alaska,* Fairbanks

Shellfish Casserole

Yield: 2 to 3 servings

2 cups cooked rice
1 cup vegetable juice cocktail
1 7-ounce can crab meat
1 5-ounce can shrimp
1/3 cup chopped green pepper

Salt and pepper to taste
2 tablespoons melted butter
1/2 cup slivered almonds
1 cup soft bread crumbs

Combine rice, vegetable juice cocktail, crab meat, shrimp, green pepper, and salt and pepper. Place in a buttered casserole dish or in individual casseroles. Combine butter, almonds, and bread crumbs; sprinkle over casserole(s). Bake at 375 degrees F. until bubbly and heated through, about 20 minutes.

—Gladys Parker, Fairbanks

Tagux

To make tagux you can use any kind of fish. Boil it and remove the bones. Mash the fish, along with the cooked milt (inside the male fish), if you wish. Then mix in any kind of berries. You may eat this like it is, or mix it with seal oil.

—Platonida Gromoff, Sophie Pletnikoff, and Sophie Sherebernikoff
from the *Cuttlefish*, Unalaska

The dungeness crab is common in shallow bays. However, the king crab and tanner crab, which are often called the snow crab, live in deeper waters. Shrimp of many kinds live in most areas, sometimes in abundance.

Ready to Go Fishing
Photo
Fairbanks Daily News-Miner

This little fellow is ready for his father to bring the boat to go salmon fishing.

THE ALEUT

The Aleutian Islands, which stretch out into the Pacific Ocean for fourteen hundred miles, are the home of the Aleut. The Aleut also live on the Pribilof Islands, parts of the Alaska Peninsula, and in some parts of southwestern Alaska.

Mother and Child
by April Kelley

Until the time of initial historic contact with Bering and Chirkov in 1741 and succeeding Russian influence, the Aleut culture of this area had been developing for thousands of years. Skeletal remains of the Aleut people have been found on Umnak Island which date to around 2000 B.C.

The Aleutian Islands have a harsh terrestrial and marine environment. Nevertheless, the Aleuts have developed a rich culture and traditionally have secured a well-balanced livelihood from the rich fauna of the ocean surrounding them. The Aleutian Islands themselves are the tops of submarine ridges. Some of the islands are mountains that rise twelve thousand feet above the sea floor. There is an arc of fifty-seven volcanoes along the Aleutian Islands, twenty-seven of which are active and rise two to nine thousand feet above sea level. Needless to say, these areas are vast geothermal areas. Many earthquake epicenters are in the Aleutian Trench, adjacent to the Aleutian Islands. It is a real hotbed of seismic activity, often accompanied by tidal waves that pound the Aleutian beaches.

The streams in the Aleutian Islands are short and swift. Many of them plunge from low cliffs into the sea in spectacular waterfalls. Lakes are common in ice-carved basins on some of the more glaciated islands and in craters of old volcanoes or calderas.

There is little or no permafrost in the Aleutians, although most of the high volcanoes bear icecaps or small galciers.

The climate is maritime, since it is so near the extensive open ocean areas. The temperature extremes, both daily and seasonal, are confined to narrow limits. Clouds are abundant, restricting the actual amount of sunshine received: at Cold Bay and other places in the islands, the cloudcover averages ninety percent year round. Some sort of precipitation occurs two hundred days of the year—widespread, heavy fog and low stratus clouds are common throughout the Aleutians in the summer months. Frequent high-velocity windy periods add to the harshness of the area. The winds average about seventeen to twenty miles per hour year around, and in the winter, gale-force winds with blizzard snow conditions are quite common.

Umnak Island is the first and largest island in the vast Aleutian chain of islands. The mariners from long ago called it the "Isle of Lost Ships," due to the litter of doomed vessels tossed asunder in the wind-stricken Pacific Ocean.

The home of the Aleut paints a striking, lush picture in our minds, so different from other regions of the vast and beautiful state of Alaska.

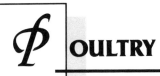

$\mathcal{P}$OULTRY

Each spring and fall in Alaska are marked by great migrations of ducks and geese heading north and south, respectively. As with all of our wild game, these creatures have been hunted and used for food by many of the peoples of Alaska, past and present.

In addition to waterfowl, other small birds such as ptarmigan and grouse are hunted in the Interior forests and tundra regions of Alaska. Although it takes a good number of them to make a meal, they are widely used, and we found many good recipes for preparing them.

Nearly every Alaskan native cultural group uses these wild birds, adding welcome variety to their diets. Usually they are simply plucked and boiled. One Eskimo method for preparing ducks is to roast them in a pan with wild onion and potatoes. Other abundant birds, such as owls, are used for food. Bird eggs, including seagull eggs, are also gathered and served as hard-boiled eggs, or in other dishes, such as pancakes.

If you have access to these birds, we hope you will enjoy some of these Alaskan poultry recipes. Feel free to experiment with domestic ducks and geese in most of these recipes: Alaskan poultry recipes are generally simple enough to adapt to whatever substitutions and creative additions you wish.

Shrimp-Stuffed Chicken Breasts

Yield: 6 servings

3 whole large chicken breasts, boned
   and halved
1¼ cups cooked shrimp, chopped
¾ cup butter, at room temperature
¼ cup chopped green onions
Salt

1 cup flour
1¼ teaspoons baking powder
1 teaspoon salt
¾ cup water
Vegetable oil for frying

Pound chicken breasts to ¼-inch thickness. In a medium bowl, combine shrimp, butter, green onions, and about 1½ teaspoons salt. Spoon the mixture onto the center of each breast, leaving ½-inch edge all around. From a narrow end, roll each one jelly-roll fashion. Fasten each with a toothpick. Cover and refrigerate for 15 minutes.

In a medium bowl, mix together the flour, baking powder, salt, and water until well blended. In a skillet, heat 1 inch of oil to 370 degrees F. With tongs, dip three of the chicken rolls into the batter, then lower them into the hot oil. Fry until golden, turning occasionally, for 10 to 15 minutes. Drain rolls on paper towels, and repeat frying with remaining three rolls. Remove the toothpicks and serve immediately.

—From *Cooking up a Storm,* Homer

Wild onion is used for seasoning geese and other wild fowl. The plant resembles garlic.

Alaskan Brew-Broiled Chicken

Yield: 4 servings

1 large frying chicken, with wings
   removed, quartered
1 small onion, quartered
2 cloves garlic
6 green onions, sliced
½ teaspoon tarragon

8 ounces or 1 cup beer
⅔ cup chicken broth
1 tablespoon tomato paste or
   barbecue sauce
¼ cup butter, melted
Salt and pepper to taste

Place chicken quarters in a shallow glass baking dish. Place all remaining ingredients in a blender or food processor and puree well. Pour the mixture over the chicken and let marinate at room temperature for 2 hours or more, turning the pieces occasionally. Pour off marinade and reserve. Cover dish with foil and bake at 350 degrees F. for about 20 minutes.

230

Remove chicken to a grill and cook over medium-hot coals, brushing with the reserved marinade until done.

Note: If desired, you can remove foil from the baking dish and continue cooking the chicken, at 350 degrees F., for 45 minutes to 1 hour, brushing with the marinade frequently and turning the pieces occasionally to cook them evenly.

—From *Alaska Airlines is Cookin,* Anchorage

Bidarka is the name of the lightweight, skin-covered marine craft that is similar to the kayak. Sometimes it had two holes for two occupants and was used as transportation along the shorelines of the islands.

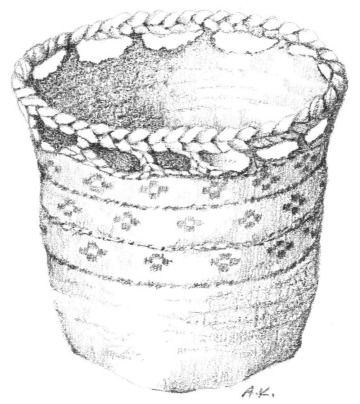

Aleut Basket
by April Kelley

The Aleuts are well-known for their beautiful basket-making abilities.

Chicken Kiev

Yield: 4 servings

4 medium whole chicken breasts
Salt
1 tablespoon chopped green onion
1 tablespoon chopped parsley
¼ pound or 1 stick chilled butter

Flour
2 eggs
1 cup fine dry bread crumbs
Oil or fat for deep-frying

Cut chicken breasts in half lengthwise, removing bone and skin. Each piece of meat should be all in one piece. Place chicken between two slices of plastic wrap; pound with a wooden mallet (or the side of a heavy, glass beer or wine bottle) to make cutlets not quite ¼-inch thick. Peel off wrap and sprinkle cutlets with salt, chopped green onion, and parsley. Cut butter into 8 sticks, placing a stick at a short end of each cutlet. Roll meat as you would a jelly roll, tucking in the sides. Press ends to seal. Dust each with flour, dip in beaten egg, and roll in bread crumbs. Chill thoroughly at least 1 hour. Before serving, fry chicken rolls in deep, hot oil or fat about 5 minutes, or until golden brown. Serve garnished with lemon wedges.

—From *Cooking Favorites of Fairbanks, Alaska,* Fairbanks

Livestock was originally introduced to Umnak Island by Russian traders almost 190 years ago to provide milk and meat for their active settlements. Nowadays, sheep, cattle, horses, and reindeer feed on the lush grasses.

Creamed Duck Breasts

Yield: 4 servings

6 to 8 duck breasts, sliced
Flour
Tarragon

Bacon fat
½ cup water
1 cup heavy cream

Roll duck breast slices in flour seasoned to taste with tarragon. Brown them in bacon fat. Put in a casserole; pour the water over, and bake at 350 degrees F. for 1 hour, until tender. Lower oven heat to 300 degrees F.; add the cream and leave in the oven for 20 to 30 minutes. Serve over bread, rice, noodles, or mashed potatoes.

For very moist duck breast, after browning in bacon fat, put the slices in a slow-cooker with the water and cream. Cook for 3 to 4 hours on the low setting.

—Brenda Wilbur, Fairbanks

232

A typical menu from parts of the Aleutians might include sea lion meat with sea gull eggs. Sea lion is a delicious cross between beef and liver, it is said. The flavor improves with the addition of a small amount of Chinese mustard. Hard-boiled gull eggs are tasty. Gull egg pie is also a treat. The Aleuts eat raw bidarkis, or gumboots, which are shelled invertebrates that clamp themselves to rocks just below tide line. They also like split, needle-like, sea urchins, called "sea eggs" by the Aleuts. The rich, yellow meat is scooped out and eaten much like a raw oyster.

Delicious Wild Duck

Yield: 6 servings

5 to 6 pound wild duckling
1 cup strong tea (2 tea bags brewed
    5 minutes in 1 cup boiling water)
¼ cup honey

2 tablespoons soy sauce
2 medium oranges, peeled and
    sectioned
2 medium oranges, halved

Roast the duck at 350 degrees F. for 1½ hours. Drain off the fat. Raise oven temperature to 425 degrees F. Combine tea, honey, soy sauce, and orange sections, and pour over the duck. Roast with the orange halves for 50 to 60 minutes longer, or until done. Baste several times during the cooking. Optional: you may put part of an apple inside the duck while roasting—discard this when done.

—Brenda Wilbur, Fairbanks

The tender leaf stalks and main stalk of the cow parsnip are eaten by the Aleuts. During the months of May and June the women gather great bundles of these stalks and bring them to the village. To eat the cow parsnip, the first finger is inserted into the hollow stalk and it is rapidly split open; the teeth are then used to assist the fingers to separate the tender parts from the exterior skin and strings of stalk. It is an operation which requires much dexterity and practice to enable one to prevent the tender parts from breaking. The main stalk is stripped of its skin, which, when young and tender, is easily accomplished. The main stalk possesses a sweetish aromatic taste. The leaf stalks are sweeter but less aromatic.

Early Fairbanks Wild Duck

Wipe the duck inside and out. Instead of stuffing, pepper and salt the cavity of the body. Wash out with salad oil and lemon juice and put in a teaspoon of tart jelly or 3 or 4 low-bush cranberries. Put into a covered roaster with ¹/₂ cup boiling water beneath; cover tightly and cook for ¹/₂ hour. Uncover, wash with a mixture of melted butter and lemon juice, and brown. Serve with Alaskan cranberry jelly.

—From the *Fairbanks Cookbook*, circa 1910, Fairbanks

Moose-Duck Patties

Yield: 6 servings

1 pound moose meat, ground
1 pound mallard duck meat, ground
2 medium onions, finely chopped
3 slices bread, ground
2 eggs
¹/₂ cup water or juice from can, if using
  canned moose meat

1¹/₂ teaspoons salt
¹/₂ teaspoon pepper
¹/₂ teaspoon celery salt
Dash of garlic salt
Flour
Bacon fat for frying

Mix meats with onion, bread, eggs, water, and seasonings. Shape into patties and dredge in flour. Fry in hot bacon fat until done, and serve with ketchup.

—From *Alaska's Cooking*, Anchorage

The natives of some of the Aleutian Islands have traditionally used heather for fuel. The women would gather great bunches by pulling it from the ground and carrying it to their houses, where it was immediately used. In rare instances, it was kept for a few days (but only because there was sufficiency of other fuel to be used in its stead) until it was dried out. It was used in the following manner: the pot or kettle containing water or food to be boiled was placed on a small stick wedged in the side of the sod chimney of the hut; a few shreds of the heather plant were lighted. It burned rapidly and had a quick darting flame, like when you burn the branches of spruce trees. The bunch of lighted fuel was held under the vessel, and as fast as it was consumed by the flame another wisp was lighted, until the boiling was finished.

The work was generally performed by the smaller girls and boys. This type of fuel was used by the people of Atka Island and eastward thereof.

Perfect Wild Duck

Paul Coray of Kenai, Alaska has experimented extensively with cooking Alaskan wild ducks and other wild birds. Here is his "best way" of roasting wild birds, taking into account individual tastes and different sizes of birds:

The oven should be at 325 degrees F. An average 2-pound bird will take about $1\frac{1}{2}$ hours at this temperature, excluding time spent in removal for basting. (Teal ducks are smaller and will take less time). Roast the bird *uncovered* for the first 20 minutes, then seal the pan with aluminum foil (which helps retain moisture). Test the bird after an hour or so, by slicing deep along the breastbone with a thin sharp knife. Examine the meat to see if there is still uncooked, deep pink, flesh. Cook longer if necessary. Remove the foil for the last 10 to 15 minutes of cooking to brown the skin. The bird should be basted during application and removal of foil, and when the bird is tested. Be sure to shut the oven door immediately when you remove the bird for these steps, so heat is not lost. This method results in a nice, juicy bird which is not overcooked or dry.

1 washed and cleaned wild duck	$\frac{1}{2}$ cup wine (red wine, or cream sherry
Salt and pepper	—even better!)
Sage	Dash of Worcestershire sauce or Liquid
Butter	Smoke (optional—only if this is to
Orange juice	your taste)

Pat duck dry inside and out with paper towels. Lightly salt and pepper the cavity. Sprinkle a little sage into the cavity. Put the duck into a small roasting pan and spread a small pat of butter along each side of breast; douse the bird with orange juice (the acidity of juice cuts the "fatty" taste which all ducks have). Add the wine, and remove to the preheated oven. Roast as instructed above. If you will be making gravy from the drippings, you can enhance it by boiling and dicing the giblets into small cubes. Sauté 2 chopped green onions in $\frac{1}{4}$ cup butter. Add the green onions and giblets to your gravy, along with a little white wine.

—Paul Coray, Kenai

Many roots were traditionally gathered in the fall and in the spring of the year. Those which were gathered in the fall were usually stored for winter use. In the spring, the roots were more difficult to find, but when the people faced starvation, roots and bulbs were eagerly sought for. On the Aleutians, the roots of the lupine (Lupinus nookatensis) was used for food. The roots were scraped until the skin was removed. The interior of the roots possess a slightly bitter taste and were eaten either raw or boiled. When eaten in excess, it produced disagreeable effects. For example, if oily foods were not eaten soon after, the presence of the woody fibers in the stomach and intestine would produce fatal inflamation. However, the roots were sometimes the only thing that hunters could obtain during long continued storms.

Pickled Duck

This recipe is more than one-hundred-years-old.

1 wild duck, cleaned
12 cloves
½ cup vinegar

⅓ cup sugar
3 bay leaves
Salt and pepper to taste

Combine ingredients in a saucepan with enough water to barely cover the duck. Let simmer until duck is tender, approximately 45 minutes.

—From the *PTA Cookbook*, Petersburg

The bulblets of Indian rice (Fritlaria kamchatcensis) are collected when full grown and put into cans and covered with seal oil, for winter use. The Aleuts, traditionally, consumed great quantities of the bulbs. During the months of August and September the women would accompany the men, who were hunting for geese on their autumnal migration pattern. The women would dig the roots of the lily and store them in huge grass sacks for winter use. The bulbs were dug up with a copper or iron rod. The soil was then shaken off and exposed to the air to dry the remaining soil, which was then removed as much as possible. The bulbs are boiled with meat or simply in water. Either way reduced them to a pasty consistency, having about as much taste as boiled starch. When eaten raw, the bulblets have a bitter taste. The bitterness lies only in the thin skin which surrounds them. It is at first difficult to acquire a taste for them. Those plants which grow in rich loose soil form a bulb which is often two inches in diameter and one inch thick.

Puffin
by April Kelley

The puffin is one of the many bird species found on the Aleutian Islands. It is happily at home on the cliffs overlooking the ocean.

Roast Wild Duck

2 wild ducks, cleaned
1 cup finely chopped celery
1 cup finely chopped onion
1 cup raisins
4 cups soft bread crumbs
2 beaten eggs

1/2 cup hot milk
1/2 teaspoon salt
Bacon strips
1 cup ketchup
1/2 cup chili sauce
1/4 cup Worcestershire sauce

Stuff the ducks with a mixture of the celery, onion, raisins, bread crumbs, eggs, milk, and salt. Place bacon strips across breasts of the ducks. Roast the ducks in an uncovered pan at 500 degrees F. for 15 minutes. Lower oven heat to 350 degrees F. and continue roasting, allowing a total roasting time of 35 minutes per pound (based on the weight of the heavier duck). Fifteen minutes before removing from oven, pour over the ducks a mixture of the ketchup, chili sauce, and Worcestershire sauce.

—From the *PTA Cookbook*, Petersburg

Ptarmigan and Cranberries

The ptarmigan is a popular, small, game bird and is also the state bird of Alaska. The combination of game birds or meats with tart, wild, berries is most typical of Alaskan cooking.

Yield: 6 servings

6 ptarmigan (1 for each person)
Seasoned flour
Fat for browning
6 or 7 green apples, sliced

1 cup cranberry sauce (made from
    lingonberries
1 cup water

Dip the ptarmigan in the seasoned flour and brown in hot fat in a skillet. Remove the ptarmigan and add the cranberry sauce mixed with water to the skillet; scrape up all the browned bits first. In a 2-quart casserole, make layers of sliced apples and ptarmigan. Pour the cranberry mixture over all, and bake in a 350 degrees F. oven until done—about 1 to 1 1/2 hours.

—From the *Nome Cookbook*, Nome

On the island of Atka, there are many well-known basket makers, who use the native wild barley grass for their beautiful creations. First they have to clean the outside leaves from the stalk. Only the two inner leaves are used in the basket making after they have been bleached by the sun.

Ptarmigan Breasts

Yield: 3 servings

6 ptarmigan breasts
½ pound bacon
Lemon pepper seasoning

3 onions, peeled and quartered
  (optional)
¼ cup water

Place breasts in a baking dish; drape bacon over breasts. Season with lemon pepper; add onions (if used) and ¼ cup of water. Bake at 350 degrees F. for 45 minutes to 1 hour.

—Matilda Davidson, Eielson Air Force Base

Several edible plants are used in the Aleutians. Among them are the following: Labrador tea, giant kelp, marestail, seaweed, siberian spring beauty, wild celery, water sedge, wild sweet potato, wintercress, beach greens, blueberries, blackberries, low-bush cranberries, dulse, fireweed, Kamchatka rockcress, cowslip, dwarf fireweed, seashore plaintain, felty leafed willow, wild cucumber, dandelions, alpine bear-berry, beach strawberries, cloudberries (not in Eastern Aleutians), trail-ing raspberry, salmonberries, bog cranberry, and black lily. Yellow pond lilies and red berried elders are eaten only as emergency food.

The Narcissus-flowered anemone, nootka lupine, and vetch are poisonous plants found in the Aleutians.

Beautiful flowers abound on the Aleutian islands in the summer. False helebore, veronica, rhododendrons, cushion type saxifrages, two types of orchids, arnica, and fernweed are only a few species. All of these many types of plants paint a striking lush picture of the home of the Aleut.

Stuffed Ptarmigan Breasts

With a sharp knife, remove the breasts from the bone and put them together, sandwich fashion, using a favorite bread stuffing for the filling. Wrap with strips of bacon and fasten with toothpicks. Bake in an uncovered pan at 350 degrees F. for about 45 minutes, basting occasionally with orange juice. Serve with a cream sauce to which you have added freshly chopped dill.

—From *Alaska's Cooking,* Anchorage

Yupik Ptarmigan Soup

Traditionally, a man or boy must catch the ptarmigan while hunting; the girls tear or pluck the feathers off. It is cut up and cleaned like a chicken. Wash the bird (unless you like the wild taste) and put it into 6 quarts of water. Boil for 5 to 10 minutes, then add 1 cup of rice and one cup of chopped potatoes. Add 1 tablespoon of salt. Mix flour and water together until pastry, then add to the pot with the bird to make gravy. Let it simmer for 5 minutes and then it is done.

Sour Cream Sauce for Roast Wild Birds

This is simple to make and excellent with roasted or plainly-cooked wild duck, grouse, or ptarmigan:

2 cups sour cream
1 tablespoon lemon juice

Few drops hot sauce
Dashes of salt and pepper

Combine ingredients in a saucepan; heat until just warmed through, and pour over cooked birds.

—Paul Coray, Kenai

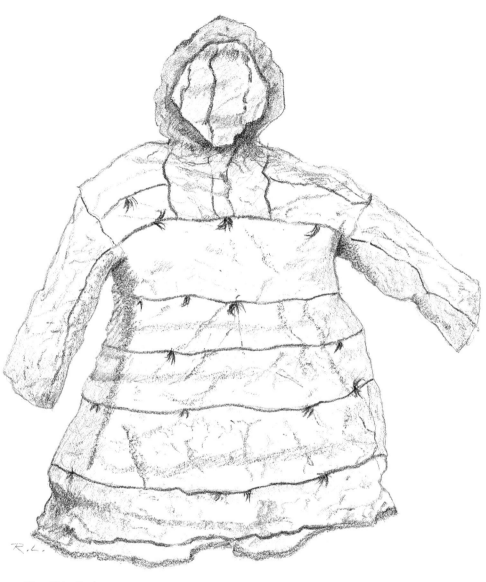

Gut-Skin Parka
by Rachel Levine

Raincoats made from the skin of seal intestines proved very weather-hardy in the Aleutian Island storms.

Special Grouse or Ptarmigan Breasts

Yield: 4 servings

Grouse or ptarmigan breasts, enough
   for 4 people
1 egg, well-beaten
Fine dry cracker or bread crumbs

2 tablespoons shortening
2 tablespoons butter
1 cup heavy cream
¼ cup sherry wine

Separate the breast meat from the bones using a sharp knife. Dip the pieces in the beaten egg, then in the crumbs. Dip again in egg, and again in crumbs. Melt the shortening and butter in a heavy skillet. Sauté the breasts until they are golden brown. Put into a Dutch oven or casserole. Thoroughly combine the cream and the sherry and pour over the breasts. Cover and bake at 375 degrees F. for 45 minutes to 1 hour.

—Paul Coray, Kenai

Cod fishing was very big until.the cod disappeared; herring salteries went empty. During World War II, the Japanese took over Attu, interring the Aleuts in concentration camps. Unalaska was bombed by the Japanese and then taken over by the United States as a military base. Most Aleuts were forced to evacuate their islands—either moving stateside or to abandoned canneries in Southeast Alaska. Sadly, they suffered at the canneries from the change of climate and lifestyle. Many died.

Wild Grouse Flamed with Gin

Cut any number of birds up into pieces, separating legs, wings, breasts, etc. Salt and pepper the pieces and sprinkle with paprika and dust or shake in a bag with flour. Melt butter or shortening in a heavy skillet and brown the pieces. Add ½ cup cold water, reduce heat, cover skillet, and simmer only until done. The birds will dry out rapidly if overcooked. Heat about ⅔ cup of gin (gin must be heated to ignite), remove skillet from heat, pour gin over birds, and—averting your face— ignite with a match. Serve when all the flames have died down.

—Paul Coray, Kenai

When the Russian fur traders invaded the Aleutian Islands in the mid-1700s, the estimated Aleut population was twenty thousand. It fell to two thousand partly because of new diseases and poor conditions. The sale of Alaska to the United States did little to improve the Aleuts: sea otters became an endangered species, and fox trapping did not enjoy a wide market.

Canadian Geese
by April Kelley

Roast Wild Goose

Yield: 6 servings

1 wild goose	2 apples, sliced
Salt and pepper	Bacon drippings
1 onion, sliced	4 slices bacon
2 stalks celery	2 cups water

Rub the inside of the bird with salt and pepper. Stuff the bird loosely with the onion, celery, and apples. Truss the bird if it is large. Place in a roaster, brush bacon drippings lightly over the bird, and sprinkle pepper generously over the breast. Place bacon slices on top of breast. Cover exposed part of bird with aluminum foil. Pour water into the roaster. Bake at 325 degrees F. for 15 minutes per pound. Remove the foil and roast until brown, if desired. Discard the stuffing and broth.

Nowadays the population of individual island villages varies from season to season, as men leave to fish during the summer months from their own boats or from other boats at Kodiak. Some people work on crab-packing boats during winter weeks, if the crab is available. In recent years the crab industry has been low. A bottom fish industry is developing that may even be greater than the crab industry.

Casserole of Elderly Goose

This is a good treatment for game birds of uncertain age, or for grouse that have been feeding on spruce needles instead of good blueberries!

1 Canadian goose or 4 large grouse	½ cup light cream
¾ tablespoon salt	2 tablespoons sauterne
2 tablespoons melted butter	2 hard-boiled eggs
1 tablespoon flour	Parsley

Pluck, draw, and skin the bird(s). Quarter the goose, or leave grouse whole. Place in a kettle and just barely cover with cold water and the salt. Bring to a boil; lower heat immediately and simmer for about 1 hour, until tender. Remove the bird(s) and boil the stock until it is reduced to 1½ cups.

Remove the meat from the bird(s) and place in a greased, 3-quart casserole. Make a sauce by melting the butter, stirring in the flour, and gradually adding the reduced broth; stir over heat until thickened and smooth. Stir in the cream and simmer sauce for 5 minutes. Stir in the sauterne and pour over the meat in the casserole. Let casserole stand for 2 hours, then cover and bake at 425 degrees F. for about 35 minutes, until the sauce starts to bubble. Remove, and garnish with the sliced whites and grated yolks of the hard-boiled eggs, and parsley. Serve with low-bush cranberry jelly.

—From the *Catholic Daughters of America*, Juneau

A seasonal occupation of the people on St. George and St. Paul in the Pribilof islands has been the harvesting of the northern fur seal. There are also reindeer herds and major sea bird colonies here. Bottom fishing industries are important to the livelihood of the people.

Stikine Duck Casserole

Yield: 8 servings

4 wild ducks, cleaned and cut into serving pieces	4 cups prepared bread stuffing (with onion and thyme)

Flour
Salt and pepper
Oil for frying

1 cup white wine
¼ cup water

Shake duck pieces in a paper bag with the flour and salt and pepper. Fry in hot oil until gently browned. Arrange some of the duck in a ring in a large casserole. In the center make a shallow nest of foil, and add the prepared stuffing. Put remaining duck around and partially over the stuffing. Baste with a mixture of the white wine and water. Bake, covered, at 325 degrees F. for 45 minutes; uncover casserole and bake 30 minutes longer.

—From the *PTA Cookbook*, Petersburg

Often when someone gets a seal, sea lion, reindeer, or large halibut, it is shared among villagers. Reindeer were transplanted to some islands like Atka in the early 1920s to add to the food ration of the people. The reindeer, a relative of the caribou, were never domesticated, as in areas on the Seward Peninsula.

Wild Duck with Sour Cream

5- to 6-pound duck, cut in serving
  pieces (or use duck breasts only)
2 tablespoons fat
Flour, salt, and pepper
1 onion, chopped

2 tablespoons chopped parsley
¼ teaspoon rosemary
¼ teaspoon thyme
1 cup dry red wine
1 cup sour cream

Dredge the duck pieces in flour, salt, and pepper; brown in the hot fat. Place in a casserole and add remaining ingredients, except sour cream. Cover and bake at 350 degrees F. for 1½ hours. Lower oven heat to 300 degrees F. Add sour cream and bake 30 minutes longer.

—From *Alaska's Cooking*, Anchorage

Baraberas are sod houses built into the ground. They gave protection to early-day Aleut hunters on hunting trips. They were originally made of upright driftwood timbers and occasional whale bones. The roof was covered with a layer of dry grass and sod. In some areas of the Aleutians they are still used, since severe winds blast the islands from time to time. The only difference between old-time shelters and the present abodes, is the use of wood paneling on the interior, electric lights, and paint.

Wild Goose and Sauerkraut Stuffing

1 10- to 12-pound wild goose
3 pounds sauerkraut, well drained

Stuff the goose loosely with sauerkraut (as dressing swells) and sew up. Place on a rack in an uncovered roaster and roast in a very hot oven (500 degrees F.) for 15 minutes. Lower heat to 350 degrees F., and roast about 25 minutes per pound of goose. When goose is roasted, drain the fat from the pan, and add water to the drippings to make a gravy.

—From the *Golden Heart Cookbook,* Fairbanks

Sea Lions
Photo
Alaska Department of Fish and Game

Sea lions on rookery on Barren Islands, Shelikof Strait. The small pups seen in foreground are tagged by biologists to study migrations and growth rates.

246

THE TLINGIT

The southeastern portion of Alaska, an area where large ice fields, numerous glaciers, and steep mountains slope down to breathtaking shorelines, is the home of the Tlingit Indians. The precipitous terrain is cut deeply by channels, straits, and fjords, creating many large islands and innumerable small islands. Needless to say, the coastal edges are typically quite rugged. Four large rivers cut across the coastal mountains: the Unuk, Stikine, Taku, and Alsek. Since there are numerous waterways, there are many easy avenues for boat travel.

Because of the proximity of the ocean, the Tlingits are strongly influenced by the maritime climate. Most of southeastern Alaska has relatively little sunshine, moderate temperatures, and abundant precipitation. As an example, Yakutat averages approximately 134 inches of rain yearly.

In response to favorable moisture and temperature conditions, an extremely lush vegetation has developed. Below the timberline, the vegetation is a thick dense forest interspersed with muskeg. Dominant tree species are western hemlock, Sitka spruce, red and yellow cedar, Jack pine, and alder. In isolated areas you will find cottonwood, mountain hemlock, birch, and other woody plants. Many kinds of grasses and berry-producing plants are generously and widely distributed.

The Tlingits occupied southeastern Alaska at the time of the first European contact with the area. The culture is highly developed into families, or clans, in their different communities or tribes at various locations in southeastern Alaska. The different communities were divided into two moieties. One was called the Wolf and the other was called the Raven. Each moiety was in turn divided into a number of clans. The membership into the clan was descended through the mother. Each clan had its own distinctive name, traditions, and crests. Marriage within a moiety was forbidden. Since no one in the clan could marry anyone else from that clan, a local clan had to associate with another clan from the opposite moiety. The local clan divisions in a village were made up of house groups. That is, a village consisted of a number of large houses of local clans. Each house sheltered a number of families—some houses were large enough to hold a dozen families!

The livelihood patterns of the Tlingit were strongly influenced by the rich supply of resources which varied in location and abundance, according to the season. The different clans held to well-defined hunting, fishing, and gathering areas. Clan property included the fishing streams, the coastal waters and shores, the hunting grounds, the berrying areas, the sealing rocks, the house sites in the villages, and the rights to many of the mountain passes leading into Interior Alaska. Many of the hunting grounds consisted of the watersheds of the rivers and streams of the southeastern part of the state.

Chilkat Dancer
by Rachel Levine

248

The Tlingit culture made use of a great variety of natural resources of both the land and sea. Fish was the principal resource, of which salmon was the most important. From the various resources available to them, they made their food, shelter, clothing, and the tools needed for their everyday existence. The fish, animal meats, berries, roots, clams, fish oil, many types of grasses and other products were made into food for immediate consumption or were dried and stored for winter feasting or trade.

Wood was the primary material for most of their artistic skills. The homes, canoes, boxes for foods and articles of value, totem poles upon which they carved their crests, and most of the implements they used in day-to-day living, were made of wood. They made a host of articles from bark, particularly the inner bark of the red and yellow cedar. The well known Chilkat blankets were made from the wool of the mountain goat and the bark of the cedar, and they were sometimes lined with the fur of the sea otter.

Historically, items for trade with other linguistic groups included furs, cedar logs and canoes, oil made from the olachen fish, bark, robes made of marmot skins, wool and bark blankets, carved utensils, shells, lichen for dyes, and copper. During the winter months from November to February, the Tlingits lived in permanent villages composed of their tribes. At other times of the year they had temporary camps associated with good fishing grounds, hunting grounds, or gathering areas.

Subsistence utilization of fish and game resources remain important to the proud modern-day Tlingit culture.

$\mathcal{D}$ ESSERTS

With a bountiful and varied wild berry crop throughout Alaska, it is natural to find many of our desserts made from these sweet and colorful fruits. Raspberries, blueberries, and "low-bush cranberries" (actually lingonberries) are usually abundant, fun to gather, and keep well in the freezer or canning jar. The different regions of Alaska offer different kinds of berries—some sweet and some not. But berries are the natural choice for creating special treats or for making good, home-style pies, cakes, and—even in Alaska—frozen desserts.

With few exceptions, no other fruits except berries grow well in Alaska. Most of the Alaskan berries we use are still gathered by hand from the wild, and the berry picking itself is often a hobby, family outing, or social meeting. One longtime Alaskan friend asserts that she gets to know a friend well by going berry picking with her. Over the years she has brought home many new friends, as well as delicious berries. Another friend "always" brings several noisy children with her when picking so she won't be surprised by a berry-munching bear! And favorite berry patches are often well-guarded secrets: asking the recipe for the pie is great, but don't dare ask where the cook picked her berries!

Desserts are so well-loved by all Americans, and the "traditional favorites"— cake, pie, and ice cream—are Alaskan favorites too. Traditional Alaska native desserts such as "Eskimo ice cream," may not be as sweet, but they are relished as special treats. Hopefully, as you enjoy these dessert recipes, you will feel the spirit of a sunny, berry-picking afternoon shared with a friend.

Norwegian Prune Pudding

Yield: 4 servings

2 cups pitted, cooked prunes
1 cup prune juice
½ cup sugar
4 tablespoons cornstarch

½ teaspoon salt
12 prune pit kernels, cut up
2 tablespoons lemon juice

Bring prunes and juice to a boil. Separately combine sugar, cornstarch, and salt. Gradually stir it into the prune mixture. Cook for 15 minutes, stirring until thickened. Add the kernels and lemon juice to the pudding. Turn into individual molds or into a large mold; chill thoroughly. Serve with whipped cream.

—Frances L. Hardy
From *PTA Cookbook*, Petersburg

Lingonberry Chiffon Pie

1 cup lingonberry juice
1 package strawberry or lemon chiffon
  pie filling mix

⅓ cup sugar
1 cooled, baked 9-inch pie shell or
  graham cracker crust

Chill ½ cup juice. Heat remaining ½ cup to boiling. Add to pie filling mix in a large bowl, and stir well. Add the chilled juice, and beat at highest speed of electric mixer until mixture is very foamy. Add sugar and beat until mixture stands in peaks—1 to 3 minutes. Spoon into pie shell and chill until set (about 2 hours). Serve plain or with whipped cream.

—University of Alaska, Cooperative Extension Service

Homemade Yeast

Scrub three medium-sized potatoes, cut into small pieces and cover with three pints of water. Tie one tablespoon of hops in a piece of cheesecloth and place with potatoes; add two tablespoons of rice. Let boil until potatoes and rice are thoroughly cooked. Remove from stove, mash potatoes and rice in liquid and add cold water to the amount evaporated by boiling, making the original amount of liquid, which was three pints. To this tepid liquid add one tablespoon of salt, one tablespoon of sugar, and two yeast cakes which have been previously soaked in a cup of warm water. Keep this mixture warm for 24 hours, at which time it will be covered with bubbles, indicating it is ready to be put away in a cool place. This yeast will keep indefinitely.

—Mrs. Miner Bruce, *Fairbanks Cookbook*, circa 1910

Alaska Low-Bush Cranberry Dessert

1 cup sugar
2 cups flour
2 teaspoons baking powder

1 cup milk
2 tablespoons melted butter
2 cups low-bush cranberries

Preheat oven to 350 degrees F. Stir together the sugar, flour, and baking powder. Stir in the milk, butter, and low-bush cranberries; mix. Pour into two greased pie pans and bake at 350 degrees F. for 30 minutes. Serve warm with Butter Sauce (recipe follows).

—From *Alaska Airlines is Cooking*, Anchorage

Butter Sauce

½ cup butter
1 cup sugar
¾ cup cream

Boil butter, sugar, and cream together, stirring constantly, until it is the consistency of syrup.

—From *Alaska Airlines is Cooking*, Anchorage

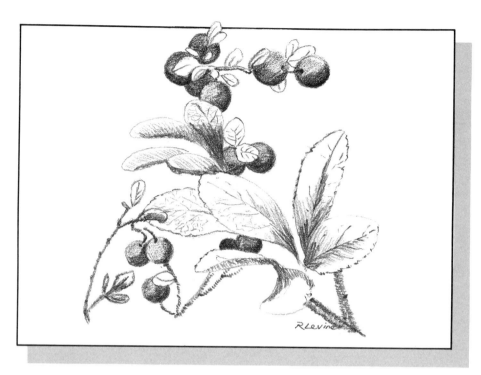

Blueberries
by Rachel Levine

Blueberry Jello

When jelly made from ripe blueberries fails to set, use it in this dessert.

1 cup homemade blueberry jelly
1 cup water

1 envelope unflavored gelatine
1 tablespoon lemon juice

Melt and heat together the jelly and ¾ cup of the water. Sprinkle gelatine over ¼ cup cold water and let soften 5 minutes. Add to hot jelly mixture and stir until gelatine is dissolved. Stir in the lemon juice. Chill to set, and serve with whipped cream.

—From the *Golden Heart Cookbook,* Fairbanks

254

Athabaskan Indian Candy

2 to 3 cups blueberries
1 cup salmonberries

1½ cups shortening
¼ to ½ cup sugar

Gently stir all the ingredients together, trying not to squash the berries. This can be served in a dish with milk, or just eaten by itself.

—From *Alaska Airlines is Cookin,* Anchorage

Cranberry Sherbet

Yield: 1 quart

1 quart lingonberries (low-bush cranberries) or regular cranberries
2 cups water
¼ cup lemon juice

2½ cups sugar
1 cup applesauce
1 cup water

Boil lingonberries in 2 cups water until soft. Rub through a strainer; add remaining ingredients and freeze. Serve with turkey or ham, or as a dessert.

—From the *Golden Heart Cookbook,* Fairbanks

Cranberry Foam

Yield: 4 servings

2 egg whites, stiffly beaten with 3 to 4 tablespoons sugar
4 tablespoons thick Alaskan cranberry sauce

Fold cranberry sauce into the stiffly beaten whites and serve immediately.

—Roswitha Miller, Ninilchik

Ninilchik Pioneer Candy

2 cups brown sugar
1 cup butter
¼ cup molasses

2 tablespoons water
2 tablespoons vinegar

Boil all ingredients together rapidly and cook to a hard crack stage, stirring frequently. Pour at once into shallow, buttered pans. Let cool and break into pieces.

—Vicky Cooper, Ninilchik

Alaska Cranberry Sherbet

2 cups fresh lingonberries
1 cup water
1 cup sugar

Juice of ½ lemon
1 egg white, beaten

Boil the cranberries in the water until tender. Strain, and add the sugar to the juice. Cool completely; add lemon juice and place in a 2-quart container. Freeze until slushy. Add the egg white and freeze until hard to turn. Remove dasher and let freeze completely.

—From the Nome Cookbook, Nome

Nome Eskimo Ice Cream

Cut up tallow or reindeer fat in thin slices. Add seal oil, and stir until well blended—keep working it until smooth. Then add sugar to suit taste and blueberries or moss berries. The mixture will remain white in color.

—Bessie Osaruk, Nome

Christmas Ice Cream

1 pound Alaskan low-bush cranberries
2 cups water
2 cups sugar
¼ cup lemon juice
1 teaspoon grated orange peel
2 cups cold water
½ cup sugar

¼ teaspoon salt
1 cup milk
3 egg yolks, beaten
½ teaspoon almond extract
Green food coloring
2 cups whipping cream, chilled

Cook cranberries in 2 cups water until the skins break, about 10 minutes. Rub the berries through a sieve to make a smooth pulp. Stir in the sugar, lemon juice, peel, and 2 cups cold water. Pour half the mixture into a serving container and freeze until firm.

Mix the sugar, salt, milk, and egg yolks in a saucepan. Cook over medium heat, stirring constantly, just until bubbles appear around the edge of the mixture. Cool to room temperature. Stir in almond extract and the food coloring. Pour into a refrigerator tray and freeze until slushy and partially frozen, ½ to 1 hour. In a chilled bowl, beat the cream until soft peaks form. Spoon the partially frozen mixture into another chilled bowl and beat until smooth. Fold in the whipped cream. Spread over the frozen cranberry mixture and freeze until firm. Add the rest of the cranberry mixture and freeze until ready to use.

—Karen Encelewski, Ninilchik

Krummel Torte

4 egg yolks
1 cup sugar
6 tablespoons bread crumbs
1 teaspoon baking powder

½ cup chopped walnuts
1 cup pitted dates, chopped
4 egg whites, stiffly beaten

Preheat oven to 300 degrees F. Beat yolks, add sugar gradually. Add bread crumbs, baking powder, walnuts, and dates. Fold in stiffly beaten egg whites. Pour into a greased, 8-inch-square cake pan and bake at 300 degrees F. for 1 hour. Serve with Vanilla Sauce (recipe follows), or whipped cream.

—From *Nome Cookbook*, Nome

Vanilla Sauce

1 cup sugar
2 tablespoons cornstarch
2 cups boiling water

4 tablespoons butter
2 teaspoons vanilla

Mix the sugar and cornstarch. Gradually stir in the boiling water and boil for 1 minute, stirring constantly. Stir in the butter and vanilla. Keep warm until ready to serve.

—From the *Nome Cookbook*, Nome

Rusk Custard

1 package Swedish rusk or about 25
  graham crackers, crushed
1/2 cup sugar
1/2 cup melted butter
4 egg yolks
2 cups milk

1/2 cup sugar
1 tablespoon cornstarch
1 teaspoon vanilla or other flavoring
4 egg whites
2 tablespoons confectioners' sugar

Preheat oven to 350 degrees F. Mix rusk crumbs with 1/2 cup sugar and the melted butter. Put half of the mixture into a buttered 9-inch baking pan, pie plate, or small casserole. Mix egg yolks, milk, sugar, cornstarch, and vanilla until very smooth; pour over crumb mixture. Beat egg whites with the confectioners' sugar until they are stiff, and spread over the custard. Top with the remaining crumb mixture. Bake at 350 degrees F. for about 30 minutes. Chopped nuts may be added, if desired.

—From the *Golden Heart Cookbook*, Fairbanks

Blueberry Pudding #2

1 pint Alaskan blueberries
3 tablespoons sugar
2 tablespoons butter
1 cup sugar
1 egg, beaten

1 cup milk
2 cups flour
1 teaspoon baking powder
1 teaspoon vanilla

Preheat oven to 350 degrees F. Sprinkle blueberries with 3 tablespoons sugar and place in a deep, buttered 10-inch pie plate or shallow casserole. Mix remaining ingredients as a cake batter and pour over blueberries. Bake at 350 degrees F.

for about 40 minutes. Turn from the dish, with the fruit on top, and serve with cream or a spice sauce.

—From the *Golden Heart Cookbook*, Fairbanks

Rum Pudding

Yield: 6 servings

2 tablespoons or 2 envelopes
   unflavored gelatine
$1/2$ cup cold water
3 cups whipping cream

5 eggs, separated
3 tablespoons rum
5 tablespoons sugar

Soak gelatine in cold water for 10 minutes. Whip the cream. Using clean beaters, beat the egg whites until stiff; fold into the whipped cream along with the rum. Beat egg yolks to a foam with the sugar and add to the cream mixture. Dissolve gelatine by heating gently over hot water, then fold it in thoroughly. Chill until set, and serve with any red berry sauce.

—From the *Golden Heart Cookbook*, Fairbanks

Finnish Whipped Berry Pudding

Yield: 6 servings

1 cup low-bush cranberries or regular
   cranberries
$1^{1}/2$ cups water
4 cups water

1 cup farina (cream of wheat)
$1^{1}/2$ cups sugar
$1/2$ teaspoon salt

Boil cranberries in the $1^{1}/2$ cups water until soft; strain out the juice. Combine juice with remaining ingredients and cook until it is quite thick. Cool, then whip until very light, either with a wire whip or a beater. Any other berries may be used.

—From the *Golden Heart Cookbook*, Fairbanks

Royal Rhubarb Dessert

4 cups rhubarb, cut into 1-inch pieces
1/4 cup sugar
2 tablespoons quick-cooking tapioca
1/2 teaspoon salt
1 11-ounce can mandarin oranges, drained

1 cup rolled oats (quick or regular)
1/4 cup flour
1/3 cup brown sugar
1/4 cup melted butter

Combine rhubarb, sugar, tapioca, and salt. Mix, and let stand 30 minutes, stirring occasionally. Stir in mandarin oranges, and place in an 8-inch square cake pan. Preheat oven to 350 degrees F. Combine remaining ingredients and sprinkle over rhubarb mixture. Bake at 350 degrees F. for 40 to 50 minutes.

—From *Alaska Airlines is Cookin,* Anchorage

Caramel Pudding

1 cup white sugar
2 cups hot water
1 13-ounce can evaporated milk
1/2 teaspoon salt

6 tablespoons cornstarch mixed with cold water
1 teaspoon vanilla

Slowly melt the sugar in a heavy frying pan until it is caramelized, about 1 hour. Add 2 cups hot water, and let stand on the stove until dissolved. Add evaporated milk and salt; bring to boiling point. Stir in cornstarch mixture and cook until thickened. Remove from heat and add the vanilla.

—Betty Doyle, Nome

Mama's Cranberry Pudding

4 cups low-bush cranberries
2 cups water
1 1/4 cups sugar

1/4 teaspoon salt
2 tablespoons cornstarch mixed with 2 tablespoons water

Add water to berries and bring to a boil; simmer for 20 minutes. Add the sugar

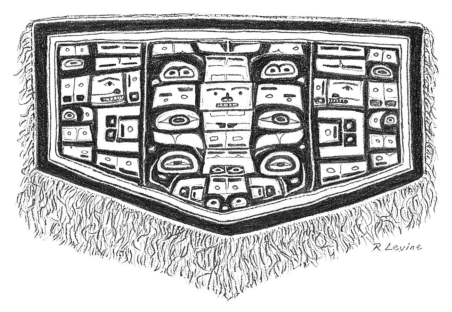

Chilkat Blanket
by Rachel Levine

and salt, and cook slowly for 10 minutes. Add the cornstarch mixture, and heat until thickened. Chill and serve. This is good with all Alaskan meats.

—Virginia Doyle "Bunny" Heiner, Fairbanks

Alaskan Carrot Cookies

2 cups sifted flour
2 teaspoons baking powder
¼ teaspoon salt
1 cup shortening
¾ cup sugar

1 cup raw grated carrots
½ teaspoon orange extract or 1 teaspoon grated orange rind
1 egg, beaten

Preheat oven to 400 degrees F. Resift flour with the baking powder and salt. Cream the shortening and the sugar; add grated carrots, flavoring, and egg. Work in the dry ingredients. Drop by teaspoons onto greased cookie sheets and bake at 400 degrees F. for 10 to 12 minutes.

—From the *Golden Heart Cookbook*, Fairbanks

Raspberry Jam Bars

1 cup flour
1/4 teaspoon salt
1 teaspoon baking powder
1/2 cup butter
1 1/2 eggs, beaten
1 tablespoon milk

1 cup (or more) thick raspberry jam
Additional 1 1/2 eggs, beaten
1 cup sugar
1 teaspoon vanilla
1/4 cup butter, melted
2 to 3 cups shredded coconut

Preheat oven to 350 degrees F. Stir together the flour, salt, and baking powder. Cut in the butter until mixture is crumbly. Add 1 1/2 eggs and milk. Pat into the bottom of a 9-by-11-inch baking pan, making the sides a little thicker so they extend upward. Spread on a thick coating of the jam, and cover with a mixture of the remaining ingredients. Bake at 350 degrees F. for 30 minutes. Let stand 15 minutes and cut into small squares.

—From the *Golden Heart Cookbook*, Fairbanks

Berliner Kranze

Yield: 3 dozen

1/4 cup shortening
1/2 cup butter
1/2 cup sugar
1/4 teaspoon grated orange rind

1 egg, beaten
2 cups sifted flour
1/4 teaspoon salt

Cream shortening, butter, sugar, and orange rind until fluffy; add egg, beating well. Add flour and salt to creamed mixture. Chill dough for 1 hour. Break off small pieces of dough and form into long rolls the length and size of a pencil. On an ungreased cookie sheet, form a circle with each piece and bring ends through in a single knot, leaving 1/2-inch end on each side. Brush tops of cookies with meringue (see recipe below) and sprinkle with coarse sugar crystals (colored ones may be used). Preheat oven to 400 degrees F. Bake for 10 to 15 minutes.

—From the *Golden Heart Cookbook*, Fairbanks

Meringue

1 egg white
2 tablespoons sugar

Beat egg white until stiff with a wire whisk, adding sugar slowly.

—From the *Golden Heart Cookbook*, Fairbanks

Cheechako Oatmeal Jelly Cookies

Yield: 2 dozen cookies

2/3 cup shortening
1 cup brown sugar
2 eggs
2 teaspoons vanilla
1 1/2 cups flour

2 teaspoons baking powder
1 teaspoon salt
2 cups rolled oats
1/2 cup evaporated milk
Jelly

Preheat oven to 375 degrees F. Cream together the shortening and brown sugar. Beat in eggs and vanilla. Stir in the dry ingredients alternately with the evaporated milk. Drop by heaping teaspoons on greased baking sheets, and press a hollow in each with the back of a teaspoon. Bake for 12 minutes at 375 degrees F. Fill each cookie with 1/2 teaspoon jelly.

—From *Alaska Airlines is Cookin,* Anchorage

Chocolate Sour Cream Cookies

1/2 cup shortening
2 squares (2 ounces) unsweetened
   baking chocolate
1 1/2 cups sugar
2 eggs
1 cup sour cream

1 teaspoon vanilla or almond extract
1 cup chopped nuts
1/2 teaspoon baking soda
1/2 teaspoon salt
2 3/4 cups flour

Preheat oven to 350 degrees F. Melt chocolate and shortening together; add sugar and beat well. Beat in eggs. Add sour cream and flavoring. Stir in the dry ingredients. Drop by teaspoons on greased cookie sheets. Bake at 350 degrees F. for 10 minutes. These may be frosted with a simple confectioners' sugar icing.

—From *Alaska Airlines is Cookin,* Anchorage

Apple Spice Bars

Yield: 3 dozen bars

½ cup shortening
1 cup sugar
1 egg
1 teaspoon vanilla
2 cups flour
2 teaspoons baking powder
1 teaspoon salt

1 teaspoon cinnamon
1 teaspoon nutmeg
2 tablespoons cocoa
½ teaspoon baking soda
⅔ cup milk
1½ cups diced raw apples
Confectioners' sugar

Preheat oven to 350 degrees F. Cream the shortening and sugar until fluffy. Add the egg and vanilla. Sift the dry ingredients and add to the mixture alternately with the milk. Add the diced apples. Pour into a greased and floured 9-by-13-inch baking pan, and bake at 350 degrees F. for 25 minutes. When cool, cut into bars and roll in confectioners' sugar.

—St. Matthew's Guild, Fairbanks

Potato Cake

Yield: one loaf cake

1 cup shortening
2 cups sugar
4 eggs
1 cup mashed potatoes
2 cups cake flour
4 tablespoons cocoa

1 teaspoon mixed spices—cinnamon,
   nutmeg, and cloves
3 teaspoons baking powder
½ cup milk
1½ teaspoons vanilla
1 cup walnuts, chopped

Preheat oven to 350 degrees F. Cream shortening and sugar. Mix in the eggs, and then the potatoes. Sift flour with cocoa, spices, and baking powder. Add dry ingredients alternately with milk to the mixture. Add vanilla and nuts. Bake in a large, greased loaf pan at 350 degrees F. for 45 minutes.

—From the *Golden Heart Cookbook*, Fairbanks

Boiled Raisin Cake

Yield: one 8- or 9-inch cake

1 cup raisins
1 cup boiling water
½ cup butter

¼ teaspoon salt
¼ teaspoon mace
2 cups flour

1 cup brown sugar
1/2 teaspoon cinnamon
1/2 teaspoon nutmeg

1 teaspoon baking soda
3 eggs, well beaten
1/2 cup chopped nuts

Cover raisins with boiling water and let simmer on back burner of stove. Add butter, brown sugar, and spices; let cool. Preheat oven to 350 degrees F. Add the flour sifted with the baking soda, then mix in the eggs. Stir in the nuts. Bake in a greased 8- or 9-inch cake pan at 350 degrees F. for 1 hour.

—From the *Golden Heart Cookbook,* Fairbanks

Paystreak Cake

Yield: one 2-layer cake

4 eggs
1 cup sugar
1 1/2 cups all-purpose flour
1/2 cup cold water
1/2 teaspoon baking soda

1 teaspoon cream of tartar
1 teaspoon vanilla
1/2 cup chopped nuts
Melted sweet chocolate

Preheat oven to 375 degrees F. Grease and flour two 8-inch, round cake pans. Beat eggs for 5 minutes, then gradually add sugar, beating well. Add 1 cup of the flour and beat, then mix in the cold water. Sift or mix remaining 1/2 cup flour with the baking soda and cream of tartar, beat into mixture, then mix in the vanilla. Spread batter in prepared cake pans and bake at 375 degrees F. for 25 to 30 minutes. Let cool 5 minutes, then remove cake layers from pans. When cool, fill layers 1-inch thick with buttercream (recipe below) and spread remaining buttercream on top of cake. Top with chopped nuts and drizzle with melted chocolate.

—From the *Golden Heart Cookbook,* Fairbanks

Coffee Buttercream

1/2 pound (2 sticks) unsalted butter, at
    room temperature
1 cup confectioners' sugar, sifted

2 egg yolks
1/2 cup cold, strong coffee
1 teaspoon vanilla

Cream butter and sugar thoroughly. Add yolks and beat again. Beat in coffee a few drops at a time, then the vanilla.

—From the *Golden Heart Cookbook,* Fairbanks

Blueberry Upside Down Cake

one 9-inch square cake

¼ cup butter
1 cup brown sugar
1 cup uncooked blueberries
1¼ cups unbleached white flour
2 teaspoons baking powder
½ teaspoon salt

½ cup sugar
1 egg, beaten
½ cup milk
1 teaspoon vanilla
¼ cup melted fat

Preheat oven to 350 degrees F. Melt the butter in a 9-inch, square baking pan, add the brown sugar and spread with the blueberries. Sift or stir together the flour, baking powder, salt, and sugar. Combine the egg, milk, vanilla, and fat; mix with the dry ingredients. Pour this batter over the mixture in the baking pan. Bake at 350 degrees F. for about 45 minutes. Turn out on serving plate while still warm.

—Lola Tilly, Fairbanks

Oatmeal Cake

Yield: one 9-by-13-inch cake

1½ cups boiling water
1 cup oatmeal
1 cup butter
1 cup sugar
1 cup brown sugar
2 eggs
1½ cups sifted flour

1 teaspoon baking soda
1 teaspoon baking powder
1 teaspoon cinnamon
¾ cup butter
¼ cup evaporated milk
1 cup brown sugar
1 cup chopped nuts

Stir boiling water into oatmeal and let cool. Preheat oven to 350 degrees F. In another bowl, cream the butter, sugar, and brown sugar. Add eggs and beat again. Add the cooled oatmeal mixture and blend. Stir together the flour, baking soda, baking powder, and cinnamon; add to the creamed mixture and blend. Spread in greased 9-by-13-inch cake pan. Bake at 350 degrees F. for 40 minutes.

For cake topping, heat together the ¾ cup butter, evaporated milk, and brown sugar over medium heat until smooth. Stir in nuts and mix. Spread over top of baked cake.

—From *Alaska Airlines is Cookin,* Anchorage

German Poppy Seed Cake

Yield: 1 tube cake

1 cup margarine or butter
1½ cups sugar
4 egg yolks
⅓ cup poppy seeds
1 teaspoon baking soda

1 cup sour cream
2 cups sifted cake flour
2 teaspoons vanilla
4 egg whites, stiffly beaten
Confectioners' sugar

Preheat oven to 350 degrees F. Cream the margarine and sugar. Add egg yolks and poppy seeds, and beat. Add baking soda and sour cream; stir in flour and vanilla. Fold in the stiffly beaten egg whites. Pour into an ungreased tube pan, and bake at 350 degrees F. for 1 hour. Invert until cold. Sprinkle with confectioners' sugar.

—From *Alaska Airlines is Cookin,* Anchorage

Rhubarb-Strawberry Coffee Cake

Yield: 1 cake

3 cups fresh rhubarb, cut into 1-inch
    pieces or 13 ounces frozen rhubarb
1 pound frozen sliced sweetened
    strawberries
2 tablespoons lemon juice
1 cup sugar
⅓ cup cornstarch
3 cups flour
1 cup brown sugar
1 teaspoon baking powder

1 teaspoon baking soda
1 teaspoon salt
1 cup butter or margarine
1 cup buttermilk
2 eggs, slightly beaten
1 teaspoon vanilla
¾ cup brown sugar
½ cup flour
¼ cup butter or margarine

In a saucepan, combine the rhubarb and strawberries; cook 5 minutes. Stir in lemon juice. Combine the sugar and cornstarch; add to berries, cooking and stirring until thickened. Set aside to cool.

In a mixing bowl, stir together the flour, 1 cup brown sugar, baking powder, baking soda, and salt. Cut in the butter. Separately beat together the buttermilk, eggs, and vanilla; add to dry ingredients and stir only until moistened.

Preheat oven to 350 degrees F. Spread *half* the batter in a greased 9-by-13-inch baking pan. Spread the cooled rhubarb-strawberry filling over the batter. Spoon the remaining batter in mounds over the top. Mix together the ¾ cup brown sugar, flour, and butter until crumbly; sprinkle over the top. Bake at 350 degrees F. for 40 to 45 minutes.

—From *Alaska Airlines is Cookin,* Anchorage

Sourdough Blueberry-Sauce Cake

Yield: 1 8-inch square cake

1 cup sourdough starter (see page 102)
1 cup flour
$^{1}/_{2}$ cup nonfat dry milk
1 cup blueberry sauce
$^{1}/_{2}$ cup sugar
$^{1}/_{2}$ cup brown sugar
$^{1}/_{2}$ cup shortening

2 teaspoons baking soda
1 teaspoon cinnamon
$^{1}/_{2}$ teaspoon each of salt, nutmeg,
   cloves, and allspice
1 egg, well beaten
$^{1}/_{2}$ cup chopped walnuts

   Combine starter, flour, dry milk, and blueberry sauce in a covered glass bowl, and let it set in a warm place while you prepare the rest of the cake mixture. Preheat oven to 350 degrees F. Cream the sugars, shortening, baking soda, and seasonings; add the egg and walnuts. Combine the sourdough mixture and the creamed mixture, and beat for 1 minute. Spread in a greased 8-inch, square cake pan, and bake at 350 degrees F. for 30 to 50 minutes. Note: the batter will have an unbecoming blue-gray color which will become a rich golden brown when baked.

—Mary Hawkins, Ninilchik

Blueberry Shortcake

$^{1}/_{2}$ cup butter
4 cups pancake mix
1$^{1}/_{3}$ cups milk

Melted butter
Sugar
2 to 3 cups blueberries

   Preheat oven to 450 degrees F. Cut butter into the pancake mix. Add the milk and stir lightly with a fork. Turn a bit more than half of the dough into a well-greased, shallow 9-by-12-inch pan and press out to the edges. Brush with melted butter and cover with waxed paper, extending over sides of the pan. Grease the pan and spread remaining dough on top, patting it out to within $^{1}/_{2}$ inch of sides of pan. Brush with melted butter and sprinkle lightly with sugar. Bake at 450 degrees F. for 25 to 30 minutes. Lift off top layer with paper. Slip lower crust onto a platter and cover with sweetened berries. Place top crust over berries and cover with more berries. Serve plain or with cream.

—From the *Nome Cookbook*, Nome

Pear Upside Down Cake

Yield: 6 or 8 servings

4 tablespoons butter, at room
  temperature
¾ cup brown sugar
6 canned pear halves
¼ cup shortening
¾ cup sugar
1 egg

1 teaspoon lemon juice
2 teaspoons grated lemon rind
1½ cups sifted cake flour
2 teaspoons baking powder
½ teaspoon salt
½ cup milk or syrup from canned pears

Preheat oven to 375 degrees F. Mix the butter and brown sugar and put into an 8-inch, square cake pan. Arrange pear halves over this, cut side down. Cream the shortening and sugar. Add the egg, lemon juice, and lemon rind, and beat until fluffy. Sift the flour, baking powder, and salt together, and add alternately with the milk. Pour the batter over the pears and bake at 375 degrees F. for 45 minutes or until cake tests done. Serve flipped on a platter.

—St. Matthew's Guild, Fairbanks

Carrot Pie

Pumpkins don't grow well in most parts of Alaska, but carrots do!

Yield: 1 pie

2 cups cooked carrots, mashed
1 cup sugar
2 eggs, beaten
1 teaspoon salt
1½ cups milk

1 teaspoon nutmeg
1 teaspoon cinnamon
½ teaspoon ground ginger
½ teaspoon ground cloves
1 tablespoon butter, melted

Mix all ingredients together until very well blended. Pour into an unbaked, 9-inch pie shell. Bake at 425 degrees F. for about 50 minutes, until a knife inserted one inch from the edge comes out clean. Center will look soft but filling will set as it cools.

—From the *Golden Heart Cookbook*, Fairbanks

Forget-Me-Not
by April Kelley

Forget-Me-Not, Alaska's state flower.

Blueberry Pie

Yield: 8-inch pie

3 cups blueberries
2/3 cup sugar
4 tablespoons flour
1/4 teaspoon salt

1/4 teaspoon cinnamon
1 cup evaporated milk
1 unbaked 8-inch pie shell

Preheat oven to 450 degrees F. Crush berries slightly and mix with the dry ingredients. Add evaporated milk and pour into the pie shell. Bake at 450 degrees F. for 10 minutes, then at 350 degrees F. for 30 minutes more. Serve with whipped cream.

—From *Alaska Airlines is Cookin,* Anchorage

Melt-in-Your-Mouth Cranberry Pie

Yield: 1 pie

2 cups low-bush cranberries
1/2 cup sugar
1/2 cup chopped nuts
2 eggs

1 cup sugar
1 cup flour
1/2 cup melted butter
1/4 cup melted shortening

Grease a 9-inch pie plate. Spread cranberries over the bottom and sprinkle with the 1/2 cup sugar and the nuts. Preheat oven to 325 degrees F. In a bowl, beat the eggs; add the 1 cup sugar, flour, melted butter, and melted shortening. Beat well and pour over cranberries. Bake at 325 degrees F. for 50 to 60 minutes, or until golden. Serve this tart and delicious pie with ice cream or whipped cream.

—Mariel Wilbur, Fairbanks

Easy Raspberry Ice Cream Pie

Yield: 1 pie

1 small package raspberry flavored
    gelatine
1¼ cups boiling water

2 cups vanilla ice cream
2 cups wild raspberries
1 baked 9-inch pie shell

Dissolve gelatine in boiling water. Stir in the ice cream and raspberries. Pour into pie shell and refrigerate until set.

—Brenda Wilbur, Fairbanks

Sour Cream Rhubarb Pie

Yield: 1 pie

Pastry for a 2-crust pie
2 egg yolks
¾ cup sour cream
1 cup sugar

⅛ teaspoon salt
½ teaspoon cinnamon
2 tablespoons flour
2 cups chopped rhubarb

Line a 9-inch pie plate with pastry. Preheat oven to 475 degrees F. Mix egg yolks and sour cream; mix in remaining ingredients, and pour into unbaked pie shell. Top with pastry to make a 2-crust pie. Bake at 475 degrees F. for 12 minutes. Reduce heat to 250 degrees F. and bake for 30 minutes longer.

—Brenda Wilbur, Fairbanks

Alaska Blueberry Pie

Yield: 1 pie

1 cup sugar
2 tablespoons cornstarch
⅔ cup cold water
3½ cups fresh or frozen blueberries,
    divided
1 tablespoon butter

1 tablespoon lemon juice
1 teaspoon grated lemon rind
1 cup heavy cream
Confectioners' sugar to taste
9-inch baked pie shell

Combine sugar, cornstarch, water, 2 cups of the blueberries, butter, lemon juice, and lemon rind in a saucepan, and cook until thick. Fold in the remaining blueberries and cool the mixture completely. Chill. When ready to serve, whip the cream and sweeten to taste with confectioners' sugar. Spread cream over pie shell, and spoon in the blueberry mixture leaving the cream uncovered around the edges.

—Elsie Cresswell, Kenai

Potlatch Hats
by April Kelley

Potlatch hats were worn traditionally at many celebrations and potlatches.

Fresh Raspberry Pie

Yield: 1 pie

4 cups fresh raspberries
1½ to 2½ tablespoons quick-cooking
  tapioca

1 to 1¼ cups sugar
Pastry for a 2-crust pie

Preheat oven to 425 degrees F. Spread the tapioca and a little of the sugar in an unbaked, pastry-lined pie tin. Combine raspberries with remaining sugar and fill the pie shell. Cover with the second crust and bake at 425 degrees F. for 15 minutes. Decrease heat to 350 degrees F. and bake for 20 to 30 minutes longer. This same recipe can be used for rhubard or blueberry pie.

—St. Matthew's Guild, Fairbanks

THE HAIDA

The beautiful portion of Alaska in which the Haida live is much the same as the Tlingits. The southeastern coastal strip is broken by deep bays and inlets, and heavily wooded with conifers. Sheltered coves, into which fresh-water streams empty, provided the Haida with ideal locations for villages where a society based on a mountain barrier to the east and rough seas to the south isolated their region from the main currents of cultural development on the continent and gave opportunity for the creation of an original and independent way of life.

Haida War Canoe
by April Kelley

Haida war canoes plied the waters around southeastern Alaska to protect their areas.

The Haida and Tlingit are two distinct linguistic groups. The social structures, however, are similar. The moieties were the Eagle and the Raven. Each moiety was divided into clans. The livelihood patterns were historically influenced by the rich supply of resources, which varied according to the season. The major resources available to all people of southeastern Alaska are: fish; salmon, halibut, cod, olachen, herring, trout, and snapper: sea mammals, sea otter, seal, sea lion, whale, and porpoise: shellfish; a variety of clams, mussels, cockles, and snails. Other resources of the beach scene include varieties of kelp and seaweed. Some of these were eaten, while others were used for various purposes.

Winter months found the Haida in their permanent villages, which composed their tribes. Like the Tlingit, they had ceremonial houses. Spring, summer, and fall they were scattered in their fishing, hunting, and gathering areas.

The Haida were outstanding carvers. Because the country provided an abundant supply of tall, red cedar trees, they excelled in carving very high columns. The Haida carvers used the whole width of the tree trunk and carved heads over wide shoulders and hips. The surfaces of Haida totems are covered with intricately arranged figures of several sizes. Small animals and imaginary creatures were carved in the ears and between the limbs of larger ones. A Haida carver seldom repeated the arrangement of limbs and never repeated two figures, as did other linguistic groups. There was an infinite variety in forms, rhythm of lines, and contrast of masses.

Subsistence utilization of fish and game resources remain important to the proud modern-day Haida culture.

PRESERVED FOODS

Food preservation has perhaps been more important to Alaskan life and Alaskan cooking than to any other land. Because of climate, long distances between sources of food, and great dependence on wild foods, much of what was eaten in Alaska's early days was preserved in some way. Even for city-dwelling Alaskans, fresh foods were gathered or shipped in for a brief time in summer, and much had to be kept for the long winter. Sometimes this meant a moose carcass frozen in the back yard, or whole frozen fish dipped in water to give a coating of ice and stacked like cordwood. It also meant beautiful jars of jams or pickles to brighten winter meals, perhaps berries and greens preserved in seal oil and buried in the cold ground. Food preservation was, and continues to be, important to all Alaskans.

In Alaskan meals, the sweet preserves such as jams and jellies are not confined to breakfast. They appear on the table at dinner and go extremely well with sourdough breads or as condiments with game meats. This underscores the importance of wild berries in our cuisine.

Since food preservation is practiced so much in our state, our Cooperative Extension Service offers endless information, advice, recipes, and educational programs to help us, even in small villages and remote areas. Most Alaskans look to them as a source of good recipes for using and preserving our local foods. We hope that you can use and enjoy the cross section of food preservation recipes you will find in this chapter.

277

Haida Dancers
by April Kelley

Traditional Haida dances are passed down through the generations.

278

Preserved Berries

Soak a butter barrel in the river to remove salt. Fill with salmonberries or blueberries and cover the top with sour dock leaves, or other suitable leaves. Cover the whole barrel with canvas and weight it with rocks. Leave it until the ground is covered with snow, then bring the berries home by dog team. This way the berries are not eaten until winter, when they are needed most.

—Ruth Towner, Nome

The basis of Haida subsistence was the presence of two fish, the salmon and the halibut, which could be dried and kept for long periods of time. At the fishing areas they were prepared and dried by the women and at the end of the season carried back to the winter village by the canoe-load. During the summer season wild vegetables and fruits were also gathered, some to be eaten at once and others to be dried for winter use. After returning to the village, short trips for food in season were always taken and shellfish were part of the daily diet. When a village was preparing for a great feast these food-gathering activities were intensified, for several hundred guests need great quantities of food.

Alaska Cranberry Conserve

4 cups low-bush cranberries
2 cups water
1 pound raisins
¹/₂ pound walnuts

1 orange
¹/₂ lemon
5 cups sugar

Boil the berries in the water until they stop popping. Grind together the raisins, walnuts, orange, and lemon, and add to the cranberries. Add the sugar and boil for 20 minutes. Pour into clean, scalded glasses and seal with paraffin.

—From the *Nome Cookbook,* Nome

Blueberry Marmalade

Yield: 8 6-ounce servings

1 pound ripe blueberries
1 medium orange
1 medium lemon
¾ cup cold water

⅛ teaspoon baking soda
5 cups sugar
1 bottle liquid pectin

Crush berries. Cut the orange and lemon in quarters and remove the rind. Lay the skins flat and scrape off ½ of the white part. Cut rind into shreds. Add water and soda to rind and simmer, covered, for 10 minutes, stirring occasionally. Cut surface membrane from orange and lemon and cut out the sections. Add these, plus any juice, to the cooked rind and simmer, covered, 15 minutes or longer. Add berries. Into a large kettle add the fruit, solidly packed, and flood each cup with juice (or water if necessary) to make 3 cups. Add the sugar, bring to a boil uncovered, and simmer 5 minutes. Remove from heat and stir in the pectin. Pour quickly into clean, scalded glasses to within ½ inch of top. Cover with ⅛ inch of hot paraffin.

—From the *Nome Cookbook*, Nome

Tanana Red Currant Jelly

Pick over carefully red currants and remove the stems. Place in a porcelain-lined kettle, and crush enough to give a little juice so it will not burn. Cook slowly until the juice is soft, then turn into a heavy bag and press out all juice. Strain several times, if necessary, to make it clear. Measure juice, and to each pint add 1 pound of sugar. Put sugar into oven to heat, but do not let it burn. Put the strained juice into a kettle, let it boil 20 minutes; add the hot sugar, and stir until the sugar is dissolved and the juice is clear again. Pour into glasses and let stand until set. When fruit does not jell it is usually because it is over-ripe. The fruit should not be gathered after a rain nor should it be washed.

Mrs. J.A. Sutherland, *Fairbanks Cookbook* circa 1910, Fairbanks

Transportation in southeastern Alaska, historically, was by canoe and the "Grease Trails" leading to the Interior. The canoes were made from red cedar, hewn from a single log and ranged from ten to seventy feet in length. Their seaworthiness was often praised by the men in broad-

beamed, high-decked sailing vessels that tossed their way along the coast. The "Grease Trails" connected southeastern Alaska with the Interior and the Athabaskan Indians. The routes were used for trading, for the different environments on the east and west sides of the mountains offered products that each group desired from the other. Dried fish, shellfish, and olachen grease (from which the trails take their name) from the coast were exchanged for mountain-sheep horns, caribou skins, ermine skins, mountain-goat horns, and wool—all materials important in the economy of the coast.

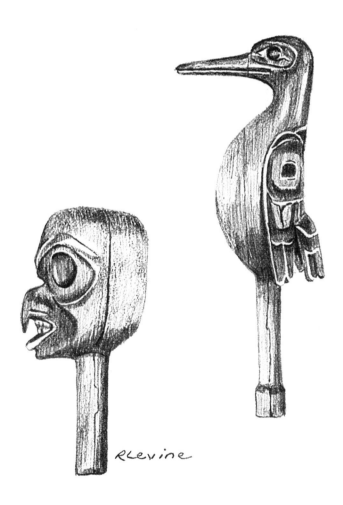

Ceremonial Rattles
by Rachel Levine

Alaska Apple Butter (using dried apples)

1 pound dried apples
2 quarts water
2 quarts high-bush cranberries
6 cups sugar

1 teaspoon cinnamon
1/2 teaspoon cloves
1/4 teaspoon salt
1 lemon, grated rind and juice

Soak the dried apples in the water for 1 hour. Add the high bushcranberries and cook until soft. Put the pulp through a sieve or food mill. Reheat and add the sugar, salt, and spices. Cook until clear. Remove from heat and add the lemon juice and grated rind. Spoon into jars and seal.

—University of Alaska, Cooperative Extension Service

A unifying factor in the Haida, Tlingit, and Tsimshian linguistic groups is the basic concept of the universe and the relationship with the supernatural as expressed in all the arts. Very small dishes in the forms of birds or animals were carved, partly for the pleasure of creation and also to be used on special occasions for the serving of small portions of rare foods at feasts. One of the great characters in northwest mythology is the raven, who is represented on such dishes as well as in many other forms of art. The Haida exquisitely carve argilite, a carbonaceous shale found in nearby areas.

Cranberry Almond Jelly

1 pint Alaskan low-bush cranberries
1 cup water
3 1-pound cans unsweetened
   applesauce

7 cups sugar
1 package powdered pectin
1 1/2 tablespoons almond extract

Place berries and water in a blender and blend until the mixture is of a fine consistency. Strain. To the juice, add remaining ingredients, following the instructions for currant jelly on the pectin box.

—Diane Covey, Ninilchik

In the winter season, historically, when there was leisure for visiting, the feast was important as a mode of entertainment as well as a means of showing wealth. Large serving dishes were carved of solid blocks of wood. Delicate little grease dishes took the forms of birds and small animals. Great ladles for serving food were carved of mountain sheep horn and the food was eaten with spoons of mountain goat horn with handles designed in a vertical structure like the totem poles. All this grew out of the need and the desire to share surplus food with others, and out of this generous gesture developed all the striving for social position through control and show of wealth. Invitations to a feast could be issued a year in advance if a potlatch was connected with it, or at a week's notice if only the nearby villages were involved. Preparations for a feast took the time and energy of everyone in the family of the sponsor, and often of the whole village. During the previous season the women had dried salmon and halibut as they were caught. They had also collected extra quantities of vegetables and fruits such as camas, brake fern roots, salal berries, and huckleberries. These were stored in large wooden boxes and baskets.

Haida Totem Pole
by Marionette Donnell Stock

Rhubarb Jam

Clean rhubarb and cut into ½-inch pieces. Cook together equal amounts of sugar and rhubarb. Season with ginger, and let simmer until brown, 3 to 4 hours. Put into sterilized jars and seal.

—Marion Blossom, Ninilchik

Blueberries were cooked to a certain consistency and then poured into wooden vessels, historically. The mass was covered with skunk cabbage leaves. In recent years, five gallon gasoline cans from which the tops have been removed are used. If the cans are not lined, the portion of the cooked mass in contact with the sides of the can turns black and is not considered desirable for food. During the picking season, the women and children gathered as many berries as they could pick, sometimes staying in the forest for days at a time. It was not uncommon during the picking season to hear women shout to drive away the bears, who were also fond of the berries.

Frozen Raspberry-Salmonberry Jam

3½ cups mixed berries (raspberry and salmonberry)
6 cups sugar

1 cup water
1 package powdered pectin

Mix berries and sugar; let stand for 5 minutes or more. In a saucepan bring the water and pectin to a boil; let boil for 1 minute, and add to the fruit mixture. Stir for 5 minutes and put in jars or freezer containers. Refrigerate for 24 hours, then freeze. To use, just remove from the freezer and serve—mixture does not freeze solid.

—From *Alaska Airlines is Cookin,* Anchorage

The soapberry is one of the many sorts of berries found in south-eastern Alaska. It is preserved dried or canned—but not in oil. When it is used, it is put into a wash bowl, a dish pan, or wooden chopping bowl and beaten vigorously with the open hand into a creamy foam which resembles strawberry ice cream; however, it is light as foam. Both men and women mash the berries with their hands, their sleeves rolled up to their elbows. Swishing hands are buried in the mass to beat the product into creamy foam. When one tires at the job, another takes a turn at it. They keep it up until it is ready to eat. Care must be exercised having the hands free from oil or the product will not foam. Half a dozen people can sit around a bowl of soapberries, each helping himself with a spoon as often as he likes. The berry is cooked in water and preserved by canning. Sometimes it is dried in the sun after cooking. When prepared for eating, about two tablespoons of berries are mixed for a family. Sometimes, a little sugar is put into the foamy mix. Orange or strawberry juice can be added, but in former days, nothing was added.

Seal Species
by Rachel Levine

Uncooked Berry Jelly

3 cups berry juice
4½ cups sugar

1 box powdered pectin
½ cup water

Add the sugar to 1½ cups berry juice and stir thoroughly. Add the powdered pectin to the ½ cup water and heat almost to boiling, stirring constantly. Pour the pectin mixture into the remaining 1½ cups berry juice and stir until the pectin is completely dissolved. Let pectin mixture stand for 15 minutes, stirring occasionally. Combine the juice and pectin mixtures and stir until all the sugar is dissolved. Pour into containers and let stand at room temperature until set, which may be from 6 hours to overnight. Store in a refrigerator or freezer and use within 3 months.

—University of Alaska, Cooperative Extension Service

Carrot Marmalade

Yield: 8 one-half jars

5 cups scraped carrots, medium-finely
   chopped
½ teaspoon salt
4 cups sugar

2 oranges
Juice of 3 lemons
1 cup water

Boil or steam the chopped carrots until tender. If carrots are boiled, drain well. Wash and peel oranges, putting one peeling through the food chopper and cutting the other one into fine strips. Place these in water and boil until tender. Pour sugar over hot cooked carrots, allowing sugar to melt. Then add the orange pulp (chopped), the lemon juice, water, and cooked orange peel. Cook until the syrup is thick and the fruit is clear. Pour into hot, sterile jars, and seal.

—From the *Golden Heart Cookbook,* Fairbanks

Rhubarb Conserve

Yield: 8 one-pint jars

3 oranges
8 cups chopped rhubarb
8 cups sugar

1 1-pound can crushed pineapple
1 cup nuts

Cut whole oranges, including peel, into small pieces. Combine with the rhubarb, sugar, and pineapple; let stand overnight. Cook mixture until it is thick, and add the nuts. Pour into sterilized jars, and seal.

—From the *Golden Heart Cookbook,* Fairbanks

Rhubarb
by Rachel Levine

The inner bark of the western hemlock was used as food by the Haida, Tlingit, and Tsimshian Indians. The bark is gathered when the sap is flowing, sometime around the first of May. The time during which it is useable extends for about two months. The bark is removed skillfully with a metal tool. The outer bark is removed carefully and then the inner bark is taken off in small strips. After removal from the tree, it is baked in a crude oven, depending upon the location. A crude oven can be made by digging a hole about four-feet-deep in gravel. It is lined with rocks. A fire is built on the rocks to heat them, and, after the coals have been removed, it is lined with skunk cabbage leaves. The strips of fresh bark are then placed on the leaves and after as much bark as can be conveniently handled is put into the pile, it is covered with skunk cabbage leaves, on top of which is placed a layer of about four inches of gravel. A fire is built on top of the gravel to cook the contents of the oven. After the bark has been cooked, it is removed from the oven and pressed into layers about one inch in thickness, and then it is dried and stored. It is prepared for eating similar to the preparation of seaweed.

Mincemeat Made from Native Meat

6 pounds game meat (moose, caribou, bear, or Dall sheep)
1 tablespoon salt
2 quarts molasses
1 quart apple cider
6 quarts tart apples, washed, cored, and chopped

2 to 4 pounds raisins
3 tablespoons cinnamon
2 tablespoons allspice
1/4 cup salt
2 tablespoons ground cloves

Simmer meat and 1 tablespoon salt in a small amount of water, until meat is so tender that it begins to fall apart. Set aside to cool, saving the broth. Put the molasses into a kettle and boil slowly for 15 minutes. Add the cider, apples, raisins, and the meat. Add some of the broth and fat from cooking the meat. Season with the cinnamon, allspice, salt, and cloves. Let the mixture cook slowly for about 4 hours, stirring occasionally. Taste for seasoning and add more spices, if desired. Store in Mason jars or use a stone crock, putting a clean white cloth under the crock cover. Keep in a cold place. This is not a canning recipe. Mixture may be canned by pressure canning only.

—From the *Golden Heart Cookbook*, Fairbanks

High Bushcranberry "Catsup"

Yield: approximately 3 pints

12 cups fresh high bushcranberries
1 cup water
3 cups onions, finely chopped
2 cups vinegar
4 cups sugar
1 tablespoon ground cloves

1 tablespoon cinnamon
1 tablespoon allspice
1 tablespoon celery salt
1 tablespoon salt
1 teaspoon pepper

Cook the cranberries in the water until soft, then put through a food mill or sieve. Add the onions, vinegar, sugar, and spices; boil until the mixture thickens to a ketchup consistency. Pour into sterilized jars and seal. Serve this with poultry, meats, or baked beans.

—University of Alaska, Cooperative Extension Service

Candied Rose Hips

A real Alaskan substitute for other candied and dried fruits in cookies, cakes, and puddings.

1½ cups rose hips, halved and seeded
½ cup sugar
¼ cup water

Boil the rose hips for 10 minutes in a syrup made from the sugar and water. Lift fruit from the syrup with a skimmer and drain on waxed paper. Dust with sugar and dry slowly in the sun or in a very slow oven, adding more sugar if the fruit seems sticky. Store between sheets of waxed paper in a closely covered container until ready to use.

—University of Alaska, Cooperative Extension Service

Ptarmigan
by April Kelley

The ptarmigan is the Alaska state bird.

Crispy Pickle Slices

6 pounds medium-size cucumbers
  or zucchini
1 pound small white onions
2 large cloves garlic (optional)
1/3 cup plain (uniodized) salt
2 trays ice cubes

4 cups sugar
3 cups white vinegar
1 1/2 tablespoons mustard seed
1 1/2 teaspoons mixed pickling spices
1 teaspoon celery seed
1/2 teaspoon turmeric

Wash cucumbers or zucchini, slice off both ends and discard. Slice about 1/8-inch thick into a large mixing bowl. Peel onions and slice 1/2-inch thick; add to the mixing bowl. Peel the garlic, and stick each on a wooden pick to easily remove later; add to cucumbers. Add salt and mix well. Cover the mixture with ice cubes, and set aside for 3 hours.

Drain the vegetables well and remove the garlic. In a large kettle, combine all the remaining ingredients and heat to boiling. Add the sliced vegetables, and heat over medium-high heat for 5 minutes.

Ladle into clean, hot jars to within 1/2 inch of top. Wipe tops of jars clean. Put on lids and screw firmly. Process in a boiling water bath for 5 minutes (start timing as soon as jars go into the boiling water). Remove.

—Virginia Doyle "Bunny" Heiner, Fairbanks

Pickles
by Rachel Levine

Watermelon Rind Pickles

Yield: 8 one-half pints

For many years in Alaska's Interior, watermelons were a rare treat to be enjoyed down to—and including—the rind.

3 quarts peeled watermelon rind
3 quarts cold water
3 tablespoons salt
3 tablespoons alum

1 quart white vinegar
9 cups sugar
¼ cups whole cloves
2 2-inch sticks cinnamon

Soak rind for 24 hours in a solution of 2 quarts of water and the salt. Drain and let stand another 24 hours in a solution of 1 quart water and the alum. Drain and add fresh water to cover; let stand another 24 hours. Bring to a boil and cook until rind is tender. In a large kettle combine vinegar, sugar, and spices (tied in cheesecloth). Add drained rind and cook about 20 minutes, or until clear. Pack the rind into hot, sterile jars. Boil syrup for 15 minutes, and fill jars with hot syrup. Seal jars.

—Phelpsie Sirlin, Fairbanks

Pickled Puffballs

1 pint puffball mushrooms
½ cup vinegar
½ cup sugar
½ cup chopped onions

1 teaspoon salt
1 teaspoon celery salt
Dash of cayenne pepper

Wash puffballs—they need not be peeled. Put all ingredients into a kettle and simmer for about one hour, stirring occasionally. This is delicious as a relish served with native meats.

—From the *Golden Heart Cookbook*, Fairbanks

Great Cranberry Relish

4 cups low-bush cranberries
4 cups sugar

2 sweet apples, diced, with seeds removed
2 sweet oranges

292

Grind all ingredients with a meat grinder. Cranberries grind more easily when frozen, and they do not have to be fully ripe. Put in jars and freeze or refrigerate.

—Ruth Towner, Kenai

Puffballs
by Rachel Levine

Frozen White Relish

1 cup heavy cream
1 tablespoon prepared horseradish
1 teaspoon lemon juice
½ teaspoon salt
2 tablespoons minced parsley
1 tablespoon chopped pimiento

Whip the cream until stiff; fold in remaining ingredients. Freeze, stirring once or twice. Serve with baked fish or ham.

—From the *Golden Heart Cookbook,* Fairbanks

Rhubarb Relish

Yield: 5 one-half jars

1 quart chopped onions
1 quart chopped rhubarb
1 tablespoon salt
1 teaspoon allspice
1 teaspoon cinnamon

1 teaspoon cloves
³/₄ teaspoon crushed red pepper
1 pint vinegar
4 cups brown sugar

Simmer all ingredients together until mixture is thick. Pour into sterilized jars and seal.

—From the *Golden Heart Cookbook,* Fairbanks

Uncooked Relish (for meats)

Yield: 14 pints

2 medium-sized heads of cabbage.
8 carrots
6 or 8 red bell peppers
12 medium-sized onions
¹/₂ cup salt

3 pints vinegar
6 cups sugar
1 teaspoon mustard seed
1 teaspoon celery seed

Grind cabbage, carrots, red pepper, and onions in a food chopper. Add the salt and let stand two hours. Drain and mix with the remaining ingredients. Pack into jars, but do not seal. Keep in a cold place.

—From the *Golden Heart Cookbook,* Fairbanks

Alaskan Cranberry-Orange Relish

Yield: approximately 4 cups

1 quart or 1 pound Alaskan low-bush cranberries
1 large orange (including the rind)
1 cup sugar

Put the fruit through a food chopper and add the sugar. This will keep refrigerated for about one month. To make in a food processor: cut the orange into wedges and chop medium-finely in the processor, using on-off turns. Add the berries and process again until they are medium-finely chopped. Stir in the sugar.

Totem Pole
by Rachel Levine

Raw Cranberry Relish

1 pound raw low-bush cranberries
2 oranges, peeled, white membrane removed, and rind reserved
2 cups sugar

Grind cranberries, oranges, and rind. Mix with the sugar and let stand several days before using. This is especially good with ptarmigan.

—From the *Nome Cookbook*, Nome

ℬ ibliography

Books

Brooks, Alfred H. *Blazing Alaska's Trails.* 2nd Edition. Fairbanks: University of Alaska Press, 1973.

Brower, Charles D. *Fifty Years Below Zero.* New York: Dodd, Mead & Co., 1942.

Chance, Norman A. *The Eskimo of North Alaska.* New York: Holt, Rinehart and Winston, 1966.

Chase, Will H. *Pioneers of Alaska: The Trail Blazers of Bygone Days.* Kansas City: Curton Publishing Company, 1951.

Cole, Terrence. Tanana-Yukon Historical Society. *Ghosts of the Gold Rush.* n.p.: Self Published, 1977.

Federal Field Committee for Development Planning in Alaska. *Alaska Natives and the Land.* Washington: U.S. Government Printing Office, 1968.

Heller, Christine and Edward M. Scott. *The Alaska Dietary Survey. 1956-1961.* Public Health Service Publication No. 999-AH-2. U.S. Department of Health, Education and Welfare. Public Health Service.

Hick, George. *Pioneer Prospector.* Fairbanks: University of Alaska Press. 1954.

Hope, Andrew. *Raven's Bones.* Sitka: Sitka Community Association, 1982.

Hughes, Charles Campbell. *An Eskimo Village in the Modern World.* Ithaca: Cornell University Press, 1962.

Jones, Dorothy M. *Aleuts in Transition.* Seattle: University of Washington Press, 1976.

Kari, James and Priscilla Kari. *Dena'ina Etnena Tanaina Country.* Alaska Native Language Center. Fairbanks: University of Alaska Press, 1982.

Krauss, Michael E. Native Peoples and Languages of Alaska. A map. Alaska Native Language Center. Fairbanks: University of Alaska Press, 1974. Revised, 1982.

Naske, Claus and Lou Rowinski. *Alaska: A Pictorial History.* Norfolk, Virginia: The Donning Company/Publishers, Inc., 1983.

Nelson, Richard K. *Athapaskan Notebook Series.* Fairbanks: University of Alaska Press, 1983.

Smith, G. Warren. "Arctic Pharmacognosia." *Journal of the Arctic Institute of North America.* Vol. 26, No. 4. December 1973.

United States Department of Agriculture. *For Wilderness Wives.* Washington, D.C. Bulletin F39, n.d.

United States Department of the Interior. Bureau of Indian Affairs. *Alaska Native Regional Profiles.* October 1978.

Van Stone, James W. *Athapaskan Adaptations*. n.p.: Aldine Publishing Co., 1974.
Van Stone, James W. *Eskimos of the Nushagak River*. Seattle: University of Washington Press, 1967.

Cookbooks

Alaska Airlines. *Alaska Airlines is Cookin*. Self Published, 1974.
Alaska Airlines. *Lighter than Air Cookbook*. Self Published, 1975.
Alaska Crippled Children's Association. Anchorage, Alaska. *Out of Alaska's Kitchens*. Ketchikan: Self Published, 1948.
Alaska Magazine Editors. *Alaska Wildberry Guide and Cookbook*. Anchorage: Alaska Northwest Publishing Company, 1982.
Alaska Sugardoes Homemakers. *The Northern Lights*. Nenana, Alaska: Self Published, 1967.
Alberts, H.W. *Uses of Plants by Indians and Eskimos in Alaska*. University of Alaska Archives. Fairbanks, Alaska.
Alderman, Hazel Hake. *Favorite Recipes from Ruralite Readers, 1954-1976*. Ruralite Services, Inc. Forest Grove, Oregon: Times-Litho, 1979.
American Legion Auxiliary. *Past President's Parley Cookbook*. Fairbanks: Self Published, 1939.
Anchorage Women's Club. *Alaska's Cooking*. Anchorage: Self Published, 1961.
Barnabus, Bessie. *A Story by Bessie Barnabus*. An unpublished interview, 1980.
Boy Scouts of America Troop #49. *Favorite Recipes from the 49th*. Fairbanks: Self Published, 1984.
Business and Professional Women's Club. *Alaska's Capital City Cookbook*. Juneau: Self Published, 1960.
Cabin Fever Quilter's Guild. *Cookbook of Our Favorites*. Fairbanks: Self Published, 1984.
Carey, Mary. *Let's Taste Alaska*. Talkeetna, Alaska: Self Published, 1982.
Cleveland, Bess. *Alaskan Cookbook for Homesteader or Gourmet*. Berkely: Howell-North, 1970.
Ellis, Eleanor A. *Northern Cookbook*. Edmonton, Alberta: Hurtig Publishers, 1967.
Epsilon Chapter of Beta Sigma Phi. *Sitka Cookbook*. Sitka: Sitka Printing Co., 1949.
First Presbyterian Women, First Presbyterian Church. *The Fairbanks Cookbook*. Fairbanks: Self Published, 1910.
First National Bank of Fairbanks. *Golden Heart Cookbook*. Fairbanks: Self Published, 1949.
Fishery Products Laboratory, The. *Alaska Seafood Recipes*. Ketchikan, Alaska: Self Published, 1951.
Gambell Community Education Program. *Community Education Program Cookbook*. Gambell, Alaska: Self Published, 1978.
Golden North Rebekah Lodge No. 4A. *Alaska Recipes from our Cache*. Fairbanks: Self Published, 1950.
Grosvenor, Gilbert M. "The Making of America...Alaska." *National Geographic Magazine*. Vol. 165, No. 2. January, 1984.

Gunther, Erna. *Indian Life on the Northwest Coast of North America.* Chicago: University of Chicago Press, 1972.

Homer Homemakers. *Cooking Up a Storm.* Homer: Self Published, 1976.

Kananen, Leona. *Yukon Cookbook.* Whitehorse, Yukon: Yukon Press Limited, 1971.

Kari, Priscilla Russell. *Tanaina Plantlore.* Adult Literacy Laboratory. University of Alaska. Anchorage: Anchorage Community College, 1978.

Loftus, Audrey. *According to Mama.* Espicopal Church of Alaska: Self Published, 1957.

Loftus, Audrey. *According to Papa.* Espicopal Church of Alaska: Self Published, 1957.

Marion Society of the Immaculate Conception Church. *Cooking Favorites of Fairbanks, Alaska.* Fairbanks: Self Published, 1954.

Members and Friends of St. Joseph's Hospital. *Northern Nuggets.* Fairbanks: Self Published, 1962.

Ninilchik Homemakers. *Ninilchik Community Cookbook.* Kansas Circulation Service, 1978.

Officers Wive's Club. U.S. Naval Station. Kodiak, Alaska. *What's Cooking in Alaska.* Kodiak: Self Published, 1952.

Petersburg PTA. *PTA Cookbook.* Petersburg, Alaska: Self Published, 1955.

Pioneers of Alaska Auxillary #7. *Homemade Kitchen Magic.* Ketchikan, Alaska: Self Published, n.d.

Rainbow Girls of Alaska #5. *Cooking with Anchorage #5.* Anchorage: Self Published, 1950.

Rampart Dog Musher's Association. *Doggone Good Recipes.* Kansas: Fundcraft Publishing, 1983.

St. John Berchman's Church. *A Book of Recipes.* Iowa: G & R Publishing Company, 1984.

St. Matthew's Guild of St. Matthew's Espiscopal Church. *Favorite Recipes.* Fairbanks: Self Published, 1944.

Siberian Yupik Cookbook. n.p.: Eskimo, Indian and Aleut Printing Company, Inc., 1973.

Students of Shishmaref Day School. *Eskimo Cookbook.* Easter Seal Society for Alaska Crippled Children and Adults. Anchorage: Self Published, 1952.

Toastmistress Council #12. *Here's a Toast.* Fairbanks: Self Published, n.d.

Unalaska City School District. *Cuttlefish.* Unalaska, Alaska: Self Published, 1981.

University of Alaska Coorperative Extention Service. *Sourdough.* Publication #61, 1974.

University of Alaska Cooperative Extention Service and United States Department of Agriculture. *Rhubarb Recipes.* Publication #64, 1980.

Wildflower Garden Club. *Cookbook.* Juneau: Self Published, n.d.

Women's Society of Christian Service of the Methodist Church. *Nome Cookbook.* n.p.: Self Published, n.d.

Index

303

304

307

308